THE CINEMATIC TANGO

THE CINEMATIC TANGO

CONTEMPORARY ARGENTINE FILM

Tamara L. Falicov

WALLFLOWER PRESS

LONDON & NEW YORK

First published in Great Britain in 2007 by
Wallflower Press
6a Middleton Place, Langham Street, London W1W 7TE
www.wallflowerpress.co.uk

A catalogue record for this book is available from the British Library

ISBN 978-1-904764-92-2 (pbk)
ISBN 978-1-904764-93-9 (hbk)

Book design by Elsa Mathern

Printed by Replika Press Pvt Ltd (India)

CONTENTS

ACKNOWLEDGEMENTS

There are many people who have supported this project from its nascent beginnings; it was they who helped me cultivate the seed of an idea until it blossomed into a fuller flower. This project was the outgrowth of my dissertation, and for this reason I will acknowledge my main advisor and dissertation committee members. Professor Daniel C. Hallin has been an infallible mentor, astute advisor and personal friend. Other committee members who have provided invaluable advice, feedback and moral support have been Randal Johnson, Ellen Seiter, DeeDee Halleck and Michael Monteón. Other *compañeros* in Argentina and the US who have read drafts, sent me articles and provided insight about Argentine cultural politics are Octavio Getino, who was my host under a Fulbright grant in 1997–98, Claudio España, Diego Curubeto, Daniel 'Parana' Sendros, Estrella Joselevich, my *tío* Pablo Jaes, Andrea Goldstein, Alba Kaplan, Nieves Consuelo, Tapia Morales, Paula Rodríguez Marino and Atilio Roque González. Thanks to those members of the film community in Buenos Aires who volunteered their time to be interviewed. My hope is that their unflagging commitment to maintaining their national treasure is as accurately reflected in these pages as can be. Thanks to Anne Geiberger for her copyediting skills, and my colleague Matt Jacobson for helping me with the frame-grab technology. I also must acknowledge Annie Martin, who helped guide me through the editorial process and who acted selflessly. Special thanks go to Yoram Allon, editorial director at Wallflower Press, who fortunately understood this book project, and with whom it has been a pleasure to work. Thanks also to Jacqueline Downs, assistant editor at Wallflower Press, for her very helpful editorial suggestions. David Oubiña also provided invaluable feedback in his evaluation of the manuscript.

This study is dedicated to my family: to my mother, Celia Haydée Jaes Falicov, who inspired me to pursue an advanced degree and who I admire and love dearly; to my wonderful sisters, Yael and Anna, whom I can always depend on and who make me smile – my Mom and sisters have always been my 'cheerleaders' and never-ending sources of morale boosting; to my relatives in Buenos Aires who inspired me to undertake this study in the first place – the late Bobe Fanny Zisman de Jaes who was my 'rock' when I lived in Buenos Aires, for Tia Beba, who has always been a source of love and support, and to the late Julio and Sarita Perelstein, who lived such rich and compelling lives; and to the everlasting memory of my father, Raúl Esteban Falicov, who always believed in me. I know he would be proud.

To new but no less important members of my family – I am so fortunate to have found my companion, best friend and love, Stephen Steigman. I thank him for his editorial support, and general good sense of humour and patience with this project. I also would like to thank my father-in-law, Bill Steigman, who has become a second father to me. His interest in this project, moral support, legal advice and wonderful suggestions have brought joy to my life. I cannot omit other sources of new-found encouragement: thanks and much love go to Linda and Ellen Steigman, Lillian Kersh, Phyllis Dansky and Aunt Barbi Miller – I could not be more grateful.

In terms of institutional support, I would like to thank the Fulbright Commission in Argentina for facilitating my stay in 1997–98. The Communication Department at the University of California, San Diego also deserves recognition for assisting me financially in various forms as a graduate student. A Kimbell Grant provided by the Department of Theater and Film at the University of Kansas greatly aided the completion of this project. I also must acknowledge my colleagues at the University of Kansas for their encouragement: Cathy Preston, Tony Rosenthal, Chuck Berg, John Tibbetts, Michael Baskett and other colleagues in my department. I delved into the National Archives to complete chapter two with the financial support of an NEH Summer Stipend. Kathy Porsch at the Hall Center for the Humanities at the University of Kansas played an integral part in obtaining this financial support.

Some of the contents included here have been published in the following publications and have been granted permission to be reprinted here. A section of chapter one is published as 'Hollywood's Rogue Neighbor: The Argentine Film Industry during the Good Neighbor Policy, 1939–1945' in *The Americas: A Quarterly Review of Inter-American Cultural History*, vol. 63, no. 2, October 2006, 245–60. A portion of chapter two has been published as 'Film Production in Argentina under Democracy, 1983–1989: *The Official Story (La historia oficial)* as an International Film' in *Southern Quarterly*, vol. 29, no. 4, Summer 2001, 123–34. A section of chapter three appeared as 'Argentina's Blockbuster Movies and the Politics of Culture under Neoliberalism, 1989–1998' in *Media, Culture, and Society*, vol. 22, May 2000, 327–42. An expanded version of this section was published as 'Television for the Big Screen: How *Comodines* Became Argentina's First Blockbuster Phenomenon' in Julian Stringer (ed.) (2003) *Movie Blockbusters*, Routledge, 242–54, of which portions are reprinted here. An earlier version of part of chapter four was published as 'Los Hijos de Menem: The New Independent Argentine Cinema, 1995–1999', *Framework*, vol. 44, no. 1, Spring 2003, 49–63.

INTRODUCTION

Film industries in Latin America as well as other parts of the world (except the United States – Hollywood – and Hong Kong industries) are state-supported entities funded in part to sustain national cultural production. State cultural policies have been defined, in the words of Randal Johnson,

> in terms of the notion that culture is an integral part of development and that as the ultimate guarantor of a nation's cultural unity and identity the state has a legitimate responsibility to protect society's cultural memory and heritage, to defend its cultural values, to stimulate cultural production, and to ensure that culture is not defined exclusively by market criteria. (1993: 105)

Moreover, film industries, apart from being part of the national patrimony, are also seen as industries that need state assistance, due to the overwhelming competition from the United States, in order to sustain employment in this sector. This study examines the film industry in Argentina, specifically focusing on the films produced from the 1940s to 2006. Although this is a case study of a country with specific film policies that differ from those of other Latin American countries as well as those of countries outside Latin America, it also represents a broader exploration of economic, political and cultural trends that all national cinemas face in terms of development and financial sustainability.

Historically, the study of national cinemas has concentrated on the national image and narrative over the political and economic aspects of production, exhibition and distribution of films. National images and stories are reified as markers of nationhood, perhaps because these differences more easily distinguish one country from another. Susan Hayward (1993a), in her study of French national cinema, discusses the various ways in which differences in national cinemas are enunciated, such as narratives, genres, codes and conventions, among others. It can be argued that national cinemas can also be defined in terms of their funding structures, that is, by what national cultural policies are enacted and which groups (such as individual director-producers versus large television companies) are given access to state subsidies. This, too, can be a marker of difference. Ideally, however, national cinema studies should consider a holistic approach in examining a nation's cinematic past and present.

National cinema studies, according to Tom O'Regan, situate the cinema simultaneously as a natural object in the film world (its production and industrial context), as a social object connecting and relating people to each other (its social and political context) and discursively through language, genre and knowledge (its representations) (1996: 2).

My study of the Argentine film industry focuses on the political and economic dynamics of film funding over time, but it is also concerned with understanding how cultural policy shapes national film culture. Throughout the book I will discuss films thematically and visually, while situating them within a production context.

The history of Argentine cinema has been documented extensively in Spanish-language publications such as both volumes of Domingo Di Núbila's *La epoca de oro: Historia del cine argentino* (first published in 1959 and reissued in 1998). These volumes, rich in detail, focus on descriptions of films and actors, but are impressionistic and light on critical analysis. The anthology *Historia del cine argentino*, by Couselo *et al.* (1992), is more nuanced, with attention paid to larger historical factors such as the politics, economics and culture that affected various movements and trends in Argentine cinema. A final book (which proved useful in formulating my own ideas) is Octavio Getino's *Cine argentino: Entre lo posible y lo deseable* (2005). Getino takes a primarily political-economic approach to the history of the cinema in Argentina. Although he does not describe the films themselves in great detail, he does look generally at how films shifted ideologically over time due to changes in the social, political and economic landscape both nationally and globally.

Argentine national cinema is defined in this study primarily as a state-supported articulation of national culture. In the Latin American context, it is nearly impossible to produce films outside of a state-subsidy framework, although there are instances of Argentine filmmakers who work on the margins (for example, videomaker Raúl Perrone and filmmaker Mariano Llinás discussed in chapter four). The Instituto Nacional de Cinematografía (INC) (National Film Institute, changed in 1994 to the Instituto Nacional de Cine y Artes Audiovisuales (National Institute for Film and Audiovisual Arts, or INCAA) made changes in the mid-1990s to cast a 'wider net' – that is, to include first- and second-time filmmakers in their pool of recipients (which until that point had favoured the directors with a proven track record).

A state-centred definition of national film culture can be problematic in the limitations that state-supported culture might bring, such as the freedom of cultural expression. The history of Argentina, beginning in the 1930s through to the early 1980s, has amply illustrated this when government dictatorships seriously curtailed cultural discourse in cinema as well as other media. In addition, as Thomas Elsaesser rightly points out, state subsidies 'encourage aesthetic difference from the dominant (Hollywood) product, but discourage biting the hand that feeds it' (quoted in Crofts 1993: 52). At the same time, there is not much hope (at least in its current configuration) that the market will intervene broadly as exemplified by the Hollywood model. Nor, it can be argued, would members of the Argentine film community necessarily want to 'privatise' film-making, as this would necessitate that films conform to the laws of the market more than they already have to – something that art-house cinema struggles with due to its small share of the general movie-going audience. Indeed, to hold the market responsible for producing a film culture can also be limiting in appealing to wide audiences and 'ideal' consumers. However, as will be shown in chapter three, even private production companies (the four largest being Pol-Ka, Aries, Patagonik and Argentina Sono Film) are not wholeheartedly taking a dive into the marketplace (in competition with Hollywood) – they are utilis-ing state funds in making commercial films so as to minimise their financial risk.

In 1994, a financial crisis in the film industry catalysed a roundtable meet-ing of esteemed Argentine film directors to discuss strategies for survival. These were some of their viewpoints:

Adolfo Aristarain: We utilise the French and Spanish cinema laws [as models] that include a coherent system of subsidies, advances and bank loan guarantees.

Luis Puenzo: We are working so that we can definitely have a film industry. We run the risk of turning into a country like Bolivia, that produces two or three films a year, and where once in a while a film director becomes recog-nized and established. (Quoted in Batlle 1994a: 30–2)

The abovementioned quotes, which compare Argentina's film industry to those of other nations, point to an issue that Argentine cultural producers constantly face. Preserving and sustaining national culture via cultural policy legislation conflicts with complex and often contradictory notions of cultural identity in Argentina. There are at least two typologies that characterise how people de-scribe national culture and perceive national identity in Argentina. Some favour a European-influenced cultural identity that emulates a Western, industrialised, urbane culture. This perspective advocates a state-supported cultural policy in order to create cinematic 'art and culture' capable of transcending the laws of the marketplace. Often these cultural products are made for an elite audience, both nationally and internationally. Films screened at international film festivals, such as María Luisa Bemberg's *Camila* (1984) or Luis Puenzo's *La historia oficial* (*The Official Story* aka *The Official Version*, 1985) were not only high-quality films but they provided a specific, typically middle-class image for how Argentina was coming to grips with the horrific military dictatorship of 1976–83.

The other predominant discourse surrounding Argentine national culture embraces what can be typified as the 'Latin American perspective'. This world-view sees Argentina as being much like its regional counterparts, that is, as a 'developing' country with limited financial resources. In this view, Argentina, like the rest of Latin America, is regarded as being in an unequal, dependent relationship with the United States in most economic, political, social and cultural realms. The Latin American school believes that films should embody a 'Latin American' aesthetic, one marked by low-budget productions or what Cuban filmmaker Julio García Espinosa called *un cine imperfecto* (an imperfect cinema), insisting that a low-budget, gritty, non-commercial film reflects the social realities of underdevelopment, such as social inequality, economic dependence, poverty, violence and limited resources.

García Espinosa, in his famous essay first published in 1969, proclaimed that 'all technically and artistically masterful cinema in Latin America is almost always reactionary cinema' (1997: 71). This camp typically espouses a national/popular ideology in which culture created by the people (popular or folk culture) is heralded above 'bourgeois high art'. Cinema is seen as a means to reach a mass populace, and is usually embraced by leftist cultural producers with a progressive ideological bent, as opposed to conservative 'cultured elites'. Additionally, a critical form of filmmaking (that is, one in which the audience must think and not be passive) can take a more 'mass popular' slant, rather than be too intellectual or esoteric, but must be careful not to embody the ideology of 'Hollywood style' movies. Fernando Solanas and Octavio Getino, in their book *Cine, cultura y descolonización* (1973), propose the creation of a politicised national culture that is imitative of neither Hollywood nor European auteurism. Their solution from a Latin Americanist (or Third World) perspective is the creation of a 'militant cinema' that works to 'decolonise' the spectator from the dominant ideology of imperialism, in what they have dubbed a 'Third Cinema'. Fernando Birri, an Argentine filmmaker from Santa Fe, has been dubbed the 'godfather', 'father' and, alternately, the 'pope' of what was a cinema of denunciation that formed a pan-continental film movement known as the New Latin American Cinema (his work will be discussed in more detail in chapter one).

This tension between a European identity and a more Latin American identity has created problems in Argentina not only on social and cultural levels, but also in terms of legislating cultural policy. These competing definitions of culture also impact on industrial conceptions of development because each 'identity paradigm' brings with it differing assumptions about paths to development, such as what economic, political and social issues deserve priority.

While the European and Latin American worldviews could appear to polarise the cultural politics of filmmaking, there is actually a spectre that looms larger than both of them: Hollywood. Tom O'Regan notes that in the case of Australian national cinema (another film industry of roughly the same size as Argentina's), value is placed on their film production as something 'simultaneously an alternative to and a supplement of the dominant Hollywood cinema' (1996: 113). In other words, Argentina's film industry is distinguishing itself from what it is not. Stephen Crofts, in his 1993 essay on reconceptualising national cinemas, reminds us that all national cinemas are in dialectical tension with Hollywood.

In the case of Argentine national cinema, films are often thought of as inferior to Hollywood in terms of technical quality, although these conceptions are slowly starting to change. Thus, in the case of cinema specifically (as opposed to other forms of cultural production such as literature, art and dance), Argentina is compared both to Hollywood and Europe. In addition to Argentina's love affair with all things European, there is also a link with Europe in the kind of co-production help it receives and the European film festival awards that it has won. That is, Argentine cinema is supported by the European film establishment in terms of both encouragement and financial support for individual films.

Argentine cinema might be described as dancing a complicated tango, with the Hollywood film industry on one arm and European cinema on the other. While it is entangled with both partners, one more commercial, one more auteurist, it is a cinema that cannot be separated from its Latin American comrades, who are watching the awkward tango from the periphery of the dance floor. While it has historically aimed to distance itself from its Latin American neighbours by invoking its European immigration origin story, it cannot escape its position in world geopolitics, economic stability or geographic location.

To survive financially, the Argentine film industry (whose audience base is a population of 39 million) traditionally has depended in large part on taxes on movie tickets and other forms of revenue collected by the INCAA. I argue here that protectionist policy measures (taxes on movie tickets, low-interest film loans, subsidies, co-participation agreements and so on), even within a neoliberal environment, are unique to the Argentine situation, partly due to its position as a 'Europeanised' Latin American country. On the one hand, legislators and film lobbyists envision Argentina as an industrialised country with a strong state-supported culture similar to a social-democratic European country. On the other, proponents of a 'populist' perspective argue that Argentina should be categorised within the Latin American paradigm; it is seen as a subordinate, developing nation in need of industry protection.

Film industries are seen by most countries (other than the United States) as producing cultural as well as industrial goods. Therefore, issues of employment, labour unions, costs, technical support and such like, are concerns in upholding a national film industry. Argentina's film industry (considered medium-sized) has straddled the line between being a developing 'infant industry' in need of economic support and a cultural entity in need of protection. Argentina's film policy has included both the industrial and cultural definitions, but it has emphasised one over the other at different times.

The film industry has a long history of economic crises and disputes between the various sectors involved: production, exhibition and distribution. In addition to internal problems, the dominance the US film industry enjoys in the

Argentine film market went unchallenged until recently (from 1997 onwards). Since the 1950s the United States has enjoyed between a 60 and 80 percent market share in Argentina.

As I explore in chapters three and four, changes in cultural policy from the Alfonsín to the Menem administration had as much to do with varying strategies in economic policy as they did with cultural concerns. Differing conceptions of culture have historically broken down along party lines in Argentina, via the two largest political parties, the Radical Party, Unión Cívica Radical (UCR), and the Peronist Party, Partido Justicialista (PJ). The cultural platforms of these parties will be described in these chapters to provide a political and cultural context for the kind of film legislation that was passed.

By comparing state film policies across various government administrations, it is possible to understand the various ways the state can further or constrain the production of national cinema. The issue at stake for most national film industries is to what degree state support is necessary to ensure the survival of the national cinema. By the same token, film projects must be encouraged to possess a combination of entertainment created for a wide national audience and one that works in the public interest. Film industries are forms of art, culture and commerce. It is in these intersections that traditionally fixed notions of the 'national' can prove troublesome. Argentine cinema, throughout its history, as well as in its current configuration, poignantly illustrates this tension.

Film industries have a dual nature as both purveyors of cultural goods (that in the national context ideally should grapple with social issues facing the national community) and industrial entities (that should provide national employment opportunities and maintain a healthy financial footing). Often cultural and commercial objectives do not overlap, and sometimes they contradict each other, resulting in failure for film productions. Ultimately, though, it is important to bear in mind that the state is frequently 'brought in' to help sustain the separation between issues of 'national culture' and the 'market'. In theory, national culture is conceived as an artifact or an expression that should not have to follow the logic of the marketplace. However, as Nestor García Canclini (1995) has observed, with the increased commercialisation of all spheres of life, even artisan crafts displayed in national museums cannot be separated from the marketplace.

Several binary oppositions characterise the issues national film industries must reconcile: (i) national versus global markets, (ii) high art versus mass culture, (iii) broad versus niche/segmented audiences, (iv) national versus local representation and (v) urban versus rural representation, to name a few. Most national film industries must face these tensions in orienting national film policy towards domestic film spectators in addition to international audiences.

This book is divided into four chapters. Chapter one, 'From the Studio System Era to the Dirty War', examines the origins of the Argentine studio system based on the Hollywood classical model. With the use of European film equipment and immigrant will, the film industry converted from silent films to sound – the first ever in Latin America. These were made in a studio fashion, with actors who were known from *radionovelas* and *sainetes* (one-act popular skits). These genre films (tango films, comedies and gaucho films, for example) were extremely popular with working-class audiences, and with other Spanish-speaking countries in Latin America. The chapter goes on to examine the ordeal the film industry faced during World War Two and the Good Neighbor Policy. Because Argentina had declared itself neutral, the United States did everything in its power to assure that no forms of Nazi propaganda or otherwise were produced in the country, and mandated laws to stop selling raw film stock to its 'wayward' neighbour. This ultimately hampered the production of a mainly democratically-minded film sector. The success the Argentine film industry had enjoyed in its heyday was soon but a memory.

A later section of the chapter explores the 1960s through to the early 1980s, when Argentina suffered a series of military dictatorships that financially, socially and culturally crippled the country. The film industry was no exception. This part of the chapter delineates the various film movements that expressed a particular vision of Argentina between periods of democratic rule and military repression. It outlines four decades of the more important film movements in Argentina, and how the state encouraged or discouraged their activities. Young cineastes in Buenos Aires came from literary and intellectual circles to create the *Nueva ola*, or New Wave of cinema. In this time, the concept of the art-house film developed alongside the entrance of European auteur films in Argentina. While they were not recognised as important either aesthetically or at the box-office, they later became emblematic of the nation's cultural patrimony, primarily because many of these films were based on national 'Europeanised' writers such as Julio Cortázar and Jorge Luis Borges. This was due to Argentina's middle-to-upper-class urban collective desire to be European.[1]

In the province of Santa Fe, in a world away from the metropolis, filmmaker Fernando Birri and students at the first documentary film school in Latin America were producing a neorealist-inspired 'cinema of underdevelopment'. During the same decades, more militant groups that formed part of a pan-Latin American film movement dubbed the 'New Latin American Cinema' arose from under a military regime headed by General Onganía from 1966 to 1973. Later, during the most brutal dictatorship in Argentine history, known as the *Proceso* (Process of National Reorganisation), there was a much more repressive atmosphere that made it practically impossible to make underground cinema.

Chapter two, 'The 1980s: Cinema, Democracy and Film Policy with Views Towards Europe', describes the film industry in the period of 'redemocratisation' in Argentina from 1983 to 1989. The first half focuses on film production under the Alfonsín administration, and how films performed at the box office both at home and abroad. In addition, it examines the Radical Party's push to produce middle-class art-house cinema for an international film festival viewership and how cultural policy during that period favoured 'high culture' over industrial considerations, and how this translated into poor box office attendance in general. Although films carried out the Film Institute's mission to 'further the national community' in terms of social content, they only reached an educated, socially progressive segment of the population. Finally, an analysis of the biggest international success, *La historia oficial*, lends insight into how films at this time were framed to resonate with a 'universalised' middle-class audience.

Chapter three, 'Menem's Neoliberal Politics and the Birth of the Blockbuster', examines the commercial turn in state-supported filmmaking under President Menem's two government administrations. When he entered office in 1989, the country was undergoing a severe financial crisis. In an effort to rectify the problem of low attendance for national films, Menem appointed more business-oriented professionals to the helm of the National Film Institute, thereby skewing film production from a 'national-popular' conception of film production to one geared more toward a commercialised market in the urban sectors of the country. Thus, the model used for a national film industry shifted towards the commercial model traditionally embraced by Hollywood.

Aided by new cinematic legislation paved in 1994, film production in Argentina saw the entrance of new investors – television channels, themselves owned by multimedia conglomerates who were given subsidies to produce national cinema. Tie-ins, extensive advertising on television and other forms of media, and television actor participation in films based on TV programmes, converged into the first group of Argentine blockbuster movies in the country's history. Undoubtedly, this more commercial film helped revive an ailing industry, but it did so in a way that provided state subsidies to wealthy multimedia conglomerates while leaving little film financing possibilities to independent director-producers. Smash-hit films such as *Comodines* (*Cops*, 1997) and *La furia* (*The Fury*, 1997) essentially imitated the Hollywood action film, but did so with well-known television actors, thereby creating a 'star system' for national audiences rather than a 'cinema for export' in the Spanish-speaking world.

Chapter four, 'Young Filmmakers and the New Independent Argentine Cinema', concludes the study by examining recent trends in filmmaking. This was a period of experimentation in filmmaking, marked by the return to a low-budget, innovative and daring view of the nation. As a result of the popularity of film schools and a small fund for first-time filmmakers from the Film Institute, filmmakers mainly from their early twenties to their mid-thirties began to produce a cinema that moved away from traditional notions of national cinema entrenched by a few long-standing directors, dubbed the 'dinosaurs'. Films from this time depict an Argentina with social problems, namely unemployment and disaffected youth, framed within a nihilist poetic. Some films garnered international acclaim and reintroduced the nation on the world cinematic stage. Moreover, with the introduction of the Buenos Aires International Independent Film Festival in 1999, films such as *Pizza, birra, faso* (*Pizza, Beer, Smokes*, 1997), *Mundo grúa* (*Crane World*, 1999), *Esperando al mesías* (*Waiting for the Messiah*, 2000), *La ciénaga* (*The Swamp*, 2001), *Glue-Historia adolescent en el medio de la nada* (*Glue*, 2005) and *Agua* (*Water*, 2006) now had a platform from which to be exhibited and critically praised in the annals of world cinema.

This study thus looks at Argentine cinema through the social contexts of its productions with a special focus on state cultural policy toward cinema at the time. Because the majority of films were produced with the help of the state, a major question put forth by this study is to what extent state film policy helped shape many of the kinds of films produced in a particular era.

It also explores the impact of economic policy, politics and cultural mores in shaping film legislation and cultural policy in Argentina. The administrative policies implemented in Brazil, Mexico and Cuba differed from those in Argentina, yet there were similar issues at stake for these countries. For example, most of the films produced from the 1980s onward were 'quality' films, that is, films that displayed higher production values with the intention of dissemination abroad to reach film festival audiences. Thus, rather than producing a large quantity of low-budget films for domestic audiences, each of these countries produced a few films with higher budgets and more well-established actors. A broad shift occurred away from *un cine pobre* (a poor cinema) to *un cine rico* (a wealthy cinema). The phrase *un cine pobre* refers to the vision of film articulated by the New Latin American Cinema movement, the militant leftist political movement active in the 1960s and 1970s that held that cinema should be made to expose the underdevelopment and grim social realities of a Latin America in crisis. *Un cine rico*, by contrast, refers to glossy films geared toward middle-class audiences and international film festival consumption. After the crisis, discourses further divided camps into the 'low-to-no-budget filmmakers' (a renaming of *un cine pobre*) versus the 'industrial auteurs' (*un cine rico*) who jockeyed for inclusion into the 'independent' film camp. The case of Argentina clearly illustrates this shift in film production values, beginning in the period of redemocratisation.

CHAPTER I

FROM THE STUDIO SYSTEM ERA TO THE DIRTY WAR

With the advent of sound technology, Argentina was the first to produce sound films in Spanish (Di Núbila, Vol. 1, 1959). The period of the 1930s was a time of rapid industrialisation for Argentina (España 2000b). When sound technology was first introduced, two film studios replete with sound equipment were erected in 1933. With the coming of sound, the Argentines were able to take advantage of a treasured musical legacy that enjoyed widespread popularity throughout Latin America: the tango.

The first sound film, *Tango!* (1933), by José Moglia Barth, was an overwhelming success. By hiring already well-known performers from the world of theatre and tango, such as singer-actress Libertad Lamarque, theatre actor Pepe Arias, comedic actress Tita Merello and singer Azucena Maizani, filmmakers could ensure that patrons from the popular theatre and those who listened to *radionovelas* would attend the newly-developed sound cinema. Luis Sandrini, a recently discovered actor from the popular stage, was considered the first movie star due to his popularity as 'the poor kid from the barrio, immature and insecure' (España 2000b: 57).

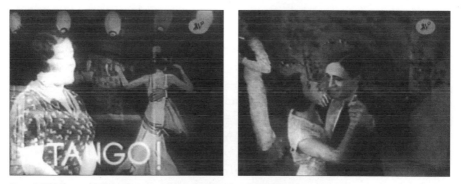

Tango! (1933): a vehicle to showcase Argentina's national song and dance

Argentina Sono Film, one of the two new studios, was founded by Atilio Mentasti and his family, Italian immigrants who began by working in the theatre and later established a cinema business that continues to thrive to this day. Sono Film began by importing film equipment from the United States with the help of RCA Victor (España 2000b). The other studio, Lumiton, was founded by a group of radio businessmen who set up a studio in Munro, a suburb of Buenos Aires. Lumiton's owners Enrique T. Susini, César Guerrico, Luis Romero Carranza and Miguel Mugica based their studio on the Hollywood model and imported Hollywood technicians John Alton, a director of photography, and Lazlo Kish, a sound designer (originally from Hungary) to work with them (Getino 2005). Both studios were privately financed, and managed to stay successful by employing actors from the popular theatre and *radionovelas*. National film production at this time followed a business model in which the state did not encourage film production or offer subsidies. This in part may explain why the majority of films produced followed a commercial model of genre filmmaking. Besides Sono Film and Lumiton, there were others such as Estudios Cinematográficos Argentinos SIDE, Buenos Aires Film, General Belgrano, Artistas Argentinos Asociados and Pampa Film, along with some shorter-lived, smaller companies. Argentina's first film processing lab, Laboratorios Alex, was founded during this time and gained fame throughout Latin America after 1937 as one of the finest laboratories to develop and print celluloid (ibid.).

The rise of popular film magazines such as *Mundo radial*, *Estrellas*, *Radiolandia* and *Cine Argentino* solidified the formation of a vibrant star system. What once solely featured movie stars from the United States and Europe slowly made way for columns and feature spreads of Argentine actors and actresses (Bermúdez *et al.* 2003). Famous starlets such as Tita Merello, Mecha Ortiz and Zully Moreno graced the magazine covers. This print culture helped to create a widespread and popular base of filmgoers.

According to Octavio Getino (2005), Argentine film during this time developed ideologically in two different ways: (i) a bourgeois style of filmmaking that was the dominant form (characterised by parlour-room melodramas and costume dramas, directors such as Francisco Mugica and Luis César Amadori, for example) and (ii) a popular (in the sense of 'the people') cinema that gained prominence not only in Argentina but throughout Spanish-speaking countries. For the latter cinema, the film scripts themselves utilised elements from the popular theatre sketch, the *sainete*.[1] By appealing to an already established working-class entertainment sector, these films were guaranteed a mass audience. Admission prices were low, and movie theatres were built in working-class neighbourhoods. Popular themes such as the tango were set in the poor urban neighbourhoods with which audiences were familiar. Among other locales used was the pampa region of the interior, where dramatic gaucho films were set. Argentine cinema in the 1930s and early 1940s was popular at home as well as throughout Latin America.

One director who exemplifies this rural setting for Argentine cinema was Mario Soffici, a prolific filmmaker who produced films in almost every popular genre. His most remarkable works were his films of the late 1930s. Shot in rural settings, these films formed part of a genre called the 'social-folkloric'. They dealt with themes of social justice, and sought to expose some of the degrading conditions that working people had to endure in the agricultural sectors of Argentina. Popular writers and directors such as Soffici took up the banner of popular nationalism and utilised the gaucho figure within a framework of realism, unlike the romanticised images of the elite. The most successful film, *Prisonieros de la tierra* (*Prisoners of the Land*, 1939), filmed in the Misiones region, depicts the exploitation of *yerba maté* (Paraguayan tea) workers in a rural town by a wealthy landowner. It is a powerful drama about a *mensú* (an indentured labourer) who works tirelessly for the patron, and is beaten relentlessly. This film documents the inhumane treatment of workers by a powerful landowner; a series of events leads a rebellious worker to exact revenge on the landowner by beating him with a bullwhip and leaving him to die drifting on a raft. Jorge Luis Borges, acclaimed essayist, storyteller and poet, described this sequence as 'one of the most powerful in memory' (quoted in Barnard & Rist 1996: 18). Other films include *Viento norte* (*North Wind*, 1937), *Kilómetro 111* (1938), *El viejo doctor* (*The Old Doctor*, 1939) and *Tres hombres del rio* (*Three Men by the River*, 1942). Soffici's film career spanned forty films, the last one made in 1961.

During this period, Argentina entered a phase in film history known as the *época de oro* (the golden age). Prevalent genres were tango films, detective films, gangster films, comedies and melodramas. Prolific directors such as Manuel Romero, who produced 53 films and wrote 178 theatre plays and 146 songs, worked for Lumiton. Most known for his genre films with a populist bent, he is most famous for his film noir *Fuera de la ley* (*Outside the Law*, 1938) and romantic comedies like *La rubia del camino* (*The Blonde on the Road*, 1938), starring Paulina Singerman and singer Fernando Borel. This film is about a wealthy, flighty woman who hits the road to flee a bad marriage to an Italian count. She meets a truck driver and becomes involved in a passionate romance. In addition to tango films such as *Historia del tango* (*History of Tango*, 1949), he made well-received women's films such as *Mujeres que trabajan* (*Women Who Work*, 1983), starring Mecha Ortiz, about an upper-class woman whose father commits suicide, forcing her to live in poverty and to work for the first time in her life (Tarruella 1993).

The success of these films and the strength of Argentine film studios created a source of tension for the US film industry. Jorge Schnitman (1978) postulates that for this reason the United States decided to produce Spanish-language films for Latin American consumption. However, these films did not prove to be very successful with local audiences. Another issue at stake was documented by Gaizka S. de Usabel (1982), in which Mexicans, Cubans, Brazilians and Argentines began protesting English-language sound cinema in the 1930s on the grounds that it threatened their national languages. In Cuba, representative Gabriel Ariza introduced a bill urging a ban on English sound films. *La Prensa* of Buenos Aires noted that American talkies were 'a danger to Argentine culture'; thus, it was logical that the United States produce films in Spanish, thereby respecting the national language of these countries. Usabel notes that 'if English antagonised the Latin American people, Hollywood was ready to provide them with Spanish-language films' (1982: 85).

For these reasons US companies set up film studios to produce Spanish-language films both in the United States and abroad. In 1929, Paramount studios set up production in Joinville, France, where Spanish-language films were made with Latin themes in the hope of capturing the Latin market. Other strategies were implemented such as employing famous Latin movie stars and celebrities for US films. For example, the famed tango singer Carlos Gardel was asked by Paramount to shoot films in Spanish. Gardel made eight films before his untimely death in 1935. Paramount invariably profited from films such as *Luces de Buenos Aires* (*Buenos Aires Lights*, 1931) and *Tango Bar* (1935); one film executive noted that 'since his death, the value of his pictures has increased so tremendously, that perhaps 30% of Paramount's 1935 business can be traced directly to his pictures' (quoted in Usabel 1982: 96). Between 1930 and 1936, no fewer than 113 Spanish-language films were produced by North American companies (Pinto 1973: 423).

While ultimately they were a short-lived phenomenon, Hollywood Spanish-language films served as an opportunity for Latin American film technicians from Argentina and Mexico to go to Hollywood and train there. Ana M. López (2000), in her study of transnational filmmakers in Latin America, describes how director Carlos Hugo Christensen left his native Argentina and directed films in Chile and Venezuela before returning to his homeland. He later fled Perón's Argentina and lived in exile in Brazil, where he was able to continue his career in filmmaking. Thus, the movement of directors and talent across borders further complicates the notion of a purely 'national cinema' and how images are represented.

Through the early 1940s Argentine filmmakers continued to produce notable films that are recognised today as prime examples of the 'golden age' of Argentine cinema. In 1942 Lucas Demare's *La guerra gaucha* (*The Gaucho War*) was a grand success at the box office. Based on the poetry of Leopoldo Lugones, this film depicts, in the words of film historian Domingo Di Núbila, 'the guerrilla war fought in the northern mountains when the valiant gauchos, at the point of their lances, held the Spanish Army that came to crush the newly declared Argentine Independence' (1959: 9–10). This film was produced by the newly-formed studio, Artistas Argentinos Asociados (AAA), made up of directors such as Demare; theatre actors Enrique Muiño, Francisco Petrone and Elías Alippi; a young film actor, Angel Mangaña; producer Enrique Faustin, and financially backed by the owner of another studio, San Miguel. This studio, based on the

United Artists ownership model, continued to produce well-received films such as Hugo Fregonese's *Pampa barbara* (*Barbaric Pampas*, 1945), a film also set in the pampas.

Argentina's studio system continued to produce high quality films of the melodramatic, gangster, comedy, tango and gaucho genres until the film industry's decline in 1946. The rise of Perón and his sanctioned film legislation and censorship were major factors.

The US Good Neighbor Policy was another factor in the general decline of economic and political stability in Argentina. During World War Two, the United States created this political, economic and cultural policy aimed at improving hemispheric relations between the US and Latin America. The objectives of the Good Neighbor Policy were twofold: (i) to insure that nations in Latin America were joined in the Allied war effort and were not associated with the Axis or Communist sympathisers; and (ii) to allow the US access to Latin America as a source of raw materials and a market for goods, including films. Because Argentina did not side with the Allies, instead preferring neutrality, it was castigated by an economic boycott. Beginning in 1941, the US sold only small rations of raw film stock to Argentina, and eventually refused to sell it altogether. The film industry in Argentina, at the time considered the most profitable and advanced in Latin America, began to lose its hold on the Spanish-language market.

The United States, vis-à-vis the Good Neighbor Policy agency, the Office of the Coordinator of Inter-American Affairs (OCIAA) and its Hollywood counterpart, the Motion Picture Society of the Americas (MPSA), withheld film stock from the Argentine film industry because of Argentina's pro-Axis sentiments. That is, some charged that Argentina produced pro-Axis newsreels and other propaganda on behalf of the government. However, my research (2004) demonstrates that although there was one film studio – Argentina Sono Film – that produced newsreels sympathetic to the Axis, by and large, the industry remained firmly democratic and did not sympathise with the government's censorship tactics against US pro-Allied films. The Argentine government during wartime was headed by a succession of conservative military leaders who admired the Spanish fascist leader Francisco Franco and Italy's leader, *Il duce*, Benito Mussolini. While the Castillo government (1940–43) declared neutrality mainly to continue trade with both Britain and Germany, they censored Hollywood wartime films such as Billy Wilder's *Five Graves to Cairo* (1943) for its anti-Axis references. Later, government officials instituted protectionist policies such as the imposition of Argentine newsreel requirements in all movie theatres, and, finally, a screen quota was mandated in 1944 limiting the number of US theatrical releases that could be imported. After the enactment of these restrictive policies, the US acted in its own best interests: the State Department decided to limit, and later ban, the sale of raw film stock to Argentina – much to the dismay of Argentina's democratic and highly developed film industry. The

Argentine cinema has never been as highly organised or as financially successful as it was during this 'golden age', the historical moment before the US ban on the sale of raw film stock.

A final but no less important factor in explaining the US boycott against Argentina was the threat posed to the US industry by the Argentine film industry: it was powerful and could compete quite well against its Hollywood counterpart for the profitable Spanish-language market. Hollywood looked to Latin America as a potential market to replace the collapsed European market. Film historian Tino Balio writes that 'to offset conditions in the war-torn European countries, Hollywood turned to Latin America. There, although the industry had a near-monopoly, the market had never been fully exploited' (1976: 223). These external forces hastened the decline of the Argentine film industry during World War Two.

Argentina, out of all the Latin American countries, was the most promising market for films. According to *Variety*, in 1939, Argentina had 1,208 movie houses – more theatres than all of the other Latin American nations put together (Anon. 1942c). Film studios such as Argentina Sono Film, Lumiton, Artistas Argentinos Asociados and others hit their peak of popularity in 1942, when there were six majors and 15 to twenty smaller units (Anon. 1942g).[2] This film industry was the most technologically advanced in Latin America.[3]

In 1935 Argentina produced 22 sound films. In 1939, fifty films were released. Argentina was the most popular and prolific producer of films in Latin America, and was a considerable competitor to Hollywood in the Spanish-speaking world. It was the world's largest producer of Spanish-language films; each major studio could produce approximately twelve features annually (Anon. 1942b). Argentine cinema had surpassed all other Latin American film industries to become the 'first rank in the Spanish-production field and increasingly becoming a [US] competitor for Latin screen time' (Josephs 1942: 91). With the imposition of the US boycott, the scarcity of raw film stock created a profound crisis in the industry; a few film studios survived on black market dealings, but many film studios shut down. Production numbers slid from an all-time high of 56 films produced in 1942 to 24 films in 1944 (Getino 2005).

As historian Peter Smith argues, the Good Neighbor Policy was a move away from a historic pattern of United States intervention in Latin America, but it still functioned as a way to maintain US hegemony over the Western Hemisphere. As Smith puts it, 'Instead of relying on Teddy Roosevelt's "big stick", on military force and intervention, the United States could now rely on economic strength and diplomatic persuasion' (1996: 87). However, the US developed a tailored approach to each neighbour, and befriended cooperative countries such as Mexico, Colombia and Venezuela who had immediately allied with the US during the war. Argentina, in its state of neutrality, was considered a threat to US national security, and thus subject to an economic blockade of many agricultural and industrial items, film stock included. In addition, the US withdrew its ambassador and withheld diplomatic recognition until Argentina sided with the Allied cause in 1945.

The central agency to oversee international film industry relations was the Office of the Coordinator for Inter-American Affairs (OCIAA), renamed in 1945 the Office of Inter-American Affairs (OIAA), headed by Nelson A. Rockefeller. One of its strategies was to bring Latin American nations closer to the US by staging good-will tours throughout the Americas by famous actors and directors such as Orson Welles, Carmen Miranda and Walt Disney. Another objective was to distance itself from the traditional Hollywood practice of denigrating Latin American themes through insensitive portrayals of Latin American characters, themes and locales.[4]

Another aim was to work with the heads of Hollywood studios to create a series of Latin-themed films that would resonate favourably with Latin American audiences. Under the jurisdiction of the OCIAA was the Motion Pictures Division, headed by John Hay Whitney (who also served as the vice president and director of the Museum of Modern Art film library) from 1940 to 1944 and later by Francis Alstock from 1944 to 1946.

Another organisation that worked hand in hand with the Motion Picture Division was its private industry counterpart, the Motion Picture Society for the Americas (MPSA). This society, financed by a congressional grant, was made up of Hollywood directors, producers and others and served as a liaison between government and industry. It acted as a bridge between the State Department, War Production Board (WPB), Office of Price Administration, Hollywood Victory Committee, War Activities Committee and other government agencies in order to facilitate the production of pictures with Latin American content. In a report published by the MPSA in 1944–45, its duties included reviewing books and scripts with inter-American themes for film production, and to 'supervise and confer in connection with the production of motion pictures relating to the national defense and morale, and inter-American relationships and activities'. During this period (1933–45) many films with Latin themes were produced by Hollywood. By February 1943, for example, thirty films with Latin American themes or locales had been released and 25 more were in production. By 1945, 84 films dealing with Latin American themes had been produced (López 1993). Films with Latin themes were circulated both as theatrical releases (such as Disney's *Saludos Amigos* (1943) and as 16mm instructional films on public health issues. In a progress report filed by Nelson Rockefeller he stated that the Motion Picture Division had

> created a two-way exchange of non-theatrical 16mm films among the American Republics. Already both Spanish and Portuguese versions of 23 reels of such films either are ready or en route southward from the United States. Their varied subject matter ranges from the power of our war weapons to striking scientific and health studies. (1943/44)

Another OCIAA memo specifically addressing ways to target Argentina through film states,

> Through regular commercial distribution and through our program of distributing 16 mm prints through schools, colleges, civic organizations, and the Embassy, we endeavor to win the good will of Argentina by showing it in its best light and in the many varied aspects of its life and culture. Many of the subjects are concerned with military subjects, showing the power and strength of the United States. (Anon. 1942h)

Clearly the films sent to Latin America had propagandistic ends and proudly showcased the military and technological prowess of the North. According to a State Department memorandum on OCIAA's overall activity as of 1942, 'it was the greatest outpouring of propagandistic material by a state ever' (quoted in Smith 1996: 85).

As mentioned previously, the MPSA's main objectives included dispelling the caricatures and stereotypes that were the norm in depicting Latin Americans in Hollywood cinema. In a memo issued by the MPSA to the Foreign Committee in 1941, there was a list drawn up delineating the stereotypes of Latin American characters on film that were to be considered taboo to Hollywood producers. Some of the recommendations included:

1. Don't burlesque any Latin American. If comedy is required, strive to have it funny, not idiotic.
2. Don't offend the dignity of any government by ridiculing its institutions, political beliefs, officials, customs, or peoples.
3. Don't imagine that every Mexican wears a 'Charro' suit or that every Argentinian dresses as a 'Gaucho'.
4. Don't have every actor that impersonates a Latin American use exaggerated 'broken' English. It grates on the nerves of every English-speaking person in Latin America, besides which, many Americans are getting by in Latin America with a rotten line of Spanish and they don't like to be laughed at.
5. Don't use Latin American music/costumes in a Latin American scene that does not belong to the country that it represents. (Anon. 1941c: 1–2)

In a memo specifically addressing ways to better communicate with the Argentine people via film, the MPSA hired additional advisors to help 'exercise censorship of offensive scenes, dialogue, and situations' in two ways: (i) a special Latin American representative of the Hays Office would check on the scripts during production and after completion of the films to prevent any distasteful scenes being screened, and (ii) the Latin American Board of Review of the Hays Office would review all films with a South American locale (Anon. 1942h).

Another concern of the MPSA was for the welfare of the Hollywood film industry in Latin America during the war. During the period 1939–45 US war movies and other forms of propaganda were sent to Latin America as part of the Good Neighbor Policy. Although films of that nature were popular for a while, reports stating that Brazil and other countries had tired of those films alarmed the US film studios.

Films were not only sent to Latin America to help engender support for the war effort, but also to create a positive image for the United States. In the US, the Office of Censorship under Byron Price made 'a clear mandate to refuse to allow the export of pictures showing the country in a bad light' (Anon. 1942j: 42). The mandate was used in the case of Frank Capra's *Mr. Smith Goes to Washington* (1939). It was banned for export because it challenged the notion that Washington politics were morally sound at that time. It, along with films such as *The Grapes of Wrath* (1940), was seen to give an unflattering portrait of the US.

Further issues tackled by the MPSA were the Argentine government's censorship through its Dirección de Espectáculos. During the war, Hollywood films were cut and reassembled in Argentina in ways that repeatedly angered the US. According to Usabel (1982), the Argentine government censors acted under repeated pressure from pro-Axis embassies. By 1943, there were forty US motion pictures that had either been banned due to their anti-Axis nature or withheld from distribution by their producers rather than submit to deletions demanded by Argentine censors (Pryor 1943). Among the banned films were Twentieth Century Fox's *Secret Agent of Japan* (1942), banned at the request of the Japanese Embassy in Buenos Aires, and *The Invaders* (1941) by Columbia Pictures, banned at the behest of the German Embassy (1942d; 1942e). Paramount's *For Whom the Bell Tolls* (1943), a Hollywood picture sympathetic to the Spanish resistance against Franco, was banned due to pressure from the Spanish government. This film had been produced in consultation with the OCIAA. Throughout the war, the head of the Argentine censorship board cut anti-Axis references from Hollywood films. Allusions to dictators and remarks about Fascist authorities were deleted from US films (Fagg 1963).

One film, Charlie Chaplin's *The Great Dictator* (1940), caused a scandal in Argentina. On 8 January 1941 the foremost Argentine film trade paper, *Heraldo del cine*, reported that the Argentine censorship board had decided to ban this film, a step that various cultural entities had appealed to the executive power to revise. However, films banned in Buenos Aires were not necessarily forbidden in the provinces, and on 5 February the film was shown in the province of Paraná at the Cines Rex and Select. Historically, national censorship policy had never been centralised, and provinces had the power to determine if a work or cultural product such as film could be shown (Félix-Didier 2004; Sendros 2004). Thus, *The Great Dictator* was shown in the provinces before it ever played in Buenos Aires. Furthermore, Usabel notes that during the war many Argentines crossed over to Uruguay to see the film (1982: 154). In April 1942, an article written by representatives of the Argentine Academy of Motion Picture Arts and Sciences declared that *The Great Dictator* deserved to be on the top-ten list of the best films of 1942. They were dismayed that they could not list it because it was officially banned the year prior (Anon. 1941a: 1). The film was finally released in Buenos Aires in August of 1945, playing for ten weeks to sizeable audiences.

This form of censorship infuriated the Hollywood film industry and was a contributing factor in Congress's decision to enact a ban on the sale of raw film stock to Argentina in 1941. A *Variety* article stated that US picture shipments first needed to be previewed by Argentine censorship officials in New York City before they were allowed to be shipped into the country (Anon. 1942f). According to Usabel, the US authorities ignored the Castillo government's mandate and began to restrict the sale of raw film stock in retaliation (1982: 170). Robert Vogel, an executive at MGM studios and a member of the Motion Picture Society of the Americas, recalled in an interview that, generally, the MPSA tried to improve Hollywood films that were exported to Latin America (that is, make them less offensive to Latin audiences) but, additionally, they made sure that US films were not 'incorrectly exhibited in Latin America'. By this, Vogel referred to instances whereby US films, usually of the war genre, were re-edited in Argentina in ways to make the Nazi characters look like heroes and the US and Allies look weak. Vogel relays an anecdote relating to this situation:

We had a picture at MGM in which Joan Crawford played an American lady living in Paris [*Reunion in France*, 1942, directed by Jules Dassin, produced by Joseph Mankiewicz]. John Wayne, a parachutist who volunteered to serve in the British Air Force although he was an American, landed behind the scenes and worked his way toward her home. This was during the German occupation. And a couple of German officers enter the room – we are not yet at war with Germany officially – and they ask Wayne who he is and Wayne tells them he's an American volunteering to help the British, whereupon the leading German officer spits at him. And Wayne gives him one blow to the chin and knocks him down unconscious and escapes. Now, in Argentina, which was neutral in favor of Germany, they eliminated the spitting so that all that happened was that this German officer comes and looks at Mr Wayne and Wayne knocks him unconscious. And Wayne becomes the heavy. So of course I forbade exhibition of that picture in Argentina. (1991: 185)

However, in *Heraldo del cine*, there was a review of the abovementioned film in 1942, which suggests that the film was ultimately screened. Based on the review, it is clear that the re-cut version was not the one screened; nevertheless, the screened version was three minutes shorter than its original length.[5]

Billy Wilder's *Five Graves to Cairo*, produced by Paramount, would only be allowed in Argentina if the following changes were made: the Nazi officer Rommel, played by Erich von Stroheim, was to be identified as 'Brommel' rather than by his real moniker. This was an easy change to make, as the name was only mentioned twice in the film. Another line that an Argentine censor requested be omitted was the statement by von Stroheim as Rommel that 'we shall take the big, fat cigar out of Mr Churchill's mouth and make him say "Heil"' (quoted in Pryor 1943). Although the US studios reacted angrily to censorship and notified authorities that they would abandon the Argentine market, they stayed there (Anon. 1943f).

The censorship of Hollywood films was serious, but it was only one of the reasons the US punished Argentina by banning the sale of raw film stock. The US government agencies comprising the War Production Board, the Office of the Coordinator of Inter-American Affairs, the Board of Economic Warfare and the State Department decided to allocate quotas of raw film stock to various Latin American countries on a monthly basis. Argentina's quota, once reserved for purchase by Buenos Aires agents, was instead sold to Mexico and Chile. At that point, Argentina no longer had access to German film stock, and was dependent on the US supply to keep its industry alive. When this boycott went into effect, it had deleterious effects on the film industry. Only the two most powerful film studios, Argentina Sono Film and Lumiton, had enough reserves to last a full year of production. Countries such as Brazil and Chile had a black market for film stock, but this was an expensive endeavour.

I would argue that on the one hand, there was a legitimate reason to fear that the Argentine government under Castillo's leadership was cooperating with the Axis powers. It remained on friendly terms with Germany, Italy and England in terms of trade and diplomacy. On a cultural level, there was evidence of pro-Axis ties to Germany in such newspapers as *El Pampero*, *La Fronda*, *El Federal*, *Cabildo* and *Clarinada*, the latter of which was also anti-Semitic.

On the other hand, in the case of the film industry, the studio system in Argentina was flourishing in the 1930s to 1940s and was not dependent on state support. In other words, government policy had little bearing on the content of the films because they were not subsidised in any fashion. In researching the possible link between the production of pro-Axis propaganda and the Argentine film industry, there has only been one clear indication of evidence that Argentina Sono Film, the oldest film studio in Argentina, was producing short newsreels sympathetic to the Axis. The newsreel *Noticieros Panamericanos*, discussed below, was exhibited in Chile and Paraguay as well as in Argentina. In a 1941 article for the *Hollywood Reporter*, Vincent de Pascal writes,

There have been charges in several Argentine publications that Argentina Sono Film: (i) is financed by the German Embassy through its fiscal agency here, the Banco Germanico; (ii) that its newsreel, *Noticieros Panamericanos* has a distinct Nazi flavour, frequently shows the German ambassador, the bigwigs of the Banco Germanico, and often shows posters advertising German railways in scenes of its films; (iii) that those at the head of the organisation, as well as its artistic and technical personnel are Naziphiles; (iv) that its pictures receive unusual amounts of publicity in pro-Nazi organs and that it patronises these sheets to a great extent for advertising its product; (v) that raw and then anti-democratic cracks are made to crop up on the dialogue of some of its pictures; and finally, (vi) it is believed, though not conclusively proven, this studio receives direct subsidies from the Embassy's Banco Germanico. Though these changes would ordinarily have been open to ruinous libel suits if not true, no attempt has been made to deny them.

The only other clear allegiance to the Axis in the film sector was film critic Miguel P. Tato (known to be the renowned 'Nestor' in the newspaper *El Mundo*), who was an overt Nazi sympathizer and in 1942 was employed as a press attaché of the Japanese Embassy (Anon. 1941/42). In 1944 he was named by the government as the supervising director in charge of production of all government propaganda shorts and documentaries. In addition, he wrote film reviews for the pro-Axis paper *Cabildo* (Anon. 1944). One other notoriously conservative film critic who allied with Argentina Sono Film during this period was Raúl Alejandro Apold, a film critic at *El Mundo* who became head of publicity at Sono Film in 1941 (Anon. 1941b). Apold was later to become the most hard-line, right-wing censor in Perón's administration. However, this was the exception rather than the rule, according to Domingo Di Núbila. He writes,

> [In 1944] Washington could be calm: now there was no danger of infiltration of fascist ideas in Latin America via the cinema. This was a tragic irony, because despite the dominant pro-German elements in the circles of power in Argentina, our cinema had always been fundamentally democratic and contributed various films to the theme of freedom. (1959: 44)

Moreover, some studio heads, such as Tito Bontana of Baires Film Studios, were labelled by the US as 'ultra-democratic' because they refused to work with any company dealing with the Axis. Botana stated in a 1942 interview: 'We have even placed a British company on our private blacklist because it was handling an Axis product, and we won't advertise any of the company's other non-Axis merchandise as long as it carries the other' (quoted in Anon. 1942a). In addition, there were reports that many Argentine producers were opposed to government neutrality but felt helpless to speak outright. One producer, who remained unnamed, stated,

> It is unfair to consider us all totalitarian-lovers simply because our government decided to remain neutral. The majority of us are opposed to that policy, but there is little we can do about it individually. We producers should not be penalised for our government's policies, but we believe – on the other hand – that we should get an even break with other Latin American countries

such as Brazil and Uruguay in the shipment of vitally essential materials. And raw film stock to Argentina's motion picture industry can mean saving or losing a $25,000,000 investment. (De Pascal 1942)

Overall, it was not Argentine feature films themselves that could be labelled Nazi propaganda, but rather some pro-Axis, Argentine-made newsreels and some German film imports that were screened in a few movie houses in Buenos Aires. Some of those theatres were the German studio UFA House, the Teatro San Martín, the Teatro Alvear, the Astoria and the Cineac Theatre. Usabel notes that in the interior, pro-Axis movies represented only one percent of films shown during World War Two. In Buenos Aires, only 12 movie houses out of the capital's 624 showed any pro-Axis films (1982: 153). Furthermore, to put this exhibition of German films into perspective, a 1943 study showed that in that year, there was a ratio of 65 US films to one German film shown in Argentina (Anon. 1943e).

One task of the Coordination Committee of Argentina within the OCIAA was to set up blacklists and 'grey lists' of movie theatres that showed pro-Axis films, as well as other anti-democratic companies. In Buenos Aires, Hollywood distributors received the official US blacklist, which contained twelve thousand names of Argentine exhibitors, producers, labs, distributors and theatre owners with whom the Americans were forbidden to conduct business (Anon. 1943c). This Coordination Committee, working with the Motion Picture Division of the OCIAA, would secure the cooperation of the Treasury, State Department, Board of Economic Welfare and other interested agencies in enforcing the ban. For example, Kodak Argentina was advised not to sell raw film stock to Argentina Sono Film, since their newsreels *Noticieros Panamericanos* were being screened at the Cineac, a blacklisted theatre owned by Juan López Hojas (Anon. 1942h).

Thus, due to some inconsistencies within the Argentine film industry (for example, some theatre owners were sympathetic to the Axis while the majority of film producers sided with the Allies; the way in which the government itself applied censorship to US films), the US State Department had to carefully weigh the pros and cons of selling raw film stock to Argentina. A 1944 State Department memo from Norman Armour, US Ambassador to Argentina, sums up the debate well:

> There may conceivably be some question as to whether or not it is completely fair to the national producing industry to use the raw stock situation as a lever to secure sympathetic treatment for American pictures in terms of censorship from the Argentine Government. If the aim is entirely one of helping to win the war, and if an embargo can be expected to aid in achieving that aim, it is undoubtedly justifiable, regardless of who may be hurt in the process; If on the other hand, the concept of commercial advantage is a part of the picture, and if an embargo would result primarily in benefit to American

commercial interests at the expense of an Argentine industry, the measure may be considerably more difficult to justify. (Armour 1944)

Armour expresses concern about a conflict of interest that could occur by instituting a ban that could potentially foster the collapse of Argentina's film industry and, in essence, help the Hollywood film industry maintain its edge in Argentina's market.[6] Clearly, he articulates the tension between politically undermining an industry that may have produced or exhibited 'enemy' propaganda, and abetting US economic interests by securing a non-competitive market for Hollywood films. He goes on to characterise this strategy as a 'present opportunity, heaven-sent in that patriotism and self-interest call for support of the same action – an embargo on raw stock for a competitor who is becoming more and more active, and whose very life depends for the moment on a single source of supply'. Ambassador Armour concludes the memo by stating his fear that Argentina would see this boycott of raw film stock as a commercial move rather than an ideological one. While debates emerged in various memos, ultimately the agency decided to impose an embargo and thus punish Argentina until 1946.

The United States punished Argentina at the same time that it lauded Mexico for its participation in the Allied cause. Mexico's film industry, until this time, had been trailing Argentina in terms of the technical quality, as well as the quantity, of its films. During the war, however, the Mexican film industry flourished, due in part to its special treatment by the United States. Mexican films increased in output and flowered into what is now called Mexico's golden age of cinema, from the 1940s to the 1950s. According to *Variety*, the desire to position Mexico as the most prolific and popular film producer in Latin America was no secret:

A terrific US pressure is being exerted to eliminate Argentina as the world's greatest producer of Spanish-language films, and elevate Mexico into the spot. Action is part of the squeeze being exerted by this country to blast Argentina from its friendly attitude towards the Axis. Francis Alstock, film chief of the Committee of Inter-American Affairs, is constantly in and out of Mexico helping the industry. WPB has cracked down hard on the volume of raw stock being shipped to Argentina, and is lavish with Mexico. (Anon. 1943b)

In 1942 the Mexican film industry produced 49 films. By 1944, its production had increased to 78 films. As previously mentioned, Argentina's production in the same year slid down to 24 films, a 50 percent decrease from its 1942 level of 56 (Schnitman 1978). In 1944, Florence Lowe, a film critic for *Variety*, commented that

The WPB is still awaiting word from the State Department on what the 1944 quotas to the various countries should be. You will recall that about a year ago, the allotment for Argentina was cut way back because of her flirting with the Axis and Mexico received a 'super-colossal' footage. (Lowe 1944)

Reports stated that rather than continuing to receive 40 million feet of film from the US, Argentina would receive 50 percent less in 1943. This represented the deepest cut in Latin America. In contrast, Mexico would be 'well taken care of' (Anon. 1943a). An interdepartmental memo from the Motion Picture Division of the OCIAA listed the reasons why the Hollywood film industry should aid the Mexican film industry technically, materially and financially. One reason was as follows:

> The fact is that Mexico will never be a competitor of the American companies no matter how much help is given to the Mexican industry. But if better Spanish-speaking pictures were made through the help extended to the Mexican industry, it should result in larger audiences, new theatres, and a strong and better motion picture situation in Latin America. It should strongly stimulate and develop the market for American pictures. It should help them become more profitable. The American company which helps the most may reap the greatest benefit. (Bohan 1942)

Other reasons offered related to tax incentives given to Hollywood that would make it risk-free to invest in their Mexican counterparts. Finally, according to Merwin L. Bohan, the plan might have resulted 'in developing Mexican talent, the best of which might be utilised in America' (1942).

Other efforts by the OCIAA to assist the Mexican film industry included donating film equipment to help build film studios. In a memo by OCIAA representatives John Hay Whitney and Francis Alstock, they stated that in order to avoid a monopoly of film studios, the OCIAA would help 'consolidate the interests of the Azteca and Stahl studios, and the other unit to be the Clasa studios'. In addition, they committed to help set up a finance fund for Mexican motion pictures and promised to send Hollywood film experts to help train Mexican technicians. Finally, the OCIAA offered to 'negotiate with the American Moving Picture industry for the commercial distribution of Mexican pictures in those countries and territories requested by the producers of the Mexican Committee', the body who met with representatives of the OCIAA (Whitney & Alstock 1942).

Film scholar Román Gubern explains why the United States aided the Mexican film industry (while debilitating Argentina):

> The OCIAA policy to favour the Mexican film industry has a double advantage from the point of view of United States interests. From an ideological perspective, an Allied country was a better guarantee of suitable motion picture content; from an economic point of view, reducing the importance of

the Argentine film industry in Latin America spared North American film companies a competitor from some sectors of the Latin American film market, and it gave North American entrepreneurs the opportunity to participate in the development of the film industry in Mexico. For instance, in 1945, 49 percent of the stock of Churubusco studios (the most important in Mexico in the 1940s) was owned by RKO. (1971: 95)

Thus, Mexico was seen by the Hollywood studios as a potentially lucrative place to invest in order to diversify their holdings.

Argentina's film industry declined primarily because it had to buy film stock on the black market from Chile and Brazil at inflated prices, thus incurring higher production costs.[7] At the same time, US films were entering Latin American markets at an unprecedented pace, in part due to the shrinkage of Europe's film markets, as previously mentioned, which had virtually shut down during the war. In 1945, eight large US distribution companies accounted for 62 percent of all films released in Argentina (Schnitman 1978). For this reason, there was clearly more at stake in systematically weakening the film industry than simply the threat of Nazi propaganda. In 1943, John B. Nathan, the managing director of Paramount for Argentina, Chile, Uruguay and Paraguay, stated that 'the quality of Argentine pictures is steadily improving, and they are getting better reception from the public, especially the interior, where they are taking playing time away from the Hollywood product' (Anon. 1943d). In short, this political pressure mounted by the US State Department and other agencies stunted national film production. From that point on, the once-powerful Argentine film industry was never able to recover its position as the most prolific and popular film industry in Latin America. The US was able to use its economic power and dominance to stifle what it perceived to be a political-economic threat.

Argentina declared war on the Axis on 27 March 1945, about two weeks before the war ended. Despite this, the US maintained its boycott of raw film stock until mid-1946, when the OCIAA was disbanded (Maranghello 2000). The budget for the OCIAA's first year of operation was $3.5 million; by the end of the war it was $45 million. As Rockefeller reflected in 1945, 'The United States came in with a program of truth in answer to enemy lies' (quoted in Smith 1996: 83). The Motion Picture Society of the Americas was the first of the war-born agencies in Hollywood to be created, in April 1941, and the last to be dismantled, on 28 February 1946.

This is what historian Ronald C. Newton (1992) has typified as the 'Nazi menace' in Argentina, which was used to justify the US government's isolation of the Argentine film industry. By refusing to supply it with raw film stock, the US seriously undermined the key to the film industry's survival.

In researching archival documents from the State Department and other film industry trade magazines and memos, one can conclude that the economic power of the Argentine film industry played a significant role in the motivation behind US actions taken against Argentina during World War Two. While it is true that the Argentine government was censoring US films, the United States retaliated to such an extent that it created a space for debate on how far to starve the film industry.

By 1944, the Argentine film industry was on the verge of collapse. This was due in large part to the external policies imposed upon it, but there were also internal problems that impeded its long-range success. In 1944, the main conflict to arise among the industry sectors was a dispute between Argentine producers and exhibitors. Producers demanded that a percentage of Argentine films be required to screen at movie theatres. The exhibitors, however, benefited most by exhibiting imported cinema and thus were opposed to any quota system. These existing internal management problems compelled film industry professionals, particularly from the producers' and exhibitors' realms, to appeal to the federal government to enact film policy measures in order to protect their interests. In 1944, Col. Juan Domingo Perón, then secretary of labour under the Castillo government (1943–46), sided with producers and mandated national film quotas as the first institutionalised film policy in Argentina.

The national screen quota was formulated as follows: each of the more than 2,500 first-run theatres in Buenos Aires was required to exhibit one national film every two months. The rest of the theatres around the city were obligated to screen one national film a month. Those theatres outside of the city and in other parts of the country had to project national films two weeks out of five. However, problems surfaced when production capacity could not satisfy the requirements of the quota. Producers, who were now officially guaranteed theatre exhibition, quickly produced many poor-quality, rapidly made, low-budget films, known as 'quota quickies'. Second-rate production companies arose that were responsible for creating these 'B' movies. However, by the mid-1950s, only a handful of companies – Argentina Sono Film, Artistas Argentinos Asociados, General Belgrano and a few small studios – had withstood the test of time and were still in operation.

Although this screen quota was clearly a nationalist effort at aiding the Argentine film industry by assisting national producers to screen their films, it also worked to further exacerbate tensions between the Argentine and US film sectors. The imposition of the screen quota not only affected Argentine exhibitors, but also US distributors and exhibitors, who were impeded in their business of selling Hollywood films in Argentina. In an airgram telegraphed memo from the American Embassy in Rio de Janeiro to the State Department dated 10 August 1944, Hart Preston comments, '[Quota system] Decree would mean fortune for local film industry if had raw film stock. Production almost stopped due to lack of raw film stock. Because United States furnishes all film, we've been able to uphold this decree for months. Then last month, Kodak and Dupont through stupidity or embassy mix-up shipped two million feet [to Argentina].' Thus, both the United States and Argentina were battling for film industry territory by mandating decrees or laws to try to punish or spite the other side. President Ramírez's policy was a nationalist move to protect the Argentine film industry, but it was also most likely in retaliation for the embargo on raw film stock set by the United States. While the US may have felt threatened by the import quota, this move did not in fact diminish the chances that big-budget Hollywood films would get exhibited. As director Héctor Olivera stated in a 1995 interview, 'Import quotas do not hurt the large US movie studios, as they lobby to get their films exported abroad. It is the small US independent film companies that suffer, as these films receive limited distribution.'

In a similar protectionist move, on 5 January 1944, President Ramírez issued a decree mandating that eight minutes of national newsreels be shown per film screening in Argentina. This further angered the US State Department because it meant that no longer could the US send their newsreels. Moreover, it meant that more pro-Axis newsreels could be screened at the government's bidding. Dean Acheson, head of the State Department, wrote to Norman Armour on 7 March 1944, stating that 'the Department considers that this decree not only impairs the value of the concession on motion pictures schedule in Schedule I of the trade agreement between the United States and Argentina, but is contrary to the spirit of Article II of the agreement ... The American companies may therefore find their revenues from newsreels reduced – if they can place them – or they may be forced eventually to withdraw from the market.'

In March 1944 General Ramírez had resigned and General Farrell took the helm with General Juan Perón as the vice president. By 1946 Perón had been voted into power, and during his first term continued the trend towards nationalist protectionist policies for the film industry. In addition, he began to nationalise newspapers such as *La Prensa* and other forms of mass media. The film industry maintained some fiscal autonomy, but censorship policies loomed large over the film industry during Perón's two governmental administrations.

In 1947, an agreement was struck between the producers and exhibitors whereby a surcharge of ten cents on each ticket was allotted toward film production. The price was raised incrementally until 1955, when it increased to seventy cents per ticket in all of the movie theatres in the country for that year. In addition, a system of film loans was established in 1948. Some loans were in the form of 'development', which included loans by the Banco Industrial to cover 70 percent of the cost of the film when it was completed. The other type of loan, called the *especial* ('special'), would also provide loans of up to 70 percent as long as the film's content relayed 'themes related to the Argentine experience' (Maranghello 1992: 92).

In 1950, lawmakers passed an import quota in the hope of promoting national film exhibition throughout Argentina. In that year, fewer foreign film licenses were issued. Only 131 films were allowed in, the lowest figure in Argentine film exhibition history (Maranghello 1992). However, the plan proved a failure; instead of creating more opportunities for national film exhibition and production, the film-going public was reduced by 30 percent, thereby creating even more financial problems for exhibitors.

Problems related to censorship also contributed to the decline of the industry. Because films were monitored closely in terms of content during Perón's administration from 1946 to 1955, many films were not well made due to changes in the script or propagandistic themes. Films were being produced, thanks to the mandatory exhibition law, but severe restrictions were placed on film scripts. From 1943 to 1955 cinema content was monitored by the head of a new state department that formed part of the Press, Distribution and Special Events entity.

In 1947 Raul Alejandro Apold led the distribution subsection. Known as the 'czar of Argentine film' because of his harsh censorship measures, Apold transformed the film industry into a bastion of government propaganda. Actors and screenwriters who did not conform to the Peronist nationalist party line were blacklisted, and some suffered repercussions for petty reasons, such as posing a threat to First Lady Eva Perón's acting career. For example, the most famous starlet of the day, Libertad Lamarque, was exiled to Mexico because she had angered Eva Perón. Famed film director Luis Saslavsky, who opted to make films based on European novels rather than Argentine nationalist ones, fled the country.

With the exception of a few quality films by Hugo del Carril, Leopoldo Torre Nilsson and Fernando Ayala, the film industry under Perón entered a state of crisis. The studio system suffered rapid decline, marked by the closures of twelve studios. For this reason, only 15 films were released in 1957, the lowest figure in two decades. Gustavo Castagna writes that 'the disappearance of the twelve studios, the retirement of principal players in the film industry, the arrival of television, and the increased absence of a public that no longer formed a line to see an Argentine film did not create an encouraging panorama at the end of the 1950s' (1993: 249).

Two years after Perón's 1957 deposal by a military junta, concerned film lobbyists convened with Congress and demanded that a national film body be created to administer and regulate cinematic activity in a systematic fashion. In 1959, the Instituto Nacional de Cinematografía (INC) (National Film Institute) was established on the basis of the new cinema law (62/57). The INC was established to oversee the following activities:

1. the development of Argentine cinema as an industry, business, art and medium of communication and education;
2. the guarantee of freedom of expression for the cinema, similar to that of the press;
3. the creation of an organisation dependent on the Minister of Education and Justice would be transferred to the Director General of Entertainment;
4. the categorising of films for exhibition in terms of quality, according to

two categories: 'A', which meant that the films received mandatory exhibition, and 'B', the films were not obligated to be shown;

5. an approval system of rating the film theatres and a determination of the exhibition cycles and the percentage of payment that exhibitors would receive per national film;

6. a rating system for films to protect underage children;

7. a film development fund which received revenues from a 10 percent tax on box office admissions as well as a tax on film imports;

8. the authorisation of economic benefits for the industry (bank credits, tax credits, special loans for film projects, film equipment, etc.);

9. the distribution of 'A' category films to the exterior. (Calistro 1992: 109)

The creation of other laws helped fortify the national film industry, but it did not solidify the political instabilities that plagued the INC management from 1957 to 1967. In this ten-year period, ten directors of the INC were hired and fired. Because the directors were constantly subject to the scrutiny of the film community and the popular press, they were routinely accused of mismanagement and dishonesty in financial transactions. This scepticism of the leadership within the film production sector, as well as a general societal mistrust in state institutions, would continue throughout the history of the National Film Institute. In addition to the INC, a new state-run film school, the Centro de Experimentación y Realización (CERC) (Centre for Film Production and Experimentation as it was named until 1999) was created to train young filmmakers and technicians.

With a clearly structured set of state-supported film measures and a training ground for film professionals, film producers were now able to rely on the state for financial and organisational support of the film industry. In practice, however, the filmmakers to benefit most directly from the new law were the established film directors such as Enrique Carreras, Julio Saraceni and Enrique Cahen Salaberry, who had worked during the studio era making musicals, comedies and other genre films. The lesser-established filmmakers who did not make films according to the dominant studio aesthetic were often classified with a 'B' status and thus failed to achieve exhibition.[8]

First-time filmmakers who were training under an increasingly fragmented studio system gained experience on their own through the creation of film societies in which short films were made and screened as an experimental art form. At this time there were no film schools, and very few opportunities to apprentice with a large studio. In 1956 the Association of Experimental Film was created, as well as the Association of Short Film Directors. In addition, this year marked the opening of the documentary film school in Santa Fé, at the behest of Fernando Birri. Two years later, Birri and his film students produced the critically acclaimed film *Tiré die* (*Throw Me a Dime*).

Although young filmmakers such as Birri were not given access to large film loans for feature films, the INC did create a fund for the production of short films (*cortometrajes*). These short films were inexpensive to make and helped new film directors develop their own artistic sensibilities and film aesthetics. An allocation of three percent of the film fund was directed toward short film production, and more than 250 films were made between 1958 and 1963 (Calistro 1992). These films were never shown publicly due to film exhibitors' refusal to screen them, and the issue of rating them kept state administrators from taking decisive action. Despite the lack of institutional support, the creation of a film culture based on *cortometrajes* helped spur on a young film movement during the 1960s known as the 'Generation of '60'.

From the late 1950s and throughout the 1960s, young Argentine bourgeois film directors were experimenting with new kinds of film language, creating an elite form of cinema often based on the metaphysical writing of national authors such as Jorge Luis Borges and Julio Cortázar. There was an urge to develop a more artistic and contemplative form of cinema, not unlike the *nouvelle vague* cinema coming from France at the same time. By creating their own cinematic language, these filmmakers were in effect breaking away from established filmic conventions of the studio era, or the *ciné de papá*. Only one of these Argentine filmmakers, José Martínez Suárez (who trained at Lumiton), came from a studio system background; the rest were trained in literature, journalism and one – Lautaro Murúa – as an actor. With the development of portable film equipment, films were shot outdoors with hand-held cameras utilising the city of Buenos Aires as backdrop. Stories of urban alienation from a middle-class youth perspective dominated the screens of this young cinematic subculture. Aside from those already mentioned above, these were filmmakers such as Manuel Antín, Simón Feldman, David José Kohon, Rodolfo Kuhn and others who began their careers making short films but later expanded to feature-length pieces.

Besides working on short films and organising their own screenings, young filmmakers were part of the *cine club* movement in the late 1950s and 1960s, which viewed films from Europe around that time (including auteur films by such directors as Ingmar Bergman, Michelangelo Antonioni, Alain Resnais and Federico Fellini). In addition, the arrival of specialised film journals from Europe and the United States, such as *Cahiers du cinema*, catalysed the formation of intellectual Argentine cinema journals such as *Gente de cine* (1951), *Cuadernos de cine* (1954) and *Tiempo de cine* (1960). This helped foment a young film subculture that was marginalised by the more traditional studio system (what little survived) and by the National Film Institute (INC), who felt that the films were not commercially viable enough. A few well-established filmmakers such as Leopoldo Torre Nilsson (considered the 'godfather' of the '60s generation')[9] and Fernando Ayala (co-founder of the Aries film studio with Héctor Olivera in 1958) did appreciate what the new filmmakers were trying to accomplish and worked to provide exposure for them.

One way these filmmakers eventually did gain attention and respect was through international film festivals, where many films from the Argentine new wave were well received. For example, the short film *Buenos Aires* by David José Kohon received a prize at a festival in Austria for young filmmakers in 1959, as well as the top prize for short films at the Mar del Plata film festival in Argentina the same year. Rodolfo Kuhn, director of the feature-length film *Los jovenes viejos* (*The Elderly Youth*, 1962), remembers his participation in the fourth annual Mar del Plata International Film Festival in 1962:

> The two jurors were representatives of the traditional and conformist Argentine cinema (very similar to the Spanish cinema supported by Franco's fascists). My film and other contemporary films signified for them a dangerous corruption through a different kind of cinema. The '60s generation' was born in Argentina, and for those stodgy jurists, the Mar del Plata film festival was a political battleground for local film politics transplanted to an international arena. This battle was in part headed by the traditional producers who were in league with multinational interests and the theatre chain exhibitors. (1984: 67)

Thus, while cultural elites in Argentina wanted the prestige that comes with hosting a film festival, there were those in the film industry who saw auteur cinema and what has been described as 'thinking people's films' as an unsound business venture due to the limited number of interested spectators. Simón Feldman, film director and author of a book on the *Nueva ola*, noted that 'the principal error' made in ensuring the movement's survival was 'our incapacity to structure a viable economic channel (*salida*) to the problem of distribution and above all, in the exhibition of our finished films' (quoted in Castagna 1993: 262). Director Leopoldo Torre Nilsson had no illusions about the kind of audiences that supported this new wave of Argentine filmmakers:

> Our public is divided in two. There is a minority that has grown a lot and really supports the cinema; they go constantly and like good films. I don't know if there are a sufficient number of such people. The people who like bad cinema do not go regularly now ... The quantity of people who want to see a vulgar film may be, for argument, a million, and the people who want to see good cinema only 150,000. That means we will have to work with these 150,000 because the other million cannot be guaranteed as an audience. The problem our industry has in the future is to continue making good films, economically adjusted to this small audience and its potential overseas sales. (Quoted in King 2000: 83)

Because of its limited audience, this group of filmmakers felt marginalised by the main studio still in operation, Argentina Sono Film, and its powerful producers. In addition, the National Film Institute did not welcome this group as the new successors of the film industry. More commercial films that were independently produced, such as those starring popular singers Ramón 'Palito' Ortega, Leo Dan, Antonio Prieto, or comedians such as Jorge Porcel, continued to dominate the interests of the veteran film establishment. Gustavo Castagna argues that the *Nueva ola* was marginalised not only by the film industry, but also the general public: 'They were a generation that passed almost unnoticed by the general filmgoer' (1993: 262). Therefore, he contends, the movement was a failure. Film historian and critic Sergio Wolf (1998), as well as other Argentine film critics, blame the 1960s film movement as a contributing factor to the demise of the 'grand era of filmmaking in Argentina', the studio system era. They believe that the rupture the *Nueva ola* made with the old system marked the beginning of a flawed trend of 'auteur' cinema that led to the death of a successful commercial industry.

In spite of this negative assessment, many *Nueva ola* films are now regarded as part of an important movement in national cinema history. Films elevated to the pantheon of Argentine national cinema classics include Lautaro Murúa's *Shunko* (1960) and David José Kohon's *Tres veces Ana* (*Three Times Ana*, 1961). This is ironic, given that at the time these auteurist films were made, they were not supported by the studios or the public, but were only later added to the canon of the national patrimony.[10] In contrast, the formulaic studio musicals by Ortega and others, while popular in their time, have been relegated to the side in much the same way that Elvis Presley's movies are played regularly on US cable television but are not considered high-quality films. This phenomenon illustrates the tension between the film industry and film art: although studio films were considered an acceptable and commercially lucrative form of cinema at the time, in retrospect, critics and historians have generally dismissed them. This phenomenon is applicable to many art film movements throughout the world, which, once relegated to the margins, eventually occupied a larger space in film history. In recent decades, the commercial studio films, once dismissed as 'low-brow' or ideologically bankrupt, have been re-examined and re-evaluated by film scholars interested in both genre and studies in popular culture.

Concurrent to the *Nueva ola* film movement was a different kind of film production, which also worked outside of the studio system. It began in the late 1950s and in a university setting in the Argentine province of Santa Fe. In 1956 filmmaker Fernando Birri moved back to his birthplace after studying at Rome's Centro Sperimentale and working for such great Italian film artists such as Vittorio De Sica and Caesare Zavattini. In 1956 Birri founded a documentary school at the University of Santa Fe (La Escucla Documental de Santa Fe), the first of its kind in Latin America. There he taught the tenets of Italian neorealist filmmaking and photography, a style that he felt best resonated with the impoverished conditions in rural Argentina. Birri is arguably the most famous social realist documentary filmmaker in Argentina. He worked with students at the school in developing projects that exposed rural underdevelopment in Santa Fe and its environs.

What started as a photography project to record the manner in which local poor children ran alongside trains begging passengers for money (in Argentine slang, '*Tire dié*' or 'Throw me a dime') became a 33-minute documentary film that gained fame for its gritty realism. It was also remarkable in the way in which the eighty students worked in groups and befriended the families of the children over a two-year period. The initial screening took place at the university and was open to all of the film's participants. According to Birri (1987) the audience members asked for the film to be screened three times that night.

The film, *Tire dié* (1959), and Birri's later film *Los inundados* (*Flooded Out*, 1961), were notable, in the words of Zuzana Pick, for their 'participatory and interactive approach to social inquiry', which was 'set apart from models sanctioned by the National Film Institute' (1993: 105). Both films were recognised worldwide in film festivals, but met with disapproval from the National Film Institute. *Los inundados* was a fictionalised comedy film, based on a short story by Santa Fe resident Mateo Booz. It depicted the popular culture and ways of life of rural people living by the riverbanks in Santa Fe who faced seasonal flooding. The film was less of a social protest than a way to recuperate the culture of the provinces. All too often, films made in Argentina depicted life in Buenos Aires. Birri began a project to decentralise filmmaking from the 'head of Goliath' to the provinces. He also called for a cinema that was 'nationalist, realist, critical and popular' (1986: 79) in contrast to the innocuous and generally escapist films being produced by the studios.

The INC, wary of a film with a folkloric and critical edge, banned *Los inundados* and refused to let the film travel to film festivals. The film was invited to screen at Cannes, but the Film Institute sent *Setente veces siete* (*Seventy Times Seven*) by Leopoldo Torre Nilsson instead (Dagron 1986). However, a copy managed to leave the country, and won the Special Jury prize at Karlovy Vary, Czechoslovakia, and the Best First Film award at the Venice Film Festival in 1962. In 1963, Birri left Argentina for Italy and later went on to become the director of Cuba's newly inaugurated film school, the School of the Three Worlds, from its inception in 1986 until 1992.

During the 1960s and throughout the 1970s, the Film Institute continued to loan money to producers and give special loan status to films in the 'national interest'. In response to the burgeoning popularity of television and its negative impact on film exhibition, a law was passed in 1963 to encourage screen space for Argentine film producers. Dubbed the 'six-to-one' law, it required the exhibition sector to screen one national film for every six foreign films. The hope was that this decree would help to stimulate local production by ensuring exhibition. However, because of the dissatisfaction expressed by local exhibitors, as well as by the United States film cartel, the Motion Picture Export Association (MPEA), the decree was withdrawn. In fact, MPEA president Eric Johnson visited Argentina to persuade lawmakers (Schnitman 1978: 165). Thus, the United States film industry forcefully resisted any Argentine legislative restrictions. International export had always been an integral part of the US marketing strategy, but it increased in importance with the decline in domestic theatre attendance that occurred with the rise of television viewing.

US film studios, rather than compete against television, gradually decided to collaborate with the new medium, a trend that was facilitated by the 1948 Paramount decision stipulating that US film companies were no longer allowed to engage in vertical integration; that is, film studios could no longer own film theatres as a means of shutting out any competition. Because this form of vertical integration was banned, film studios diverted money from movie theatres to television production.

In the case of Argentina during the 1960s, the development of three television channels in Argentina greatly affected cinema attendance all over the country. All three of them were initiated around the same time, and all with financial support from US television channels. Channel 9 was transmitted in June 1960 with help from NBC, Channel 13 in October 1960 with assistance from CBS, and in the following year Channel 11 emerged with the aid of ABC (Sirvén 1988). Theatre attendance dropped from 77 million in 1959 to 35 million in 1961. In 1959, 201 theatres operated in Buenos Aires; by 1962, that number was reduced to 140 (Schnitman 1978). However, unlike the US situation, television stations were switching from private to state ownership as late as the 1980s. Until this time, there was relatively no integration between film and television production and exhibition. Although television stations began to purchase film rights to screen films on television, the prices were very low and thus did not benefit national film producers.

In 1968, under the Onganía regime, a military dictatorship, Law 17.741 was added to the existing 1966 Emergency Film Law (16.955/66); in this legislation, all import quotas were abolished, thereby allowing 'the free introduction of films into Argentina in quantities limited only by the domestic market receptivity'. Other provisions were added such as a new category of films called 'special interest', for films made under the close supervision of the Film Institute. A screen quota was installed, but with the flexibility of allowing exhibitors to select the films they wanted to fulfill the quota requirements. Additionally, Article 13 of the 1968 cinema legislation stipulated that a national film 'that attacks the national life style or the cultural pattern of the community' would be denied the right to exhibition (Avellaneda 1987: 35). Other parts of the law warned that 'all films that compromise national security or that somehow affect the country's relations with friendly nations, or that damage the interests of the state's fundamental institutions' would be banned (Dagron 1986: 89).

From that point until 1973 the government had a succession of military leaders who could not retain power due to economic and political crises that arose principally due to their mismanagement. Social unrest wreaked havoc on the nation's stability, inflation skyrocketed, wages were frozen and foreign companies were encouraged to buy national companies in what J. Niosi called an 'open country' economic policy (quoted in Schnitman 1978: 169). During this era, a group of young, radical filmmakers worked outside of the state's close supervision of film production and produced clandestine leftist Peronist films, such as Fernando Solanas and Octavio Getino's *La hora de los hornos* (*Hour of the Furnaces*, 1968) and Jorge Cedrón's *Operación masacre* (*Operation Massacre*, 1972). Militant leftist film collectives such as Grupo Cine Liberación (Liberation Cinema Collective, composed of Solanas, Getino and Gerardo Vallejo) and Cine de la Base (Grassroots Cinema Group, headed by Raymundo Gleyzer) created a militant cinema screened in union halls, at people's homes and to leftist student organisations as agitprop cinema. In 1971, while Perón was exiled in Spain, Solanas and Getino stated that 'our film collective is trying to be (*pretende ser*) the cinematographic arm of General Perón' (Rosado 1992: 146).

This form of 'guerilla filmmaking' was influenced not only by the radical Peronist urban guerrilla movement, the Montoneros, but also by the New Latin American Cinema, which promoted a continent-wide grass-roots cultural movement that organised congresses throughout Latin America (often in conjunction with film festivals) and espoused a militant political and cultural approach to filmmaking. This type of filmmaking documented the social conditions of working people or those in poverty-stricken conditions throughout Latin America. In addition, filmmakers utilised cinematic techniques from the post-war Italian neorealist film movement that some filmmakers learned while studying film there. Rather than have the lives of the oligarchy or the middle classes be the subject of their films, these young, militant filmmakers advocated that films document Latin American reality (or what Fernando Birri deemed 'underdevelopment') in gritty, rough, low-budget, 'imperfect' forms. This cinema in itself was a political act, and promoted film that was not meant to be viewed passively.

Solanas and Getino also wrote 'Towards a Third Cinema' (1969), a seminal essay that remains one of the key texts of the Latin American cinema movement. The concept of 'Third Cinema' is a reaction to what Solanas and Getino categorise as the two dominant cinemas, 'First Cinema', or classical Hollywood cinema, and 'Second Cinema', or the European auteurist cinema that sprang up in the 1960s. Both types of cinema are rejected for their bourgeois leanings, the first because it aims solely to entertain, and the second for its indulgence in individual artistic creation. Instead, a 'Third Cinema' is a 'cinema outside and against the System, in a cinema of liberation ... *The camera is the inexhaustible expropriator of image weapons; the projector, a gun that can shoot 24 frames per second*' (Solanas & Getino 1997: 43, 50).

This text served as a complement to their 260-minute documentary *La hora de los hornos*, a pièce de résistance that took the filmmakers three years to complete. In this period 150 workers, union leaders and intellectuals were interviewed, and over 200 hours were recorded. Grupo Cine Liberación defined filmmaking as 'guerilla activity'. Strict disciplinary norms, carefully defined methods, tight security, interchangeable skills, the ability to innovate and to take advantage of the enemy's weaknesses were all factors in their programme. The footage, for example, had to be constantly disassembled and reassembled in order to throw hostile lab technicians off track. Zuzana Pick, in her exhaustive study entitled *The New Latin American Cinema*, notes that 'in a very short time, this documentary became a paradigm for Third World Filmmaking. Its production was only one aspect of a much broader project, an attempt to outline the organic links between theory and praxis.' (1993: 56) The film is divided into three parts: Part I is called 'Neocolonialism and Violence' (95 mins); Part II, 'An Act of Liberation' (120 mins), is divided into two sections, 'A Chronicle of Peronism' and 'A Chronicle of Resistance'; Part III is entitled 'Violence and Liberation' (45 mins).

La hora de los hornos is shot in black and white and contains a diverse mix of documentary footage intercut with black screen and graphic slogans. The first part of the film utilises a quick-paced montage and the use of black screen to punctuate different themes such as violence, neocolonialism, the history of Argentina and the lives of the poor and marginalised in Argentina, counterposed to wealthy national elites and agrarian oligarchs. Solanas, who directed the film, relies on a minimalist soundtrack composed of drum beats, industrial sounds, sirens and other sound effects that are layered with voice-over narration, worker's testimonials and other voices. The dynamic, agitprop slogans written on the screen infuse the film with a sense of urgency, quoting from Third World revolutionary icons such as Che Guevara, Franz Fanon and Aimé Cesaire as well as homegrown thinkers and nationalist politicians Raúl Scalabrini Ortiz and Perón, among others.

Some slogans, intended to raise consciousness and ultimately mobilise armed revolutionary struggle, are placed squarely in the centre of the screen, reminiscent of Sergei Eisenstein's *Stachka* (*Strike*, 1924) or *Bronenosets Potemkin* (*Battleship Potemkin*, 1925). At other times, bold words like *liberación* (liberation) or *impunidad* (impunity) move and multiply in a mode recalling neon advertising. These slogans are intercut with documentary footage of police brutality, a group waving flags and other images invoking collective mobilisation against an oppressive system. Laura Podalsky notes that Solanas, who had an advertising background, used those same techniques to condemn the rise of consumer culture in Buenos Aires during the 1960s (2004: 221–2).

In the tableau called *'El país'* ('The Country') scenes feature long shots of the rural land intercut with faces of indigenous and mestizo Argentines framed in close-up after the camera physically zooms in. Simultaneously, an authoritative voice (female or male) iterating multiple statistics reveals how few resources are apportioned to *el pueblo*, the poor underclass shown on screen. This voice-over technique is the same employed at the beginning of Birri's *Tire dié*, a clip of which is included in Part I of the film. In addition to utilising realist documentary techniques borrowed from Italian neorealism, Solanas fuses this with more experimental techniques influenced by Jean-Luc Godard.[11] Using an eclectic mix of documentary film footage and cinematic techniques (newsreel sequences, interviews, documentary material, reconstructions of scenes, extracts of other films, still photographs, intertitles, freeze frames and the contributions of direct cinema), *La hora de los hornos* remains one of the most famous militant treatises on revolutionary struggle in the annals of Third World film history (Mestman 2003).

What made this film innovative was that the very act of seeing the film was in itself a revolutionary act. The film screenings themselves were held in a clandestine fashion, not in movie theatres in Argentina, because the military government censors would have banned the film immediately for its political content. Instead, the film circulated outside of the commercial sector in the form of screenings at people's homes, union halls, university classrooms and the like. The film was viewed in secret and not advertised to the general public. The format itself was conducive to revolutionary discourse; there were sections in the film (Parts II and III) where instructions on the screen encouraged that the film be shut off and time taken for discussion about the ideas presented in it. For this reason, the spectator was compelled to interact and engage with the subjects at hand. As Robert Stam argues, 'The two-dimensional space of the screen gives way to the three-dimensional space of theatre and politics ... Rather than a mass hero *on the screen*, the protagonists of history are *in the audience*' (1990: 254).

In one historical incident, the film incited people to stage a spontaneous demonstration. At its European premiere at the International Festival of New Cinema in Pesaro, Italy, in 1968, viewers took to the streets. As Uruguayan producer and distributor Walter Achúgar remembers,

> When they screened [the film], director Fernando Solanas was carried out into the streets on the shoulders of the crowd in a spontaneous demonstration of support. As the festival repeatedly spilled out into the street, there were many confrontations with the police. I remember tearing out telephones and throwing them at the police through the windows of the second story of the festival office. I remember fleeing en masse down the narrow cobbled streets of Pesaro with the police in hot pursuit. (Quoted in Burton 1986: 228)

This film is emblematic of a politically- and socially-charged period in Argentine history, and one in which the Left engaged in guerilla tactics against a military regime that had outlawed Peronism. Filmmakers Solanas and Getino agitated for Perón's return, and even flew to Spain to complete a lengthy documentary of his speeches.

By 1973, Perón had returned from exile and won landslide elections. He headed the country for a year, until his death in 1974. This year was one of great hope for the film industry. Film censorship was relaxed, and a new film law ensured more funding for filmmakers (Avellaneda 1986). During Perón's brief tenure, there was a surge of well-crafted testimonial films reflecting leftist

La tregua (1974): one of Argentina's most celebrated family dramas

Peronist sentiment that could be made and exhibited without major government imposition. Films such as Héctor Olivera's *La Patagonia rebelde* (*Rebellion in Patagonia*, 1974), Sergio Renán's *La tregua* (*The Truce*, 1974) and Ricardo Wullricher's *Quebracho* (1974) were popular successes at home as well as in film festivals abroad, where they were hailed as representatives of quality national filmmaking. Renán's family drama *La tregua* (based on a novel by Uruguayan Mario Benedetti) brought in 2.2 million domestic viewers and was nominated for Best Foreign Film at the Academy Awards that year.

A reversal in government views on censorship had occurred in 1973 when filmmaker Octavio Getino took the helm of the Film Ratings Board. He was responsible for allowing the release of previously banned films such as *Il Decameron* (*The Decameron*, 1970) by Pier Paolo Passolini, *État de siège* (*State of Siege*, 1972) by Costa-Gavras, *Ultimo tango a Parigi* (*Last Tango in Paris*, 1972) by Bernardo Bertolucci, *Operación masacre* by Jorge Cedrón and *La hora de los hornos* by Solanas and Getino.

During this vibrant period of filmmaking, many national films were commercially oriented at the same time they distinguished themselves for their national-popular themes, such as *Nazareno Cruz y el lobo* (*Nazarene Cruz and the Wolf*, 1975) and *Juan Moreira* (1972), based on rural folk tales and gauchoesque literature. Directed by Leonardo Favio, these films represented a break from his more auteurist films such as *Crónica de un niño solo* (*Chronicle of a Boy Alone*, 1964) and *El dependiente* (*The Dependent*, 1967) – films that were stylistically inspired by Leopoldo Torre Nilsson, his mentor. *Nazareno Cruz y el lobo* brought

Juan Moreira (1972): the community spirit of the folk tale finds popularity on the big screen

in all-time high viewership for a national film, with 3.4 million, and *Juan Moreira* attracted 2.5 million viewers.[12] *Nazareno Cruz y el lobo* was based on a popular eponymous *radionovela*, and its cast comprised popular television actors who were known Peronists, such as Juan José Camero. Both films could be characterised as a populist form of cinema with a folkloric and working-class sensibility.

In June 1974 Juan Perón died, leaving Vice President Isabel Perón, his wife, to succeed him as president. This was a time of upheaval and polarisation between leftist and Marxist guerrilla groups, such as the Montoneros in Buenos Aires and the Ejército Revolucionario del Pueblo (ERP) (People's Revolutionary Army) in Tucumán, and right-wing military groups, old guard unionists and the Catholic Church. Isabel Perón and her assistant José López Rega were themselves active in the formation of paramilitary right-wing death squads such as the Argentine Anticommunist Alliance, or 'Triple A'.

By 1975 the economy was spiralling rapidly downward as part of the political instability, and the country was embroiled in what was practically civil war. The government agencies under 'Isabelita' reverted to the censorship decrees instituted from 1966 to 1973 by General Juan Carlos Onganía during his military dictatorship. The most infamous censor in the history of Argentine cinema, Miguel P. Tato, was employed during Isabel Perón's administration to cut, ban and supervise the scripts submitted to the INC for thematic approval. Besides the stringent censorship laws, an atmosphere of apprehension and general distrust pervaded all realms of society during these unstable years. Censorship was intensified by the self-imposed restrictions that gripped filmmakers and other artistic creators. Film director Héctor Olivera stated:

> Today [1975], if we were to make the film *La Patagonia rebelde* again, even if Tato would permit us, we wouldn't go ahead and make it, because we don't have the desire to make a film with that level of dramatic content when the circumstances in Argentina right now are so volatile ... with the country so shaken up (*convulsionado*) that even without censorship, one chooses to self-censor oneself. (Quoted in Avellaneda 1986: 131)

Paramilitary groups targeted Peronists and other political filmmakers during this time. Many feared for their lives and fled the country. In December 1974 the Triple A firebombed several movie theatres for showing the Norman Jewison film *Jesus Christ Superstar*. A bomb attributed to the Triple A also destroyed the home of Gerardo Vallejo, a leftist Peronist filmmaker, who fled to Panama and later Spain. The Triple A also 'invited' Fernando Solanas to seek refuge in France, Octavio Getino in Peru and later Mexico, and Jorge Cedrón in France (Dagron 1986: 95). Other artists who received death threats were Norman Briski, noted actor and Peronist, and actress Nacha Guevara. The actor Héctor Alterio, who was invited to Spain for the San Sebastian Film Festival in 1974, chose to remain there until the democratic opening in the early 1980s. Other actors who voluntarily or involuntarily left were actors Norma Aleandro and Cipe Lincovsky, among others.

On 24 March 1976 the military staged a coup and took over the country until 1982, in one of the most brutally repressive dictatorships Argentina had faced in the twentieth century. Their reigning ideology was authoritarian and called for a form of national restructuring called the *Proceso* or the National Process of Reorganisation. Their modus operandi consisted of instilling fear in the citizenry, imposing strict censorship laws and applying brutal forms of repression, torture and death to alleged subversives. Over thirty thousand individuals were disappeared in this time period, known as the Dirty War (*la guerra sucia*).[13]

Although the authoritarianism that gripped Argentina during this period was the worst in the country's history, a strain of authoritarianism has surfaced repeatedly throughout Argentina's political history; it is not, according to Marcos Aguinis, noted Argentine writer and the secretary of culture during the democratic transition in 1983, a temporary condition:

> Authoritarianism is not a sporadic visit, but a permanent resident. It has existed in our land for a long time. It has made its mark in education, political conduct and everyday life, including hospitality, sports, the sciences and public administration. Its influence is so profound that it has blended with 'the permanent features of the national identity'. In addition, studies on the national identity are infested with concessions to authoritarianism. (1987: 7)

During this period of national restructuring, political statements or critical thought in the cultural realm were silenced by the military, and filmmakers applied self-censored to their work to avoid problems or repression. Nissa Torrents aptly describes the official mentality: 'Thought was equated with terrorism and art with subversion' (1988: 102). The military considered the sphere of cultural production to be a transgressive zone for potential 'enemies of the state'. In October 1979, Commander in Chief of the Army Lieutenant General Roberto Viola stated:

> Capture, or conquest of the mind, is the task of culture because culture is the most apt means of infiltration of extremist ideologies [via] songs of protest, exaltation of extremist artists and texts, vanguard theatres or works, the setting of poems to music, individual performances ... plastic works with strong guerilla overtones, press conferences ... and café performances in which the hidden 'message' is located in an innocent manner. (Quoted in Avellaneda 1987: 28)

The military's concern for potential violations of national security by the film industry translated into a tightly controlled National Film Institute run by a series of navy commanders. The first to take charge, a few months after the March coup in 1976, was Captain Jorge Enrique Bittleston who, according to Sergio Wolf (2001), did not grant loans or subsidies to any filmmakers or producers during his tenure. He was succeeded by Commodore Carlos Exequiel Bellio, who headed the institute until 1980. From 1981 until the collapse of the military government, Commodore Francisco Pítaro was at the helm. The INC was placed under the jurisdiction of the secretary of public information. In a 1977 handbook for filmmakers distributed by *Heraldo del cine*, a section entitled 'Guidelines from the Secretary of Public Information in Relation to the Cinema' outlines various directives regarding national film production. The state's right to censor materials is defended in the following terms:

> There is the category of film productions that completely lacks any artistic or entertainment value; those that attempt to work against the efforts to reintegrate and revitalise our community, and those that offend the sensibilities of the majority. These works are not permitted and their exhibition will be forbidden in full or partially, temporarily or permanently. (Quoted in Corti 1977: 26)

In this horrific period numerous films were banned and censored, national film quality was generally low and even more filmmakers, actors and writers fled into exile. In the filmmaking community, fear of blacklisting, torture or death forced many into exile. A few, such as filmmaker Raymundo Gleyzer and writer Rodolfo Walsh, were tortured and disappeared by the military for alleged wrongdoing.

While some filmmakers were killed, others stayed in the country but were subject to some form of artistic constraint if not blatant self-censorship. Still others continued to make films abroad that dealt with Argentine themes or, in some cases, with the experience of exile. The tension between those who stayed, or the 'AA' community (Argentines in Argentina), versus those people who left, the 'AE' (Argentines in the Exterior), has resulted in a series of debates around the 'authenticity' of experience during the *Proceso*. The film *Tangos: El exilio de Gardel* (*Tangos: Gardel's Exile*, 1986) (to be discussed more fully in the next chapter) explores the collective experience of the Argentine expatriate community in Paris, articulated though dance, letters exchanged between the homeland and abroad, song, comedy, tragedy and – of course – the tango.

In addition to Argentine films, many US and European films were also censored or banned. It has been estimated that between 1976 and 1978, a total of 180 films were banned by the Board of Film Control, on either 'political or moral grounds' (Caistor 1988: 88). In the newspaper *La Prensa* of 24 July 1980, a critic wrote, 'The film *1900* by Bernardo Bertolucci was banned and the reason given was that it worked "contrary to the moral order and the Christian ethic".' *Coming Home* (*Regreso sin gloria*, 1978), by Hal Ashby and starring Jane Fonda, was also banned, on the grounds that it 'violated the moral unity of the family'. *Piedra libre* (*Rolling Stone*, 1976) by famed national director Leopoldo Torre Nilsson, was first banned, then immediately reauthorised and then finally banned again 'for its attacks against the family, religion, morality, tradition and other fundamental values of our worldview' (quoted in AIDA 1981: 132).

Film scripts were regularly rejected by Miguel Paulino Tato. He used his power arbitrarily to ban, cut and reject outright film projects for reasons ranging from 'invalid conceptions of sexuality, and the family, and for ill-formed conceptions of optimism'. Andrés Avellaneda, a scholar of Argentine censorship, noted that 'the censors went so far as to obstruct the production of a film because "a mother does not rob to help her son", or to cut scenes because "never does a Jew win a fight with a gaucho" or "a gaucho never kills his son".'[14]

Other banned imports were *Last Tango in Paris* and Martin Ritt's *Norma Rae* (1979). By 1983, the final year of the military dictatorship, the censors were banning one out of every four films in Argentina (Aufderheide 1986). Octavio Getino, head of the ratings board in 1974, was in exile in Peru when authorities tried to extradite him in 1980 for his past authorisation to screen *Last Tango in Paris*.[15]

The Argentine films produced in that period were no longer the quality dramas that had surfaced during the populist boom of 1973–74. In his book *Cine y dependencia: El cine en la Argentina*, Getino states:

Let us remember that in 1973–74 Argentine films occupied the majority of the top slots for box office returns. According to INC statistics, in 1974 ten of the fifteen films with the top box office ratings were Argentine ... Three

years later, in 1977, due to repression and censorship borne of the new dominant politics, the top ten box office hits were void of any Argentine film: all
of them were from the US. (1990: 136)

During this period, apart from a few propagandistic films and light comedies
approved by the censors, the regime (for the most part) preferred to allow imported entertainment programming to flood the market, therefore removing political themes from the realm of cinema. In addition to comic and action films
produced domestically for a mass audience, more US films were imported than
during any other period in Argentine history (Torrents 1988). A similar scenario
can be found in the Indonesian context. Film scholar Krishna Sen (1996) writes
about the relationship between the film industry and the military apparatus in
Indonesia during the 1990s, describing how the film industry was policed inter-
nally via censorship measures, while at the same time being open to imported
film content; imports presented no threat to the Indonesian state. Similarly,
rather than restrict foreign imports, as Perón tried to do under the banner of
'cultural nationalism', this regime pacified and entertained its population with
cheap television imports and Hollywood comedies, encouraging similar fare for
locally-produced works.

In terms of domestic production, the industry was transformed into a commercial one that reproduced Argentine light sexual comedies, known as *comedias
picarescas*, from the early 1960s. Although these films were low-budget and generally of poor quality, they were popular with domestic audiences. Film scholar
Jean-Pierre Jeancolas typifies this category of cheaply-made films as destined to
be seen only by audiences in their country of origin, or 'inexportables' (1992:
141). Despite the fact that these films were too localised in content and 'too
insignificant and/or intelligible to be appreciated outside of a given country'
(ibid.), they were the most successful national films at the time. The top Argentine films in 1976 were comedies and action films: *Los hombres piensan solo en
eso* (*Men Only Think About One Thing*), starring Olmedo and Porcel, directed
by Enrique Cahen Salaberry and produced by Aries, had 108,300 spectators; *El
gordo de America* (*American Fatty*), with the same actors, director and producers, had 101,300 viewers. The third was Palito Ortega's *Dos locos en el aire* (*Two
Airborne Crazy Guys*), with 90,500 spectators. These films were ideologically in
line with the dictatorship. This was the peak epoch of the production company
Chango, owned by the actor-singer Ramón 'Palito' Ortega.[16] Ortega produced,
acted in and directed films that espoused the ideals of the military through films
such as *Dos locos en el aire* and *Brigada en acción* (*Brigade in Action*, 1977) in
which, according to journalist Adrian Muoyo, 'they aimed to show a supposed
alliance between society (*el pueblo*) and the military or police forces to confront
a "common enemy"' depicted as contraband smugglers, common criminals or
American spies (1993: 45). Another filmmaker complicitous with the regime
was Emilio Vieyra, who directed two movies in the action genre where the mili-

tary as the protagonist helps prepare soldiers for war: *Comandos azules* (*Blue Commandos*, 1980) and its sequel, *Comandos azules en acción* (*Blue Commandos in Action*, 1980).

A famous semidocumentary film considered the Argentine equivalent to Leni Riefenstahl's Nazi propaganda film *Triumph des Willens* (*Triumph of the Will*, 1935) was the box-office hit *La fiesta de todos* (*The Party for All*, 1978), by Sergio Renán.[17] The film celebrated that year's World Cup soccer victory, hosted by Argentina. A voice-over in this film, according to Sergio Wolf, explicitly echoes the sentiments of 'national cohesion' expressed by President Videla: 'There were two groups of fans: those who were optimistic, and others oppositional' (1993b: 272–3).

There was a relative thaw from 1980 to 1982; the government allowed more freedom of expression, and the military presence encroached less on daily life. At a film festival at Río Hondo in Argentina, director Héctor Olivera described the major obstacles to film production more in terms of political than economic constraints:

> Argentine cinema seems to be reorienting, from the industrial point of view. From the other point of view, that of the artistic, the situation is rather lamentable: there are few worthwhile projects, but I think that the main cause here is in *the Argentine censorship, that is the most arbitrary, absolutist, incoherent, and castrating in the West.* (Quoted in AIDA 1981: 140)

On 16 December 1980, a protest organised by the major film associations, including the film workers union (SICA) and those representing directors, producers, actors and others, publicly denounced censorship and the 'gutting' (*vaciamiento*) of national cinema. The SICA representative Aníbal di Salvo declared that 'no one can be indifferent to the uncertain situation that is affecting our film production. And nobody should ignore that, with its disappearance, we will have lost an important part of our culture' (quoted in AIDA, 1981: 147–8).

In 1981 a film allegorising the dictatorship, Adolfo Aristarain's political thriller *Tiempo de revancha* (*Time for Revenge*), was popular with audiences. It utilised symbolism in subtle and dramatic ways within the popular thriller genre to denounce the ongoing silence imposed upon Argentine society.[18] In a fascinating essay, Fernando Reati points out the dominant tropes that were found within Argentine national cinema during the dictatorship. He argues that in various films and literary works there are allusions to self-censorship (such as Aristarain's protagonist in the abovementioned film, who cuts his tongue out to avoid repercussion). This kind of self-imposed silence was a form of survival. According to Reati, 'after seven years of political terror, the retreat into a secluded domain of private life became a survival technique' (1989: 130n).

Argentine film critic Sergio Wolf (1993a) has explored a common theme that plagued the collective unconscious during the dictatorship period. This is the notion of being trapped or confined to a space. An example is the famed *Tiempo de revancha*, in which the main character, Bengoa, crawls into a cave to fake a work accident. Other films include Sergio Renán's *Crecer de golpe* (*Suddenly Grown Up*, 1976), which portrays caged animals, and *La invitación* (*The Invitation*, 1981), directed by Manuel Antín, where there is a reoccurrence of the verb *to hunt*. Wolf notes that there are noticeable absences in film of the time of such tropes as the road trip or journey – a metaphor that usually signifies change or self-discovery. This was a not a value endorsed by the military regime. The only exception to the rule is Eliseo Subiela's *La conquista del paraíso* (*The Conquest of Paradise*, 1980), which was looked upon with suspicion by the censors, but ultimately let go. Wolf notes that the censor Ares 'wanted to censor parts of the film because he didn't like it, but could never figure out what it was about it that bothered him' (1993a: 276).

The era in Argentina's history from 1983 to 1989 is known as the *apertura*, or the period of redemocratisation. The military junta finally crumbled in 1982 after a disastrous attempt to gain popular support during the Malvinas (Falklands) War. When the military withdrew in 1983, it bequeathed $45 billion in foreign obligations to civilians (Adelman 1994). Elections were openly held for the first time in almost a decade, and Radical Party candidate Raúl Alfonsín was elected president in December 1983.

CHAPTER 2

THE 1980s: CINEMA, DEMOCRACY AND FILM POLICY WITH VIEWS TOWARDS EUROPE

The period after the collapse of the military dictatorship in 1982 was marked by renewal and openness in Argentine culture. Military heads of state finally capitulated after a brutal seven years of rule. They had humiliated the nation with the ill-fated Malvinas (Falklands) War and voluntarily stepped down from power. The junta had waged an internal war against its citizenry called *la guerra sucia*, or the Dirty War, in which tens of thousands of people deemed 'subversive' were disappeared, tortured and often raped and killed. Cultural and artistic expression was closely monitored for what the military government viewed as subversive activity. Of those filmmakers and actors who did not flee the country, many were blacklisted and could not work in the arts sector during that time. Many intellectuals, including filmmakers, fled in fear and lived in exile until the *apertura*, the 'new democratic opening'.

President Raúl Alfonsín was elected to office on 25 October 1983, in the first democratic election in ten years. The Radical Party, typically supported by the middle class, had always promoted the arts, culture and education as part of the government agenda. During the transition to democracy, film production was encouraged by the state and supported by private sources of funding, and as a result the annual output almost doubled, from approximately 15 films during the dictatorship era to up to 25 films until 1989. The content of these post-dictatorship films exuded a vital force that had previously been censored. Films with social themes were once again shown and discussed freely. President Alfonsín heralded a new era of democracy by supporting an open cultural environment free of censorship. One major effort made by the Argentine government under the flowering of democracy was to reorganise the Instituto Nacional de Cine and to abolish the film censorship laws, which had been on the books since 1968, during the Onganía regime. The passage of new age-related restrictions replaced them. On 21 December 1983 the directorship of the INC was given to veteran filmmaker Manuel Antín. He remained INC head for the five years of Alfonsín's presidency, and worked closely with him on cultural policy issues.

During his tenure, Antín encouraged a wide range of artistic and commercially popular works, from art-house productions to mass entertainment films.

Under Antín, the main strategy was to mould the film industry into a public relations mechanism for the state. The goal was to promote a more positive image of a democratic Argentina liberated from the military dictatorship. The films themselves were typically emotional portraits of people testifying to the horrors of the recent era. Many proved to be cathartic, such as Alejandro Doria's *Darse cuenta* (*Becoming Aware*, 1984), Alberto Fischerman's *Los días de junio* (*June Days*, 1985) or Fernando Solanas' *Tangos, el exilio de Gardel*. Antín described the films of the *destape* (liberalising transition period) as 'psychoanalytic sessions on film' (quoted in Schettini 1988). The many films testifying to the horrors of the Dirty War were characteristic of the larger Latin American genre, the *testimonio*, which is typically a first-person narrative that testifies to a horrific event or era.

The large number of *testimonio* films produced – 16 out of 26 in 1984 alone – illustrated Argentines' need to discuss the dark period that multitudes had endured silently and under extreme fear (Leandri 1984). The forceful emergence of the *testimonio* demonstrated that Argentina was undergoing an exorcism of the recent, terrible past. Entering these films in international festivals, Antín reasoned, signified that the nation had been 'reborn' and was now ready to enter the world arena on a 'healthier, more democratic footing'. Antín stressed in interview in 1995 that this push to promote Argentine cinema abroad worked as effectively for a nation as any ambassador, and that it would help revitalise Argentina's image as a newly democratic and free country.

While critics and journalists were proclaiming the death of censorship and the rebirth of democracy, the potential limitations inscribed by policies geared towards the export of film culture were acknowledged, but not problematised. The assumption during this period was that films for export translated into a healthy domestic film industry. Also, although there was a conscious effort to create films for both domestic and international markets, it is notable that, in both 1985 and 1986, newly released Argentine films were more popular with foreign than with home audiences (Di Núbila 1986).[1] During this time, Argentine films were made for an international and national middle-class viewership, not for a domestic working-class audience.

Communication research has examined the relationship between socio-economic class tastes and domestic versus imported films and television. Joseph Straubhaar's work on Brazilian audience preferences affirms the idea that local working-class audiences prefer national products over imported ones: 'Research seems to point to a greater traditionalism and loyalty to national and local cultures by lower and popular classes, who show the strongest tendency to seek greater cultural proximity in television programmes and other cultural products' (1991: 51). In the case of Argentine national cinema, this observation also holds for films made for working-class audiences, that is, popular television spinoff films, popular comedy films, action films and other mass commercial genres.

However, the majority of films were (and still are) made for a middle-class (and in some cases upper-class) viewership. In terms of a domestic market for national films, producers run into problems because middle-class viewers on the whole tend to prefer imported films and television programmes.

In Argentina, national films are not as well attended by the middle-class sector of the population, and thus directors/producers must hope for a 'crossover' hit, or one that appeals to multiple audiences along socio-economic, age, or gender lines. Some filmmakers, such as Héctor Olivera, produced entertainment films for a broader home audience via his film studio Aries so he could subsidise his more dramatic, 'serious' art films for the more elite classes (1995).

Alfonsín's administration saw the production of an average of 23 films per year. In the same period, Argentine films won over two hundred prizes at film festivals. This was significant, especially considering that during the most recent dictatorship, many film festivals, such as Cannes and Berlin, refused to accept Argentine film entries on political grounds. The resurgence of powerful films such as *Camila* (1984), *La historia oficial* and *La noche de los lápices* (*Night of the Pencils*, 1986) had critics observing that 'the Argentine public seemed primed to use the darkened movie house like a confessional' (Aufderheide 1986: 54). Amongst the accolades garnered from numerous festivals abroad were an Academy Award for Luis Puenzo's *La historia oficial* in 1986, the first Latin American film ever to win in the foreign film category. *La historia oficial's* Norma Aleandro also shared the Best Actress Award at the Cannes Film Festival that same year.

For the most part during the Antín years, Argentine films were viewed by an educated, intellectual, middle-class audience at home; later, if a film was publicised well after gaining recognition abroad, it reached a more mainstream audience. Of all the films to be screened in the 'new' era of democracy, only one film, María Luisa Bemberg's *Camila*, broke records for attendance at home (2.1 million viewers),[2] and only a few others reached the one million mark.

There are several possible reasons for the domestic success of *Camila*. Alberto Ciria attributes the film's success both at home and abroad to a universalised theme that resonated within the parameters of local history:

> Internationally, *Camila* benefited due to a narrative schema followed by the actors that conformed to the notion of a 'well-made' film. There were also socio-political gestures within the film that one could understand without having a background or knowledge of Argentine history. The film adapted the traditional melodrama to undermine conservative values and patriarchy found in Argentine society in a very effective way. (1995: 162)

The film was successful at home and abroad, according to Ciria, because it held something for multiple audiences. The melodramatic structure was an important feature, as well as the subject matter – the famous historical tale of Camila O'Gorman, a young aristocratic woman from the provinces who falls in love

Camila (1984): an allegory for the dictatorship starring Susú Pecoraro and Imanol Arias

with a priest, elopes with him and is killed for having defied her family and the Church (a central power during the Rosas period, 1829–53). Furthermore, the film's dramatic content clearly allegorises the most recent military dictatorship in its portrayal of the Church and State as allied authoritarian bodies. The film integrates political commentary with a popular melodramatic form of storytelling. These qualities might appeal to various segments of Argentine society:

> In the domestic market, [*Camila*] could combine different market segments to create a huge success at the box office: spectators of a certain age that remained faithful to Argentine cinema, teenagers attracted to the erotic nature of the work, as well as its contemporary resonances, professionals and urban intellectuals such as feminist groups, etc. (Ciria 1995: 163)

With the exception of *Camila*, however, Argentine cinema under Alfonsín did not cater to multiple audiences and heavy movie-consumption groups such as youth.[3]

However, most of the films supported by the INC focused on contemporary aspects of national culture such as recent history, presented in an intellectualised manner, thereby reducing the audience to a small segment of the population. Films were dependent on international viewership to recuperate financial investments.

Argentine films became popular with international audiences in the mid-1980s, especially appealing to educated European and American viewers.[4] International audiences identified with these films in part because the films' historical themes were now simplified and packaged neatly for foreign consumption. In addition, a large percentage of filmmakers came out of commercial advertising backgrounds, thus creating a glossier visual format.[5] The films were produced mainly for the international film festival circuit, where filmmakers could gain prestige for themselves and Argentina as a nation.

Antín reasoned that the Argentine film industry could compensate for its small home market by showing films at film festivals, thus gaining international recognition, and by seeking alternative film financing such as international co-production agreements. According to film critic David Oubiña, Manuel Antín tried to promote national cinema abroad in order to 'recuperate a space that our cinema had occupied in the 1930s and 1940s (in all Spanish-speaking countries)' (1994: 294). However, it is important to distinguish between the films produced in the 1930s and 1940s and those made in the 1980s. First, the earlier films appealed to a mass audience. Second, they were made within a studio system. That is, various film genres were released with some consistency and used famous actors and directors – much in the vein of classical Hollywood cinema. This type of commercial film production, due to its mass appeal, was more conducive to an export industry (and larger markets in general) than the kinds of auteur cinema made in the *apertura*. This was the heyday or 'golden age' of Argentina's film industry during the 1930s and 1940s. In the 1980s, by contrast, films were directed more towards European and US markets, instead of for exhibition and distribution in Latin American countries.

Unlike those of the 'golden age', the films characteristic of the 1980s' boom were not popular genre films, with the exception of a few melodramas (*La historia oficial* and *Camila*) and some political films that form part of the larger Latin American genre, the *testimonio*. In general, countries in Europe (principally those with state-owned television channels) were the main film buyers. Antín's marketing strategy for film export was more Eurocentric than Latin American in profile.

Although Antín's rhetoric for distributing the new Argentine cinema in a fashion comparable to the industry's 'golden age' produced more hype than reality, he has received well-deserved credit for revitalising the Argentine film industry and facilitating the development of its 1980s world-renowned status. Some criticised the INC director, however, for conceptualising the film industry largely as a bastion for 'high culture'. His attitude mirrored that of many of the members of his political party, the Unión Cívica Radical (UCR). This party, in power between 1983–89, had a history of accusations by the more populist rival party, the Peronist Partido Justicialista, of elitism. Antín's attitude towards the cultivation of a national cinema reveals how the UCR viewed the support of the arts and cultural industries in Argentina.

Manuel Antín began his career in literature and theatre circles. As a young man he published three books of poetry, three plays and two novels, one of which was made into the film *Los venerables todos* (*The Venerated Ones*, 1962). This film represented Argentina in the Cannes Film Festival that year, but it never had a theatrical release because Antín was unable to secure distribution. He was part of the *Nueva ola* film movement of the 1960s. During that period he wrote two screenplays for shorter-length films directed by Rodolfo Kuhn, one of the representatives of that generation of filmmakers. Antín made his own films in a similar vein, depicting the ennui of bourgeois adolescents in an alienated Buenos Aires. Two of his best films were based on the short stories of one of Argentina's foremost writers, Julio Cortázar. *La cifra impar* (*The Odd Number*, 1961) and *Circe* (1963) were well received within academic circles, but more mainstream critics dubbed the films 'intellectualised' and 'Frenchified' (Feldman 1990: 65). Indeed, for inspiration these middle-class cine-club aficionados often looked at trends in European filmmaking such as the French *nouvelle vague* style of filmmaking, rather than the more commercial film trend in the Argentine studios at the time.

Antín's film career, inspired by international art-house aesthetics, never achieved much commercial success. Film critic Jorge Abel Martín labelled the director's style as one that is 'at moments cryptic and intellectual' and encapsulates the filmmaker's 'solitary struggle inside of auteurist cinema' (1987: 14). Although Antín generally adhered to the idea that culture was most elevated when it was 'universalist' – that is, when it embraced the Western European canonical standards – he did make some films based on the national gaucho literature, such as *Don Segundo Sombra* (1969), based on a famous novel by Ricardo Güiraldes. Antín's career spanned three decades; his last film was made in 1982. A veteran of the fine arts, he described sustaining Argentine cultural production from the point of view of preserving Western European civilisation: 'We know about the Greek and Roman civilisations through their cultural artifacts. So, in our case, if we aren't going to pass on our history through culture, how else are we going to pass it on?' (1995).

Clearly, Antín, along with the Radical Party at this historic juncture, had a well-defined cultural agenda that distinguished between 'high art' and 'popular art', a position that contrasted greatly with the subsequent Peronist cultural policies headed by President Carlos Menem in the 1990s.

The rhetoric of the Radical Party emphasised democratic values and education as central tenets of its political platform. Argentine sociologist José del Tronco's assessment of Alfonsín's administration captures the party's message of democracy, freedom of expression and education for all:

> Democracy, led by Alfonsín, signified the beginning of a new institutional stage in the political realm. Argentine populism was left behind, along with 'para-institutional' corporativism and its authoritarian colonisation of the state apparatus. The Radical government faithfully upheld this role as an institutional renovator via a discourse encouraging the awakening of a society

whose deep lethargy was a consequence of state terrorism. This social discourse of 'consciousness-raising' demonstrated the necessity of this change,
and reinforced Alfonsín's conviction that 'with democracy, one eats, one is
cured, and one gets educated'. (1996: 215)

Alfonsín's policies did not always live up to these ideals, however. In fact, many
believed that the administration privileged the middle class over the working
class. This bias can certainly be seen in terms of national cinematic representations of its populace. Peronist filmmaker Luis Barone, for example, said that
while the Radicals 'tended to show only one face of the country, the "white" side
of Argentina', Perón, by contrast, integrated the darker skinned *mestizo* population from the countryside into the public sphere (1997). Were advantages given
to film directors with the 'preferred' image of Argentina? Did Antín and his
cronies give special film loans out to friends and political clients and reject the
Peronist filmmakers, in what Argentines call *amiguismo*?[6] A review of filmmakers
approved for film loans designated with 'special interest' (*interés especial*) financing from 1984 to 1988 shows that about 50 percent of all film loan recipients
were Radicals, 25 percent were members of the Peronist party, and 25 percent
were 'independent' (that is, they were not affiliated with either party).[7]

For the most part, Antín's administration was considered democratic. If
there was any level of discrimination in terms of obtaining film loans, it was
less around partisan lines, and more along the lines of a 'quality' cinema versus a
mass commercial cinema. The former was nurtured for international audiences,
while the latter was pursued principally for the domestic market. Although quite
a few commercial, 'entertainment' films were produced between 1983 and 1989,
'serious' art-house cinema prevailed during the Antín years. In fact, of all the
films then produced and distributed, roughly 35 percent were entertainment
films (popular comedies, television spinoffs, sexploitation films, action movies
and other mass genres) and approximately 65 percent were middle-class art-
cinema fare (socially committed films, auteur cinema, dramas, historical films
and so on). Antín's filmmaking background and his philosophy, which were also
espoused by a sector of Argentine society, lend insight into the cultural policies
that were established during the Alfonsín administration.

During the Alfonsín administration, international film festivals served as a
primary vehicle to promote Argentina's national culture. Antín believed that Argentina had to be able to showcase a 'quality' cinema that reflected Argentina's
quest to regain its legitimacy as a functioning democracy. Democratic ideals were
demonstrable through the Argentine government's support for cultural expression. Yet, as is the case with most state-sponsored culture industries, the Alfonsín
government sought to foster cultural nationalism while simultaneously sanction-
ing official images of the country that emphasized Argentina's modernity.

Antín wanted to further the tradition of artistic filmmaking that had been
initiated by his predecessor Leopoldo Torre Nilsson by favouring films with a

more serious or intellectual bent, even though he did not overtly discriminate against commercial films. As a proponent of art-house cinema, Antín made sure that Argentine cinema was exhibited in the most prestigious European film festivals, such as Cannes, Berlin and Venice. Films were also shown at venues in Latin America such as the Havana Film Festival and the festival in Gramado, Brazil. However, they were less publicised in general and did not make the news as widely, even when Argentine films won top awards. Intellectuals and statesmen like Manuel Antín hoped that by gaining recognition in international film festivals, Argentina could regain its status as a cultured, democratic country, and be reintegrated in world affairs.

President Alfonsín often brought a set of Argentine films on video as a gift when visiting other foreign heads of state. Other promotional efforts by the National Film Institute included a 'Fifty-Eight Weeks of Argentine Cinema Tour' in 1985, which attracted interest in places such as Finland, Sweden, Germany and the United States. The tour had sold-out shows in Spain, and films were subtitled in English, French, German and Japanese. The image opposite was taken from the tour programme when it came to San Diego, California. Six films were screened in the two-day festival in 1988. In addition to the three films listed, the others were *Los días de junio*, directed by Alberto Fischerman, *Diapasón* (1986) by Jorge Polaco and *Made in Argentina* (1987) by Juan José Jusid.

Antín stated both in written interviews and in a personal meeting that the cinema had an ideological dimension for disseminating information worldwide. He noted how Hollywood marched under the banner 'trade follows film' during the 1920s, and how films functioned as a form of advertising for clothing, automobiles and other consumer goods. Through the cinema the United States exported a whole way of life that other nations would want to acquire through the consumption of US goods.

Antín felt that Argentina could benefit by exporting an image of the country that would appeal to foreigners. Films could show natural attractions (Iguazú waterfalls, Patagonia and so on) and cultural attributes of 'the people', such as the tango, folkloric figures such as the gaucho and other traits that historically have been 'othered' or exotic. In addition, films on the recent violent Dirty War could function to distance contemporary Argentina from the dictatorship. Promoting a certain kind of Argentine cinema abroad was one way to raise awareness about the country abroad, thereby increasing its chances to be more 'visible' as a nation. Thus while Antín was an aesthete who cared deeply about the artistic integrity of national cinema, he was also a statesman who saw the cinema as a special cultural form, and one with potential to communicate positive attributes about Argentina. Antín's use of cinema as a form of public relations or mass commercial advertising involved no little degree of irony, committed as he was to the idea of film as a pure form of art and personal expression.

Exhibiting films abroad served a dual function. On the one hand, exhibition in international film festivals helped to gain legitimacy for Argentina as a bona

Made in Argentina (1987): a film discussing those who left and those who stayed under the Proceso

fide democratic nation. At the same time, films screened abroad served as a way to sell films there. As David Oubiña (1994) observes, film festivals function both as spaces of artistic competition and as a film market. In the 1980s as now, in addition to presenting films at festivals, there was considerable effort put forth to promote films through advertising, special screenings and the distribution of promotional gifts (for example, stickers and T-shirts). This means that producers had to invest money in advertising, and/or the National Film Institute had to work actively within the distribution sector of the cinema to ensure that the films were given adequate exposure in the marketplace. Another method Antín used to secure exhibition abroad was to forge international links through a distribution wing of the film institute, Argencine (to be discussed later in the chapter), thereby gaining additional financing, as well as creating a space to promote Argentina in Europe, the United States and Latin America. This is one reason why he consistently promoted co-productions and film cooperatives.

Two film directors, Alejandro Doria and Bebe Kamin, complained in 1987 that while 'now there was the liberty to express oneself creatively, there were no economic resources to do so' (quoted in España 1994b: 43). Both suggested possible alternative sources of funding for producer-directors – co-production agreements with other countries and cooperative financing. This latter method was introduced for the first time in 1986, and was used approximately thirty times from 1987 and 1991 (Fabbro 1994). In this system, participants in the film production sector (film technicians, actors, the producers and the director) were all shareholders in the film venture. Pay was withheld until after the film was completed and distributed, and any profits realised were divided. In addition, all members of the cooperative were responsible for the film and participated in decision-making processes.

Films produced under co-production agreements in this period were often made with internationally-known stars such as Julie Christie, who starred as the English governess in María Luisa Bemberg's tale of aristocratic life in Argentina, *Miss Mary* (1986), and Bibi Andersson, who played a supporting role in Raúl de la Torre's *Pobre mariposa* (*Poor Butterfly*, 1986). Advantages to international co-production included supplemental film financing (usually from other national film institutes or state television channels) and the assurance that a distribution agreement would be reached whereby the film would be released in the co-producing country in addition to Argentina.

A roundtable discussion by prominent Argentine film critics yielded some interesting insights into the nature of co-production film financing. The film in focus was Fernando Solanas' *Tangos: El exilio de Gardel* from 1986, an Argentine-French co-production that was a prize-winning film lauded in Venice, Biarritz and Havana. This film marked a break from Solanas's past work, which was more politically radical in nature and exemplary of *un cine pobre* – films such as *La hora de los hornos* and *Los hijos de Fierro* (*Fierro's Sons*, 1972–74). Many noted how *Tangos: El exilio de Gardel* was much more stylised and 'aestheticised' than his earlier, grittier, more realist works. In discussing the nature of its production, two film critics talked about the 'nationality' of this co-produced film:

> Sergio Wolf: I would like it if we could reflect on the supposed 'nationality' of the work, despite the fact that *El exilio* was conceived, before anything, as a co-production between France and Argentina. I think, that in this respect, the film is more French than Argentine.
> Hernan Gaffet: I would say that it is even worse than that; it is an Argentine film made for the French, something that is even more serious.
> (Anon. 1986b: 26)

These critics touched upon differences between *Tangos: El exilio de Gardel* and past films, which catered less to international audiences and which had subject matters pertaining more to Argentines themselves. The critics also accused Solanas of using tango music and dance that was not truly national, but 'sterilised, very European, not expressive of our tango' (Anon. 1986b: 27). The plot of the film concerns Argentine exiles in Paris who produce a tango show for wealthy French patrons rather than for Argentine ex-patriots in the community. This quest to appease foreign co-producers has always been an issue when investors from Europe or the United States have helped fund Latin American cinema. While the power dynamic can present problems in matters of the narrative, the use of actors and the like, it remains one of the few ways Latin American filmmakers can continue to make films in their home countries (or in the case of

Solanas, while in exile in France). Marvin D'Lugo notes that Solanas is highly aware of this dynamic as 'the rehearsal [in the above-mentioned plot] self-consciously replicates as plot the very problematic of Solanas's own film as it must struggle in aesthetic, cultural and financial spheres to construct its foreign audience simply to be able to exist' (2003: 108).

The Argentine quest for European recognition and approval is a phenomenon that began with the founding of the nation-state. Uruguayan writer José Enrique Rodó (1988) called this Argentine/Uruguayan bourgeois desire for European praise *Arielismo*. Another term for this phenomenon is 'the mirror effect', or *espejismo*. Culturally, Argentina has always been a Latin American nation in search of a European identity, due in part to its Creole forefathers' aspiration for a large European immigrant population as well as its grandiose and Eurocentric desire to be a European country within Latin America. The cosmopolitan capital of Buenos Aires in particular has been considered by some to 'exist only to the extent that Europe looks at it. The city was born in this play of mirrors, in this complicity of reflection' (Dujovne Ortiz quoted in Pick 1989: 64). The fact that a film was re-released after its success abroad – like *La historia oficial* and others – attests to this national 'outer-directedness', to use sociologist David Reisman's terminology.

While many European co-productions targeted elite audiences, there was also a spate of films made with the United States that catered to a completely different audience. From 1984 to 1991, many low-budget 'B' movies were co-produced between the Argentine film studio Aries, headed by film directors Fernando Ayala and Héctor Olivera, and the US film director Roger Corman. Corman's company, Concorde-New Horizons Pictures,[8] produced nine films in Argentina, with such titles as *Cazador de la muerte* (*Deathstalker*, 1983), *Reina salvaje* (*Barbarian Queen*, 1984) and *La muerte blanca* (*Cocaine Wars*, 1985).[9] These low-budget entertainment films were made in Argentina mostly because of the low production costs involved, and in some cases because the INC granted Olivera/Corman film loans with the 'special interest' designation.[10] Therefore, it was not just 'high art' that was being co-produced during this period, but rather a combination of commercial and artistic work directed towards different audiences.

Two kinds of filmmakers typically applied for a film loan through the INC. One was a producer tied to a film production company, or film studio, and the other was an independent filmmaker, who was usually also his or her own producer. In the period 1984–88, of the 109 directors who shot films (this figure does not mean that all the films were previewed or even finished) 63, or 57.7 percent, were their own producers (Torrents 1993).

In applying for a film loan (*credito*), there were two possibilities for receiving subsidies once the film had been successfully completed and released. The 'special interest' designation meant that the producer could receive up to 70 percent of the box office take (not to exceed half of the loan given by the INC), depending on the numbers of people attending the film. If the film was not

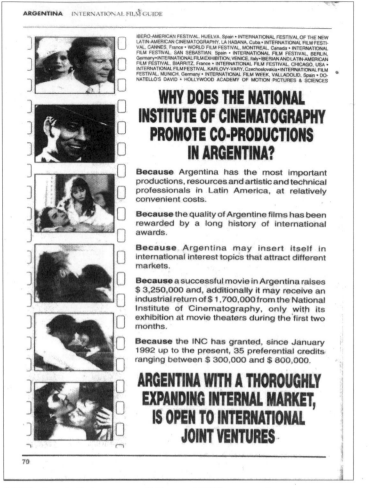

IBERO-AMERICAN FESTIVAL, HUELVA, Spain • INTERNATIONAL FESTIVAL OF THE NEW LATIN-AMERICAN CINEMATOGRAPHY, LA HABANA, Cuba • INTERNATIONAL FILM FESTIVAL, CANNES, France • WORLD FILM FESTIVAL, MONTREAL, Canada • INTERNATIONAL FILM FESTIVAL, SAN SEBASTIAN, Spain • INTERNATIONAL FILM FESTIVAL, BERLIN, Germany • INTERNATIONAL FILM EXHIBITION, VENICE, Italy • IBERIAN AND LATIN-AMERICAN FILM FESTIVAL, BIARRITZ, France • INTERNATIONAL FILM FESTIVAL, CHICAGO, USA • INTERNATIONAL FILM FESTIVAL, KARLOVY-VARY, Czechoslovakia • INTERNATIONAL FILM FESTIVAL, MUNICH, Germany • INTERNATIONAL FILM WEEK, VALLADOLID, Spain • DONATELLO'S DAVID • HOLLYWOOD ACADEMY OF MOTION PICTURES & SCIENCES

WHY DOES THE NATIONAL INSTITUTE OF CINEMATOGRAPHY PROMOTE CO-PRODUCTIONS IN ARGENTINA?

Because Argentina has the most important productions, resources and artistic and technical professionals in Latin America, at relatively convenient costs.

Because the quality of Argentine films has been rewarded by a long history of international awards.

Because Argentina may insert itself in international interest topics that attract different markets.

Because a successful movie in Argentina raises $ 3,250,000 and, additionally it may receive an industrial return of $ 1,700,000 from the National Institute of Cinematography, only with its exhibition at movie theaters during the first two months.

Because the INC has granted, since January 1992 up to the present, 35 preferential credits ranging between $ 300,000 and $ 800,000.

ARGENTINA WITH A THOROUGHLY EXPANDING INTERNAL MARKET, IS OPEN TO INTERNATIONAL JOINT VENTURES

70

A 1994 advert in *Variety* to potentially attract US film companies

'special interest', the percentage of the subsidy, or 'industrial recuperation', was lower. The idea was that the money returned to the producer could then be invested in a subsequent film project, thus providing the impetus for a continued and consistent film industry.

Definitions of the 'special interest' designation varied. One definition was 'films that stood out thematically, and that demonstrated artistic quality' (Lusnich 1994: 306); another commentator noted that it was 'unclear what the criteria were' (Raffo 1997). In some interviews, filmmakers emphasised the importance of attaining a level of technical expertise in determining the 'special interest' denomination.

The film laws (17.741 and 20.170) passed in 1968 continued to serve as legislation under the democratic regime until 1994, when new film legislation was passed. The definition of 'special interest' under the law was as follows:

a. The film contains relevant moral, social, educational or national values.
b. The film is produced especially for children.
c. The film displays interesting content and achieves a high level of film-making artistry.

Thirty-five percent of the films that attained 'special interest' status under Alfonsín were not 'national' in content, nor were they of educational interest. Instead, these films were probably given preferential status because they were films that would most likely perform well at the box office, and that could encourage the producers (many of whom were from established commercial film studios) to continue investing in film productions.

In fact, between 1980 and 1990, the National Film Institute authorised subsidies for between $20 and $25 million to national production that was mainly concentrated in the hands of three companies – the ones with the most films produced and the most commercial successes: Argentina Sono Film, Aries Cinematography and Victoria Productions. These groups obtained the majority of funding – 65 percent of the subsidies – while the remaining 35 percent were divided among more than twenty small production companies (Getino 1996).

The budget for film production during this time amounted to approximately $10 million per year, and the amount allocated for each project typically was between $150,000 and $200,000 (Anon. 1984). This was to equal sixty percent of the film's budget, with the remaining amount to be raised through private funding or alternative sources of funding. Because national film production has never been considered a lucrative form of investment, committed filmmakers have often had to mortgage their homes to raise the remaining funds to produce their films. Javier Torre, then chair of the Association of Argentine Film Directors stated in 1988 that there were '46 film directors who had put their possessions as collateral and were in danger of imminent bankruptcy' (quoted in Torrents 1993: 40).

One problem that arose from the more democratic form of issuing film loans was the smaller rate of return the institute faced. In 1998, it was calculated that between the years 1986 and 1989, there were outstanding debts to the INC amounting to $16 million. This failure to recuperate loan money was principally due to the release of a number of unsuccessful films, as well as the economic problems encountered near the end of Antín's tenure, such as hyperinflation. Patricia Moro, who at that time was in charge of film promotion, stated:

Antín tried … to help almost everyone, and quite a few were not successful, so therefore there was no way to return that kind of capital that they had received … The problem of hyperinflation did not help, as the loan/subsidy installments filmmakers received during a 16-month period would be worth one-half of its value in some cases – so this also contributed to the outstanding debt. (1998)

One of the central problems plaguing film producers in the late 1980s was obtaining access to exhibition circuits. The obstacles were twofold. Firstly, movie theatres, for the most part, were organised into chains that did not consider national cinema to be a 'safe investment'. These theatres, which were owned by Argentine nationals, acted as gatekeepers, separating films that were considered potentially profitable from those that were not. This distinction often broke down along national lines, and at one point national film producers and the film union tried to take the exhibitors to court for being "unpatriotic" and undermining a national industry (Torrents 1993: 46).

Typically, theatre exhibitors forged links with US distribution companies that worked systematically to exclude works from smaller distribution companies. Eliseo Subiela, now an established filmmaker, recalled how it took two years after completing *Hombre mirando al sudeste* (*Man Facing Southeast*, 1986) to be able to secure a movie theatre willing to release his film commercially (Torrents 1993: 43). At that time, he was able to convince two independent movie houses to show the film, and it became one of the most popular movies at home and abroad in 1987, bringing in 824,210 spectators.

Secondly, in the beginning of the economic crisis in 1987, cinema closures had a profound impact on the sustainability of the film industry. In 1960, there were 2,228 cinemas in the country, serving a population of approximately 20 million. During the Alfonsín era, 40.6 percent of the cinemas closed (Torrents 1993: 46). By 1989, only 427 theatres were still open, with a downward trend persisting into the early 1990s.

In Buenos Aires, well-established cinemas were being transformed into banks (Cine Social, Gran Sud, Once); videogame parlours (Callao and Studio); discotheques (Constitución, Atalaya and Argos); bingo halls (Alfa and Sarmiento); churches, especially of the evangelical sects (Roca, Nuevo Loria, Dante); and, in one case (Odeon), a car park (Kriger 1994). Many of these theatres would have been razed eventually to make way for the 'multiplexing' of cinemas, a phenomenon that began with the addition of significant foreign capital investment in the mid-1990s. While movie critics and writers nostalgically lamented the closure of these neighbourhood movie houses in the capital and its surrounding suburbs, very little was said about the rampant closures of movie theatres in the rural areas of Argentina, where cineplexes were unlikely to be built.

In addition to the general economic malaise that affected the film industry, changes in home entertainment technologies also negatively impacted on theatres. First, the rise of the VCR contributed to the demise of movie theatres. By 1982, an estimated 50,000 homes had VCRs. This marked the beginning of the home video revolution, one outgrowth of which, video piracy, went unchallenged until 1986. That year, large video companies invested in high-tech equipment to dub tapes and distribute nationwide to established video dealers.[11]

Changes in the television industry, such as the privatisation of various television channels, helped to increase TV audience viewership figures, which tended to have a negative impact on theatres. Under the military dictatorship, all private television stations, such as Channels 9 and 13, were confiscated and made the property of the state.

The rise of cable television in the democratic period also worked against movie theatre ownership, as many Argentines, especially those with limited resources, could not afford to spend money at the movies, but could watch entertainment programming at home for minimal cost. This strained the production of cinema, as ten percent of funding for film production was to come from a tax on box-office receipts. Changes were desperately needed to either bring people into the movie theatres or revise the system of collecting funds for the production of national cinema.

Heraldo del cine noted how the severity of the financial situation within the industry was symptomatic of the crises affecting the country as a whole. External debt, inflation and recession marked this downward spiral. The economic plan stressing austerity measures did not boost productivity and consumption (Anon. 1987b). The Association of Film Distributors, a group composed of small independent companies, wrote an open letter to *Heraldo* addressed to domestic and international film companies, stating that 'regrettably the film business has not been shielded from the ruinous situation facing the country, the effects reflected in the film audience figures (which in some cases has dropped fifty percent compared to last year). In addition, the closures of many neighbourhood movie theatres, ones in the suburbs and in the interior of the country have also contributed to the downturn' (quoted in Anon. 1987b: 1).

In 1988, the national economic situation was worsening, and even fewer people were spending money at the movies. In that year, film attendance figures hit the lowest number in two decades, at 28 million spectators (Getino 1995). INC director Antín attempted to rectify the situation by raising the public's consciousness about the interconnections between moviegoing practices and national film production finance. On 30 October 1988 he, with the support of President Alfonsín, declared 'National Cinema Day'. On that day, the purchase of one movie ticket allowed the viewer to attend up to five different films in one movie theatre. The penultimate day in October was selected in honour of 'the first day democracy returned to Argentina five years earlier' (Anon. 1988b: 25). In addition, the day had cultural importance as it marked when the ban on freedom of expression was lifted for all forms of culture and media.

A ceremony took place at the Grand Rex that evening featuring such guests as President Raúl Alfonsín, his cabinet ministers, representatives from the diplomatic sector, various senators and representatives from Congress, the secretaries of state and culture, film directors and producers, screen writers and film critics. Awards were given to pioneers in Argentina's cinema history, such as Eduardo Morera, the director of famed tango singer Carlos Gardel's film shorts, and two classic film directors from national cinema's 'golden age', Antonio Ber Ciani and Luis Saslavsky.

Alfonsín made a speech praising the 'boom' in national cinema that had occurred since he entered office as president. He expressed his gratitude to 'directors, actors and filmmakers that have demonstrated to the world what it means for a committed people to have the freedom to work towards peace and justice'. The attendance rate at movie theatres all over the country increased 1,000 percent from the previous Sunday. One critic noted that the purpose for this holiday was to commemorate the cultural importance of national cinema in the transition to democracy. He agreed with Alfonsín's assessment that Argentine cinema of this era held a privileged place in history (ibid.).

In this instance, then, the numerous film festival prizes given to national cinema during Alfonsín's term created a space in the national arena for exultation and widespread praise. It is a rare instance to find so many important statesmen, in addition to the nation's president, gather and glorify a cultural form such as the national cinema. In this era, however, national cinema had a tremendous impact on international relations by helping Argentina reconstruct a palatable image for the world to see and critically acclaim.

The question remained regarding how to gain access to national cinema viewers domestically. One way that Argentine films could be exhibited outside of theatrical releasing was on national television channels. The Argentine model of film production, because it receives state assistance, resembles the European system of film financing, as opposed to the US commercial model. However, one marked difference between the European and Argentine models is that state-run television stations in Europe play an instrumental role in financing film productions.[12] The trend in Europe began with West Germany's FRG in the early 1970s and became a general phenomenon from the early 1980s on for stations such as the UK's Channel 4, France's Canal Plus, Italy's RAI and Spain's TVE.

In contrast, the integration of television and film did not begin in Argentina until the mid-1990s, an issue that has always raised considerable ire for the film community. Part of this tenuous relationship stems from the uneven trajectory that marks the history of television ownership. When Alfonsín came to power, television stations, which had suffered debts under military rule and had been nationalised since 1974, reverted only gradually to private ownership, beginning with Alejandro Romay's Channel 9. This revitalised the television industry; almost immediately, Romay began to revamp the programming sector by developing innovative in-house productions, thus helping to attract a strong base of viewers in all regions of the country. In 1985, Channel 9 received the highest audience ratings in the history of Argentine television (Anon. 1986a).

It was not until President Menem's administration that all three television stations were privatised, leaving only Channel 7 in the public sector. With these shifts in ownership, it took time for television companies to gain control of their assets before embarking on collaborative projects. INC Director Antín attempted to negotiate an equitable relationship with television companies (by imploring them to pay fair market value to screen national films on television), but he made very little headway. These problems grew more serious as television set ownership increased, growing from 5.1 million homes in 1980 to 7.1 million in 1990 (source: UNESCO statistical yearbook 1997).

In the 1970s, the majority of screen programming was occupied by *enlatados*, or inexpensive films and television shows imported from the United States. Because the programmes had for the most part recuperated their costs in the home market, the United States could export them at minimal cost.

Although, as time went on, more resources were available to produce in-house television programmes such as comedy specials, *telenovelas* and news magazine-style programmes, there was no effort to partner with national film producers to make television movies or feature films. Instead, films were purchased from national producers for very low prices, with the argument that these were the rates they paid for US films. Thus, the funds received from national television stations were so insignificant that they rarely covered even ten percent of a film's production costs.[13] For example, when Héctor Olivera's film *La noche de los lápices* aired on television, it reached an audience high of four million viewers in Argentina, a figure representing more than ten percent of the population. This film, a gripping testimonial based on the true story of high school students who were kidnapped and disappeared in the city of La Plata during the military dictatorship, evidently reached more viewers when it appeared on television rather than in the theatres. However, the channel that aired it purchased the rights to air the film twice for $10,000, which translates to reaching a huge number of viewers for a mere $5,000 per screening (García Oliveri 1992).

This disparity between the film and television community was a bone of contention that compelled film lobbyists to write letters of protest to Congress, asking legislators to implement structural changes in the law. More than one account indicated that the lack of adequate payment for films was a rallying point for a mobilised sector of the film community, including film unionists, directors' organisations and producers' organisations.

At the onset of the national economic crisis in 1988, Manuel Antín appealed to the television executives of the 'free' television stations, asking them to stop broadcasting movies on the weekends, to reduce competition with the cinema. Antín's defence of this position was that in various countries in Europe, television executives upheld similar agreements; nations such as Spain banned movies on television on Saturdays, and France prohibited movies on Wednesday, Thursday, Friday and Saturday all day and Sunday night until midnight (Anon. 1988a). The INC director hoped that this kind of agreement with television would encourage people to attend movie theatres on the weekend, thus boosting revenues for the national industry.

However, in addition to the outright refusal by the television executives to discontinue airing movies on television, the suggestion proved to be unpopular with the public. In an article published in *Página 12*, a more left-leaning newspaper with a significant circulation, well-known writer Osvaldo Soriano (1988) responded to Antín's call with a scathing polemic. He charged that there were many reasons to disagree with this proposal. Firstly, by banning films on television one was necessarily discriminating against people with limited resources. He argued that taking television away from people who could not afford to attend the movies would not rectify the situation at hand. Secondly, Soriano felt that this measure was too protectionist towards national cinema, and that 'television could not be blamed for the deficiencies of film'. Finally, he asserted that European television did not ban movies to the extent that Antín claimed they did.

During the Alfonsín administration, tensions between film and television were exacerbated by the prevailing tendency of state film officials to (unofficially) label television as a degraded form of mass culture rather than to try to work to change existing television material to encourage cultural and educational programming on television. Antín's elitist attitude towards the television medium showed clearly in a 1995 interview. When asked if he believed that film and television would ever be financially integrated, he replied:

> No, there is not much hope for it, but I appreciate television for taking the worst element of the moviegoing public, so we can explore parts of the cinema that are more magical, and that are not love stories, *telenovelas*, etc., so we can fly higher.

When asked if he did not instead want to 'convert' that public into attending the cinema he was so fond of, he said, 'democratically speaking, people need to choose what they enjoy the most, what they are closer to or can afford – if they want to watch trash, I can't stop them.'

If Antín was averse to conjoining a 'mass cultural' industry such as television with the more 'pristine' film industry, the television sector had its reservations about the film industry as well. Because film was not traditionally stable or lucrative, investment in it was not attractive to television executives, either in the state or the private sector. In 1990, ATC, the state-owned channel, signed an agreement to promote film production via co-financing (Torrents 1993). The first systematic interaction between these cultural industries did not occur until legislation was passed in 1994 encouraging large television companies to cooperate with the National Film Institute in co-producing national films.

To further the INC's plan to circulate Argentine cinema abroad, a film distribution office was set up in Madrid to enable Europeans (principally) to more easily purchase and screen Argentine cinema. Argencine, as it was dubbed, acted as a distribution arm for five years (1985–90). This service was available to those producers who did not have pending agreements with larger private distribution companies, or who did not possess the financial wherewithal to distribute their products themselves. During its operation, Argencine distributed films to regions such as Western and Eastern Europe, Latin America, Asia, Africa and

Australia. Notably, the US was absent from this list. This elision could
that traditionally the US was not a significant buyer of Argentine films. Oct.
Getino, who gathered extensive information on this organisation, conclude
that 'from 1986 to 1990, 79 copies of Argentine films were sold. The major
buyers were state-run television stations, at 83 percent, for exhibition in movie
theatres, at 12 percent, and for film, television and home video use, at five percent.' Regionally, 48 copies of films went to seven countries in Western Europe,
and 15 copies to two countries in Eastern Europe. 11 copies were distributed
throughout Latin America, and the remainder were distributed as follows: six
copies in three Asian countries, three copies in one African country and two
copies in Australia (1995: 298).

Argencine was closed down in 1990 due to complaints by producers that
the organisation, being a state-run entity, did not know how to manage finances
efficiently and was unprofitable for the producers it intended to assist. After
this experiment, the National Film Institute participated in distribution only
by setting up booths at film festivals and large film markets to assist with the
promotion of Argentine cinema. Distribution is now left solely to the producers
themselves and the private sector.

Placement of the distribution wing in Europe (rather than in Latin America)
was not accidental; the National Film Institute obviously wished to target European markets. Clearly there was an economic reason for looking to wealthier
countries with a more developed public service television sector (a major buyer
of Argentine films). Another factor related to marketing films for a European
audience is the nature of the cinematic product itself. Most of these films were
produced as auteurist cinema, that is, a kind of filmmaking with a 'signature
style' that brands the director as author. Because this type of film appealed more
to an educated, middle-class audience, it could only be directed to certain segments of the population who also had disposable income. In addition, because
this filmmaking tradition had its roots in the European continent, it was only
logical that the largest consumers of art-house cinema would be in Europe.

One such film, which managed to garner film festival awards throughout
the world, including the aforementioned 1986 Academy Award for Foreign Language Film, was Luis Puenzo's *La historia oficial*. It is not surprising that the film
resonated with an international viewership, given the middle-class perspective
taken by the director/screenwriter in describing the recent painful events in Argentina's history. The film enjoyed success in Europe (partly because it shared the
Best Actress Award at Cannes) and performed relatively well in the US after the
Academy Awards. In Argentina, it had attracted a sizable viewership (889,940)
after its first release in 1985. After gaining accolades abroad, it was re-released
and attracted almost as many viewers as the previous year (828,436).[14]

Many Argentine films retold recent history in a way that had been repressed
and erased during that recent dark age. The resulting social narratives took on a
form of collective memory of the recently censored past. Tales of exile, margin-

alisation and disappearances filled Argentine movie screens. While these films served as a form of catharsis for audiences and worked to discredit the past regime, there were still facets of the dictatorship that were not criticised. Cultural critic Fredric Jameson (1988) notes that elisions and absences are as much a part of a text as the present and visible ones. Thus, films like *La historia oficial* presented historical events in a way that reflected the discourses that circulated about a historical event at that moment.

Although the *testimonios* functioned as a therapeutic device for domestic audiences, they served a different purpose for international viewers. The sets of discourses that the films themselves engaged with, whether on conscious or unconscious levels, were affected by the globalisation of the world economy. In the early 1980s, Argentina was attempting to project a new image. The films made in the *apertura* were presented in a glossy commercial style, which appealed to middle-class values but at the same time tried to maintain references to Argentine national culture. *La historia oficial*, in part because of its middle-class bias, has been dubbed the *Battleship Potemkin* (in terms of propaganda) of the Radical Party (Curubeto 1998).

La historia oficial is the tale of an upper-middle-class woman, Alicia (Norma Aleandro), who is a history teacher at a private secondary school. Her husband, Roberto (Héctor Alterio), is a wealthy businessman who gained his fortune through his compliance with the military junta. The story is set in March 1983. The Malvinas War fiasco has recently occurred, and the military is slowly losing power and legitimacy. Public demonstrations, organised by the Asociación Civil Abuelas de Plaza de Mayo (Grandmothers of the Plaza de Mayo) and the Asociación Madres de Plaza de Mayo (Mothers of the Plaza de Mayo) occur frequently and en masse.[15] Through newspaper clippings, her critical students, a leftist literature teacher, a college friend who has returned from exile and an Abuela she befriends, Alicia comes to the grim realisation that her adopted child Gaby (Analia Castro), brought home by her husband, is none other than a child born of disappeared parents. Gaby was born just as her mother, an alleged subversive, was murdered by the military. The child's bestowal on Roberto and Alicia was a form of reward that the junta gave to complicitous elites. The film attempts to expose the realities of life under dictatorship by focusing on the horrible truth the protagonist must face.

However, the film's content as a whole does not take a strong stance in blaming the military or the middle class for the atrocities wreaked on the populace. In fact, most of the films made during this period reflect an uneasiness about blaming the military for crimes committed. A culture of fear during the dictatorship inhibited any form of public expression to emerge, apart from a few courageous human rights groups who for the most part were not middle class, such as the Madres de Plaza de Mayo.[16] In addition, middle- and upper-class elites working in collaboration with the regime in war profiteering also helped to maintain the repressive state apparatus.

Films made during the *apertura* are critical of the past dictatorship, but any trace of a progressive ideology in creating a more equitable society (such as films made in the New Latin American Cinema vein) had faded. B. Ruby Rich calls this 'a shift from the "revolutionary" to the "revelatory"' (1991: 14). Instead of focusing on building coalitions and working collectively to construct a democratic way of life, films were now extolling the virtues of individual self-realisation. In an interview director Luis Puenzo states: 'I told the story from my own perspective, that of a great majority who never participated in repression but who felt complicity. It is not a heroic stance, but it was a position I was in' (1986: 17).

Alicia, the protagonist of *La historia oficial*, is, as Puenzo says in his interview, symbolic of the perspective of the middle class, who knew that class warfare was taking place, but were complacent or feared for their lives. The real-life protagonists who truly did lay their lives on the line were not members of the universally regarded middle class. However, to make this film understandable to a film festival audience, the main character acted as a stand-in for an internationalised middle class. Commenting on such a situation, Fredric Jameson writes:

> Whatever its defects and problems [Althusser's work on ideology] is positive because it stresses the gap between the local positioning of the individual subject and the totality of class relations in which he or she is situated, a gap between the phenomenological perception and a reality that transcends all individual thinking or experience. (1988: 353)

The scenes that best illustrate the socio-economic class dimensions of the protagonist's worldview are the conversations between Alicia, the upper middle-class, slim, pale-skinned, sophisticated-looking woman, and Sara, a working-class woman, dressed modestly, probably of Italian extraction, who is a member of the Abuelas de Plaza de Mayo. When Alicia first seeks out this organisation, she pretends she is looking for information on a child of the disappeared. She leaves a description of Gaby, and soon Sara is there, watching Gaby and Alicia as they walk home from school. Sara claims to be Gaby's grandmother, and Sara and Alicia begin to discuss the matter.

Their main interaction takes place at a café. The scene begins with a long shot of the coffee shop, where the viewer sees both Alicia and Sara inside through a window. There are passersby, and cars drive by, reflected in the window. Inside the café, as the two women discuss issues that could profoundly affect both of their lives forever, one can hear the sounds of traffic outside; children playing pinball or video games are seen and heard in the background. The conversation is set in a crowded urban space, perhaps to demonstrate how these issues interface with everyday life in Argentina. The café is a common meeting ground, where issues surrounding the horrors of the dictatorship are revealed.

The scene revolves around a set of photos, which serve as a mem for Sara to discuss the past. She shows what few photos remain of peared daughter-in-law – one as a child and one as an adult, posed with her husband, Sara's son, also among the disappeared. Close-ups of Sara show her talking about the photos while subtly wiping away tears as she recalls her son's wedding day. Sara describes the wedding, pointing out that 'the groom's suit was borrowed from a fellow factory worker, which explains why it doesn't fit him well'.

Sara is portrayed as a garrulous woman whose working-class status is shown by, among other things, her willingness to discuss matters of finance, a topic that is a taboo according to middle-class etiquette. She also might feel motivated to speak to avoid any uncomfortable silence. Alicia, on the other hand, is quiet except when she sees the photo of the daughter as a child, who looks uncannily like Gaby. Throughout the scene there are continuous close-ups of Sara and the photographs (shot from Alicia's point of view) and then cuts to Alicia. Eventually both are crying, but they are always filmed separately, as if to show the uncomfortable rift between them. As we see Alicia crying and dabbing her eyes, Sara's hand reaches into the frame to support her. Alicia pushes her hand back and continues to sob. This prompts Sara to remark, 'You mustn't cry now. There is no use in crying.' It becomes clear that Sara has suffered more hardship than Alicia could even imagine. Sara is pragmatic and has no time for tears. As a working-class woman, she has had to face many obstacles – the kidnapping and disappearance and/or murder of her son, her daughter-in-law and her granddaughter, as well as economic hardship. She has also most likely faced harassment by police and others while demonstrating against the junta with the Abuelas every week.

Despite the film's recognition of Sara's strength, she is not treated throughout the film as a subject. Instead, she is objectified as the 'other' – someone who is unfamiliar and who is not taken as a legitimate voice due to her lack of social skills. Throughout the film, the viewer sees middle- and upper-class women discussing how other people's children went to war in the Malvinas, and how other people's children were 'subversives'. It becomes evident that it is mainly the poor who are disappearing and being killed fighting in the war, but we do not hear this from their perspective. We see the Abuelas' signs that document all of the missing men, women and children, but never do we actually see or hear a testament of those alleged 'subversives', with the exception of Ana (Chunchuna Villafañe), the exiled character who has been tortured for associating with a supposed 'enemy of the state'.[17]

The only character from a working-class background who is viewed as a subject is Benítez, a literature teacher at the school where Alicia works. Benítez is able to fit into the middle-class setting with ease due to his high level of education. He dresses simply, does not have a car, and teaches his students literature from a populist perspective. One scene contrasts Alicia's traditional teaching to Benítez's charismatic pedagogy when he reads aloud with much affectation the national novel *Juan Moreira*, a legend of the lone gaucho. Moreira is an allegory

La historia oficial (1985): Sara (Chela Ruíz, right) as a Grandmother of the Plaza de Mayo

of the last living symbol of freedom in the Argentine rural interior; an independent lover of liberty, he resists foreign intrusion and modernisation. While the students delight in the mock battles Benítez stages in his reading of *Juan Moreira*, it becomes increasingly evident that the feeling of freedom that emanates from the novel is in tension with the traditional setting of the high school.

Despite their differences, Benítez befriends Alicia, but he has no illusions about her; he knows that she is a sheltered woman who is unaware of her political and social surroundings. At one point he states: 'It is better that you do not know what is going on [currently], because by knowing, you would automatically be complicitous in this situation.' When Alicia begins to understand her indirect involvement in state transgressions and divulges her concern to him, he responds ironically: 'You simply have bourgeois guilt.' Benítez acts as a bridge between the middle-class world and the more radicalised and working-class sectors. Because he works within a dominant institution and not outside it, this legitimises his viewpoint more than other radicalised characters, such as Sara.

The Abuelas/Madres, who historically were the most vocal and active in resisting military domination, are not given a strong and definitive voice in the film. While their demonstrations are shown twice on screen, there is never any discussion of what they demand, who they are and what their political ideology is. Perhaps in part because they are not espousing middle-class feminist ideals, those of 'modern' women who have careers as well as family, they have alienated groups on the right as well as on the 'bourgeois left' when they advocate justice, an economic redistribution of wealth and real democratic change – not just equality for women and other middle-class ideals.

La historia oficial is a film about bourgeois individualism. It is one woman's story, a *Bildungsroman* in which Alicia chooses to leave her morally corrupt husband, raise her own consciousness and return her daughter to her rightful grandmother. It is a story told for a middle-class audience, in which the main characters are universalised as middle-class and successful. The film functions to enhance the middle-class viewer's subjective sense of innocence while obscuring the viewer's complicity, just as Alicia and Roberto's complicity tends to be obscured. The collective is underplayed, such as the true heroines of the film – the Abuelas and the Madres – and instead, the individual's coming to consciousness is lauded.

The historical events retold in *La historia oficial* deal with the dictatorship's slow decline and how it was able to maintain power for seven years. Alicia's obliviousness to the violence that surrounds her is symbolic of the middle class – a privileged group whose members perpetuate the actions of the military by shielding themselves from the horrible realities of the terrorist state. A symbolic motif that runs throughout the film is the strict delineation between good and evil. When Alicia is distraught over the shattering of her perfect world, she visits a priest who tells her not to question her child's origins, that Gaby is a gift from God. It becomes clear that the Catholic Church played an active role in supporting the actions of the military. The film condemns the priest by making him an immoral figure.

However, other complicitous figures are shielded from blame. Roberto and his business associates, while they are seen as shady characters, are never shown directly committing any crimes. The one military figure portrayed in the film, the general, is always seen in social settings and is never shown in the corridors of power. Therefore, while the film appears to unmask the realities of the dictatorship, the atrocities towards the disappeared and the economic violence waged on the population, these realities are actually only described on a cursory level, and there are no images of torture by the military within the film. I would argue that this absence purposefully worked to 'sanitise' the images of dictatorship so as not to *epater la bourgeoisie* (shock the bourgeoisie) and distance this style of filmmaking away from the earlier, more gritty violence seen in the militant cinema of the past (such as the police beatings seen in *La hora de los hornos*) and in doing so prevented this film from overtly denouncing the State from wrongdoing.

The Church, on the other hand, is painted as a corrupt institution. Such overt criticism might have been easier to make toward the Church, since the Church and State had become less linked after military rule. In addition, Radical Party ideology was strongly liberal and anticlerical. Moreover, it was easier to blame a group that was disempowered with the dissolution of the regime than to condemn international businessmen, the middle class and other complicitous groups.

The only physical violence shown in the film is towards the end, when Roberto beats up Alicia by slapping her and crushing her fingers in the doorjamb. The domestic violence is brought on when Roberto asks where Gaby is (Alicia has taken her to the grandparents' house) and Alicia, echoing the Abuelas, states, 'Isn't it terrible not to know where your children are?' In a fury, Roberto reacts violently, and this allegorises the violence the State commits toward its citizens. At another level of signification, this scene demonstrates how the female is abused by the male in a patriarchal society. This sets up a dichotomy of the victim/victimiser, in which the victim is not framed as an agent or proactive subject. What is elided are the ways in which proactive subjects like the Abuelas were able to transcend the binaries like male/female, public/private and so on. In addition, the way in which the dictatorship is historicised demonstrates the unwillingness of new democratic subjects to delve very deeply in the condemnation of the military, the complicitous middle class and others, such as the US government.

During the early 1980s, when Argentina was becoming part of a 'free and democratic' capitalist system, the economic landscape shifted from that of a nation under national capitalist interests or foreign capital investment (such as the British presence in the 1880s), to one controlled by transnational interests. The films of this period made a break from films with expressly nationalist content to ones produced with a 'geopolitical aesthetic' (Jameson 1982: 353). This concept offers a method of understanding how the content and forms of cultural objects function within the realm of transnational commercial culture. This is an ideology in which the middle-class is naturalised as the only class that has agency in a global capitalist landscape. No longer are there criticisms of world powers, and capitalism is embraced unquestioningly.

This film is made in a glossy style with relatively high production values. Puenzo's background in advertising (indeed, he has been called the best television commercial director in Argentina) is clearly evident in shots as when Roberto is sitting in a dimly-lit room in his house. There is a close-up of his shoes as he kicks them off while sitting in a chair, and then there is a quick cut to a close-up of his whiskey glass, which has ice cubes in it. The glass is handled by Roberto, and we see it glistening, shrouded in a bluish light. The next shot is a close-up of Roberto's profile, with his hand covering most of his face. He lets out a long sigh of resignation. Raul Beycero notes that this 'whiskey shot' fits perfectly with Puenzo's use of the 'language of advertising', or *lenguaje del cine publicitario* (1997: 28). Ultimately, using glossy commercial shots help the film conform to the established conventions of an international (read: US) style of filmmaking – an aesthetic that reinforces palatability.

One theme that *La historia oficial* barely alludes to is the way in which foreign governments were complicitous in maintaining the military junta. Where was the United States, the omnipresent surveillance force in the Western hemisphere? Although the CIA and other agencies were involved in Argentina's dealings, the films themselves, although they were critical of the military, did not extend blame to other Western governments. I would argue that for the sake of diplomacy and maintaining good public relations, films made in that era avoided blaming the United States or other countries. Santiago Colas, in his research on the connection between US interests and the Argentine government, quotes both Argentine Brigadier General Graffigna and US General Gordon Sumner:

> General Graffigna stated that 'The Southern Cone's defense is vital to the security of America, and therefore to the West' [against communist subversion] and 'We Argentines have an inheritance that comes from the depths of history: liberty, order, justice, property, family, lifestyle, faith in God. We are the custodians and protectors of the inheritance.' All of this received an important seconding from the US General Gordon Sumner, former head of one of the United States' Inter-American defense training facilities: 'Your country and in fact all of the Southern Cone, have a geographical position and strategic resources that will require the development of a role in the future ... This region in the world is terribly important to the whole free world.' (1994: 125)

Because the United States was implicated in the brutal military dictatorship, American businessmen appear infrequently during the film. One American is a regular who comes into Roberto's office, speaks in English and crassly attempts to seduce the secretary. The way he says 'next time I want you to give me a tour of the city', alludes to the prostitute-like relationship between US business and Argentina. We are not told of the specific relationship the business interests of the United States have with Argentina, although a major transaction was the sale of US weapons and other manufactured imports to the military. While the film does allude to this ugly side of the business relationship, there are no critical statements made about it. In an era of transnationalism, most of the Argentine sentiment reflected in this film demonstrates a willingness to integrate into what then US President George H. W. Bush called the 'New World Order'.

At the end of the film, the young girl Gaby is sitting in a rocking chair waiting for her parents at her grandparents' house. There is visual irony here because the rocking chair serves as a reminder of a story told earlier in the film, when Alicia relates to the priest that as a young girl, she would sit in her rocking chair, waiting for her parents to arrive to pick her up. When they were both killed in a car accident, little Alicia waited patiently, and felt a deep sense of abandonment when they never arrived. Now Gaby, in the chair, patiently waiting, feeling that same sense of abandonment, gives the viewer a sense of repetition and of a circular pattern. While Argentina is supposedly a newly democratic country that is purging itself of the dark realities of the dictatorship years, there remains a sense that issues remain unresolved. This last scene reflects an unhappy closure; that is, an uncertainty of the people, who perhaps wonder whether the new government is undergoing the same pattern of abandoning its people the way it did under the military.

While the film's purpose was to discredit the old military government and play up the new democratic system, there was still a small spark of self-conscious criticism going on. Are the same patterns of the past repeating themselves? Is real change towards democratisation taking place? While these contradictions are not resolved in the text, the political realities that followed the making of the film proved otherwise. In the end, no true justice was served. When Menem succeeded Alfonsín, he immediately pardoned the military for all its crimes. These military generals, such as junta leaders Jorge Rafael Videla, Roberto Viola and others, served time in prison, but lived in plush apartments within prison walls and were allowed to make free phone calls. The maximum time the top military officials served was four years, because President Menem signed amnesty laws in 1989 to free them. The Mothers and the Grandmothers of the Plaza de Mayo continued to march every week in the plaza, demanding true justice and real closure for the Argentine people until 2006 when they forged solidarity with President Kirchner's government.

By utilising Jameson's analytical framework as an interpretive tool, it becomes possible to untangle some of the discourses that circulated during the democratic *apertura*. Some discourses were suppressed, such as openly criticising the United States for its cooperation with the regime and strongly condemning the Argentine middle class as well as the junta, for reasons coinciding with Argentina's entry into the transnational, global capitalist system. This film exemplifies how films were framed for international art-house consumption in ways that were politically, socially and culturally palatable to the bourgeoisie.

Raul Alfonsín's presidency was a return to democratic rule after a dark era in Argentina's history. It was a period of renewal for national filmmaking; censorship was lifted and many films told dramatic tales of a recent horrible time for many Argentines. Manuel Antín, head of the INC, has been lauded for the 'boom' in Argentine cinema during this time. However, because the Radical Party esteemed 'high culture', or art geared towards the middle and upper classes, cinema became geared for prestigious film festival exhibition rather than a broad national audience.

Films like *La historia oficial* were directed towards a particular middle-class audience in order that Argentina as a nation would be recognised by the Western industrialised world. This notion of recognition or *espejismo*, is an issue that cosmopolitan Argentines have struggled with throughout its history. It is clear that the 'boom' in Argentine cinema helped to shape and sanitise Argentina's image internationally; more importantly, in films like *La historia oficial*, it constructed a middle-class image of itself, thereby affirming (and to some extent reifying) its identity within a broader international middle-class aesthetic.

Furthermore, films like *La historia oficial* were also designed for a particular middle-class audience and promoted by the state distribution arm Argencine.

While this helped to boost Argentina's image abroad, it did not help to sustain a healthy domestic industry at home. Argentine cinema at this juncture became known for its 'quality' attributes, but ultimately could not compete for high audience numbers – especially with the closures of cinemas due to increased competition from cable television subscriptions, high rates of VCR ownership and an ensuing economic crisis. The film sector, alarmed by the possible collapse of the industry, appealed to legislators to help restructure the INC's revenue streams. The legislators' efforts were realised during President Menem's administration, the subject of the next chapter.

CHAPTER 3

MENEM'S NEOLIBERAL POLITICS AND THE BIRTH OF THE BLOCKBUSTER

By 1989, the crisis of hyperinflation plaguing the national landscape since 1984 had only grown worse. The peak rate of inflation soared to previously unmatched heights in world history, to 4,923 percent (source: Secretary of Press, Presidency of the Nation – Facts and Works, 1997). The level of public anxiety skyrocketed, and food riots broke out in Buenos Aires and the provincial cities of Córdoba and Rosario. President Raúl Alfonsín, rendered powerless, resigned six months before his official term ended.

In the 1989 presidential elections, Peronist candidate Carlos Saúl Menem, ex-governor of the interior province of La Rioja, beat Radical Party candidate Eduardo Angeloz with 47 percent of the popular vote and a clear majority of the Electoral College. Menem won the election under the traditional Peronist platform, emphasising social welfare rights and solidarity with labour unions. He appealed principally to the rural and urban workers, the key actors mobilised in populist regimes throughout Latin America. During the Alfonsín era, the Peronists fiercely opposed any efforts to privatise state-run enterprises. Menem, too, in his campaign, tried to dispel any fears that he planned to shrink the State's holdings. He asserted: 'We [the Peronists] will not privatise the main state enterprises, we will make them efficient' (quoted in Petrazzini 1995: 80).

However, as soon as he was elected to office, Menem proceeded to turn his back on all his promises of welfare state intervention. When he assumed office, neoliberal policies of privatisation and economic liberalisation, vigorously endorsed by the World Bank, became the main economic strategy (Gerchunoff & Torre 1998). To try to curb the massive inflation, Menem set up emergency measures in all aspects of the economy to increase the state's badly needed revenue to pay off a foreign debt that had escalated to $62 billion. The president appointed business executives of the Argentine multinational company Bunge and Born to the cabinet.[1] Together, Menem and the company forged close ties with global corporate elites in order to encourage foreign investment as a means of alleviating the massive debt. To put revenue in the state coffers, Menem embarked upon a sell-off of many state-owned and state-operated institutions. Companies like the national telephone system Entel were sold to the first and lowest bidders. (Ultimately Entel was split into two phone companies, one owned by the Spanish company Telefónica, and the other owned by Italian STET.) In the following two years, Argentina would become the country with the largest number of privatisations in the world (Petrazzini 1995: 52).

Jeremy Adelman describes Menem's strategy as an attempt to dissolve the populist strain within Peronism and to conform to the global business elite's economic agenda; it was also an attempt to end populism as Perón envisioned it. Adelman states:

> Free market liberalisation, privatisation, restoration of emphasis on exports, curbing trade union power, and limits on political participation and expression of popular grievance are not just momentary responses to internal and international pressures, but the crest of a historic struggle to shatter populist alliances and their economic programmes. (1994: 66)

Menem's administration has been described as a 'neopopulist' regime – that is, he was a leader abiding by the 'New Economic Order' espoused by the global elite (similar to Fujimori's regime in Peru and Salinas de Gortari's in Mexico), but simultaneously retaining the older charismatic and authoritarian tendencies of past populist leader Perón. Rather than adhere to democratic rules of order, populist leaders have preferred to act independently of legislative bodies. José del Tronco, an Argentine political scientist, described *Menemismo* as 'mixing neoliberal reforms with clientelism' (1996: 221). Therefore, while economic policies drastically veered away from a statist model, they retained the 'old guard' power dynamics such as *amiguismo* found in paternalistic forms of leadership. Although Menem's economic policy seemed to contradict the central tenets of General Juan Perón's original vision, he was accepted as a Peronist by members of the Partido Justicialista (PJ). Juan Corradi, an Argentine sociologist, notes that

> the political identity of Peronism is not based on programmes and measures, or on conventional pork-barrel politics, but on the intangibles of collective memories, leadership style and popular culture. The marriage of deep loyalty and pragmatism, of charisma and expediency, was a feature of the Peronist movement from the beginning. (1995: 77–8)

As a consequence of Menem's neoliberal turn, the budget for the cultural wing (including education) was reduced (minimally) by 0.5 percent from 1989 to 1992. In the city of Buenos Aires, the cuts were much more drastic: in 1986, the budget for education, the arts and culture was 6.9 percent of the municipal budget; by 1992 it had fallen to 3.6 percent.[2] As a result, esteemed supporters of the president such as Peronist deputy Carlos 'Chacho' Alvarez, actor Norman

Briski and filmmaker Fernando 'Pino' Solanas all publicly criticised Menem's veer to the right and subsequently broke with the official party to form new organisations. Alvarez created El Grupo de Ocho ('The Group of Eight'), later to become a centre-left party called Frepaso. Briski ran for a deputy position in 1991 for the party Encuentro Popular ('Popular Reunion'), and Solanas won a seat in the Chamber of Deputies under the Frente del Sur ('Southern Front'). All were discouraged with how little attention was given to sustaining and nurturing the cultural realm in Argentina. According to Deputy Alvarez:

> The problem is that a cultural platform does not exist in this government. The Radicals (while far from being perfect themselves) have had cultural discourses integrated into their general platform. Instead, the Menemists use an economist [*economista*] rhetoric that is completely void of anything cultural. (Quoted in Blanco & Marchetti 1992: 2)

Fernando Solanas, disgruntled with the apparent disinterest in the arts by the new administration, worked with then-Secretary of Culture Julio Bárbaro (who was replaced soon after) to propose the creation of a Latin American cultural centre in a vacant shopping arcade called Galerías Pacifico. According to Bárbaro, this centre would be 'more substantial than the National Library' (ibid.) Instead, Menem's close friend, businessman Mario Falak, an owner of discotheques and the upscale Alvear Hotel, was given license to redevelop the Galerías Pacifico into a shopping centre.

Clearly, Menem's administration was privileging the private sector and the commercial business world over artistic and cultural territory that previously had attempted to transcend the laws of the market. In addition, Menem placed his close friends from the business world in administrative positions within the cultural sector, thus creating a corporate 'supervision' from which the artistic and cultural realms traditionally had tried to remain apart. The emphasis on commercial culture over unique, auteur-inspired work led critics to call the cultural policy of the Menem administration the 'culture of the shopping mall'.

Julio Bárbaro defined the zeitgeist as the age of rampant consumerism. He noted that 'at the moment, [culture] is defined as conspicuous consumption, which substitutes image for substance. That is to say, that my identity hinges on the suit I wear or the car I drive' (quoted in Belaunzarán & Blanco 1993: 6).

This attitude can be traced to an earlier Peronist version of cultural policy during the 1950s that privileged mass culture over the culture of intellectuals. Menem took this idea of elevating mass commercial culture and infused it with corporate sponsorship and the participation of the global corporate elite. Radical Party senator Ricardo Laferriére viewed the change in this manner: 'The Menem government adopted a cultural model copied from the North Americans, whereby cultural policy is to keep culture open and exposed to the laws of a savage capitalism' (Blanco & Marchetti 1992: 3). Thus, Argentine cultural policy started following in the footsteps of the United States, which represents a move away from its original idol, the European model. Journalists Eduardo Blanco and Pablo Marchetti note that 'distanced from the European model, where the state gives strong subsidies to support cultural production, President Menem opted to leave this sector in the hands of entrepreneurs, who do not presently invest in it' (1992: 3).

As mentioned previously, many Peronists who had once supported Menem became openly critical of his shift in allegiance. These criticisms sometimes met with violent opposition. The outspoken Fernando Solanas, for example, was preparing *El viaje* (*The Journey*, 1992), a film that alludes to Menem's policy of 'savage capitalism', when he was shot in the legs six times by armed thugs on 22 May 1991. His assailants wore fake noses and moustaches as a form of disguise, and screamed, '*Hijo de puta, ahora te vas a callar*' ('Son of a bitch, this will shut you up'), a reference to the criticisms he made of President Menem (Rosemberg & Blanco 1993). This attack served as a warning to those defenders of free speech that the threat of state-sponsored violence was not over (Newman 1991: 1–2).

Although this was clearly not an attempted robbery (the armed men did not confiscate money, the car or other valuables), the judge refused to consider the case as a political crime, and instead charged the attackers with a robbery attempt, the abuse of arms and serious wounding (*lesiones graves*). Ultimately, this event strengthened Solanas's commitment, along with others (such as actor Miguel Angel Solá, who was also threatened), to be outspoken against the new economic regime endorsed by Menem and other heads of key global banking institutions.

In the aftermath of the hyperinflationary period, the government imposed austerity measures to curb inflation and stabilise the economy. Economic Minister Domingo Cavallo proposed slashing the budget in the cultural sector. In 1989 legislation was passed, dubbed the 'Emergency Film Law', mandating that all movie ticket tax revenues that had been earmarked for film production were to be appropriated by the Ministry of the Economy. This law was repealed in 1990. During the months of deliberation when the funds were frozen, the film production sector was paralysed.

Réne Mugica, the celebrated 1940s 'golden age' filmmaker and actor, became the new head of the INC on 14 July 1989. He, along with Vice Director Octavio Getino, proposed a plan to reorient the Film Institute towards sustaining the infrastructure (for example, by refurbishing theatres and so on) rather than solely maintaining production levels. In an interview for a film magazine, Getino stated:

> The difference between our term at the INC and the previous one is that we are more concerned with helping to build an industrial project and stabilise labour for our workers. Regardless if we win film prizes or not, what matters is that people survive in the labour market. This is not solely an economic

mission, it is political-cultural (político-cultural); rather than looking so much to the exterior, it is time we begin thinking about the interests of our people at home. (Quoted in Thieburger & Dupcovsky 1990: 11)

Mugica and Getino's central tenets were (i) to revitalise the domestic market (as opposed to exports); (ii) to oversee and assert some control over the new uses of the cinema in television, home video and cable; (iii) to reinstate the screen quota; and (iv) to 'federalise' the industry through the creation of regional film centres (Lusnich 1994: 304).

Unfortunately, Mugica's administration was not effective, largely because of the economic crisis. In 1989 only 13 films were produced and national attendance was low. Octavio Getino noted:

It is the case of Argentina in 1989, where of 13 films released, only two commercial films pulled in 400,000 spectators each, while the 11 remaining did not reach that level. Adding all of their audience attendance figures together, the average was less than 80,000 viewers per film. During the first quarter of 1991, the situation was only aggravated; of ten national films, eight did not achieve the average of 5,000 viewers per film; that is, they invested $1.2 million in each one of those eight films with the state's assistance, to reach only 40,000 people in total. (1996: 170)

Getino criticised the filmmakers' dependence on state subsidies because it allowed them to 'lose touch with their public'. Thus one of Getino and Mugica's objectives was to support the creation of films that were not 'hermetic' and 'hyperintellectualised'. The INC heads hoped to revitalise an industry that would be supported by the public rather than being dependent on state monies, and thus to ensure its survival. However, at this point in time, due to the national economic crisis, the film industry was paralysed. Réne Mugica resigned from his post for political reasons.

Getino assumed the helm of a slowly sinking ship, serving from 11 October, 1989 until 23 November, 1990. A noted filmmaker and film industry scholar, he had co-directed the radical Peronist film *La hora de los hornos* with Fernando 'Pino' Solanas in 1968. He co-authored theories on 'Third Cinema' and had been a militant leftist Peronist while in exile in Peru and Mexico. Thus, Getino came from a sociopolitical enclave that considered culture to be more authentic and powerful if it was made for working people. He also favoured the production of national culture over imports and felt that Argentine culture had to include cultural production in the provinces, the rural areas and the margins, places where 'the people' lived and experienced culture, in Raymond Williams' terms, as 'a whole way of life'. This version of culture differed drastically from the more traditional 'art for art's sake' perspective, and the more middle- to upper-class view of culture as elite, fine art or 'high culture'. For this reason, Getino supported the production of more commercial, mass culture, or what has been labelled 'popular entertainment', but also recognised the importance of culture made by the people, or 'popular culture'.

During his one-year period of office, Getino tried to lessen the economic dependence of the film industry on the state. His strategy was to concentrate on its 'industrial' capabilities. Recognising the volatility of the economy, the new director tried to move away from a 'high culture' model of a cultural industry to more of an industrially based, popular form of film production. His assumptions differed from those of Manuel Antín. When asked in an interview to compare the priorities of his administration to Antín's, Getino stated:

> Instead of designating sixty percent to assisting auteur filmmakers and forty percent to recuperating the industry, as Antín did, I proposed the opposite; to focus the majority of resources in restructuring the film sector in relation to the market. (1998)

Part of this change of strategy stemmed from economic necessity. The state was providing limited assistance due to purse-tightening measures, so the INC director encouraged the production of low-budget popular films that generally drew a wider national audience.

In 1990 and 1991, the INC was able to assist with 74 film productions. Many of these productions were carryovers from the mid to late 1980s that took many years to gain financing and exhibition. In 1990 several film projects receiving loans obtained additional money to offset the devaluation that had beset them during the hyperinflationary period (DEISICA 1991: 17). Of those films, 22 percent were popular comedies, such as Carlos Galettini's parodic *Extermineitor* series (1-4) (1989–92), produced by one of the few national film studios still operating, Argentina Sono Film. The majority were art-house films made by independent director-producers, such as Eliseo Subiela's *Últimas imagines del naufragio* (*Last Images of the Shipwreck*, 1989) and Tristan Bauer's *Después de la tormenta* (*After the Storm*, 1991).

In retrospect, it seems that while Getino wished to tip the scales more in favour of producing mass commercial films as opposed to more intellectualised fare, because of the economic crisis, more commercial films were produced, in percentage terms, during the 1983–89 period (35 percent) than in the mid-1990s. Although fewer commercial films were produced, Getino emphasised their instrumentality to the survival of the Argentine film industry.

In 1991, the situation grew even more untenable, with only 17 films released. This was the worst year for audience attendance in a decade, a statistic owing in part to the closure of movie theatres. The worst year for Argentine film production was 1992, when ten pictures were made – the lowest figure since the birth of sound cinema in the 1930s (DEISICA 1993: 5). In addition, the shrinking number of cinemas in operation made film exhibition difficult. In

1992 only 278 screens remained in the whole country, with 119 of these in the capital (Anon. 1993b: 66).

A major factor in the closure of movie theatres was the widespread economic malaise that prevented the general public from attending the movies. According to one study, nearly half of the country's middle class slipped into a lower socio-economic class during the early 1990s. In the meantime, unemployment increased from 6.5 percent in 1991 to 12.2 percent in 1994 (Skidmore & Smith 1997: 11). With such a limited number of screens available, it was critical for Argentine films to be allotted screen time. However, film exhibitors traditionally preferred to screen foreign (US) films because of a greater likelihood of profit relative to their national counterparts, and this preference was only aggravated in times of economic downturn.

One measure that Getino attempted to reinstate as part of existing legislation was the screen quota. Screen quotas create mandatory exhibition laws for national film. This provision of cinema law 20.170, created in 1973, mandated that a certain percentage of national films had to be screened in movie theatres in all regions of Argentina. Exhibitors were compelled to release national movies in first-run houses ('A' theatres), as well as second-run and smaller, independent circuit theatres. In 1979 (833/79) and 1985 (2414/85), decrees were made to amend the *cuota de pantalla* (screen quota) laws to oblige metropolitan first-run theatres to screen one Argentine film every three months, whereas theatres in the interior of the country (except neighbourhood, 'popular' [working-class] cinemas) were obligated to show 33 percent national films as part of their total. The working-class neighbourhood theatres, which mainly existed in cities outside of Buenos Aires, were mandated to screen four Argentine films every three months (DESICA 1991: 11).

Clearly, the laws were slanted towards mandating exhibition of national films in the interior of the country as opposed to the capital. Furthermore, the large US distributors would exert more pressure on the first-run theatres in the capital to show US films, making it difficult for exhibitors to conform to state legislation. In addition, when the Argentine film industry was producing forty to fifty films a year, in the 1930s and 1940s, it was making films for working class audiences, which were well received in the provinces. In the 1980s and 1990s, however, films were directed more towards a middle-class, intellectual audience. Also, very few films were released each year, so exhibitors could appeal to the excuse that there were no films to screen. Therefore, the legal mandate to show national films in the interior did not really make sense either in terms of audience response or in terms of the supply of films available to film exhibitors.

Although the screen quota remained on the books, it was not really enforced until Getino attempted to revive it. He wanted to ensure that Argentine films would have a chance be exhibited; often, a film producer would have to spend years waiting to find an exhibitor willing to show it. Getino also wanted to require distributors to carry a percentage of national films in addition to foreign (that is, US) films. However, after his short term in office, no other administrator was willing to revisit this issue.

Cultural policy from the early 1990s onwards increasingly moved away from what Jorge Schnitman (1978) called 'restrictive quotas', or protectionist policies that impeded the influx of foreign films. In a 1997 interview, for example, the Film Institute Vice Director Jorge Luis Rodríguez pointed out that a screen quota was contrary to the government's free trade economic policy. In the late 1990s enthusiasm for free trade was an obstacle to government intervention on any front. During Menem's first term in office, the free trade tenets were asserted proudly; free trade was still seen as a fresh experiment. The free trade zeitgeist that prevailed under Menem, however, rendered virtually any intervention in the private sector essentially 'off limits'. The result was that protectionist policies, including the screen quota, became practically impossible to implement in an epoch when powerful business interests opposed any such legislation.

The area most at odds with restrictive quotas was the exhibition sector. Exhibitors are business people who put profit above other considerations. By the early 1990s national films were considered high-risk ventures. Therefore, state encouragement of national cinema was in opposition to the financial interests of the exhibition sector.

Although the state has traditionally not intervened as directly with the private exhibition sector in Argentina, there have been some proposals made in other Latin American countries. During the 1970s, Brazil, Venezuela and Peru had state film policies that attempted to oversee and control all aspects of film production (Burton 1978: 56). In 1970, Roberto Farias, the recently named head of Brazil's state film institute Embrafilme, drafted proposed legislation that would subsidise exhibitors for showing national films (ibid.). However, in Randal Johnson's exhaustive study of the Brazilian film industry, there is no mention of this proposal. Most likely, then, this programme was never carried out. Johnson's book does say that exhibitors were made to screen national films without financial compensation during Farias' administration at Embrafilme (1987: 183–95).

In Argentina, the issue of guaranteed film exhibition was 'resolved' in the mid-1990s by the National Film Institute's decision to purchase movie theatres to be run by them directly. Two independent theatres (one triplex, one large theatre) would exhibit only national films. This issue will be discussed more fully in the next chapter.

Getino took a 'Latin Americanist' position which stressed including the rural or folk culture traditionally disavowed by many of the nation's urban criollo forefathers, those who valued European culture over rural folk culture. He was deeply committed to creating and sustaining a 'Latin American' style of cinema – a type of film production that expressed the sensibilities of the Argentine 'people' in the populist, working-class sense of the word. Getino believed that Manuel Antín's conception of culture veered too far from the average person's experience living in the provinces. A proponent of a popular culture who emphasised tradition, rituals, language and folk history, Getino wanted to redirect the cinema to be both locally specific and commercial/entertaining so that films would appeal to a wider cross-section of the population.

To stimulate a new Argentine consciousness about rural folk culture, Getino's agenda included forging relationships with other Latin American film industries. His idea was to stress similarities among all Latin American nations, such as the Spanish colonial legacy fused with indigenous and mestizo identities, and by so doing to help Argentina see itself as part of a greater pan-American culture.

Getino hoped to promote integration with other Latin American countries so that they would be able to assist one another with trade in cultural goods as well as co-productions. In October 1989 a treaty in Caracas, Venezuela, signed by various Latin American countries created a new organisation, the Conference of Cinematographic Authorities of Iberoamerica (CACI). Countries such as Argentina, Bolivia, Brazil, Colombia, Cuba, Mexico, Spain and Venezuela participated, agreeing (1) to begin negotiating co-production treaties; (2) to establish a common market for film production, exhibition and distribution; and (3) to set up regional integration in film exchanges and funding. The hope was that Latin American nations would embark on cinematic interchanges more often than had been occurring up to that point. For some countries, these co-production agreements went on to become law; nations such as Argentina and Spain had recourse to laws outlining the ramifications of film co-production agreements (Getino 1998). Together, participants of the CACI brainstormed possible solutions to Latin America's historic problems relating to the three facets of film industries: production, exhibition and distribution. The organisation still exists (now known as CAACI to reflect the inclusion of audiovisual industries in the organisation), and from this group a pool to fund Ibero-American film productions, known as IBERMEDIA, was created in the same vein as the European film fund (Eurimages). Each country contributes an amount (calculated on a sliding scale) every year to a Ibero-American film project competition.

This effort to promote continental integration at the cultural level has continued to the present day with the efforts made in the regional trade agreement known as MERCOSUR (involving Argentina, Paraguay, Uruguay and Brazil), which passed into law on 26 March 1991.

Getino attempted to keep production levels at an adequate level, but he faced serious administrative and management problems. In November 1990, he was fired and replaced by José Anastasio, a long-standing administrator from within the Film Institute. Anastasio was, like Getino, an old Peronist. He had also produced some of famed director Leonardo Favio's films. After only a few months in office, he died of a heart attack. Guido Parisier, a businessman and close personal friend of President Menem, then became the director of the National Film Institute, staying in office from 1991 to 1995. Out of six Institute directors in a span of seven years (Antonio Ottone and Mario 'Pacho' O'Donnell succeeded Parisier briefly in 1994–95), Parisier was the director who effected the most change in the Film Institute in terms of legislative policy and institutional restructuring. Although he clearly came from a 'free market' background, he advocated sweeping changes in film legislation. For example, he created new sources of tax revenue to supplement the diminishing box-office receipts. He was a businessman and not particularly a lover of the arts, but he nonetheless championed the notion that state intervention should play a role in the survival of a national film industry.

Although Parisier's tenure was a politically volatile one, in economic terms it was a time of relative improvement. In 1991 Minister of the Economy Domingo Cavallo created the 'Economic Convertability Law', whereby the Argentine peso was pinned one to one to the US dollar. This reduced the hyperinflation, thereby stabilising the economy, but it drove costs upward. In 1991, the cost of making films skyrocketed to an average of $1 million pesos, in contrast to an average of $350,000 pesos in 1989. The cost of movie tickets increased to an average of five pesos compared to the 1989 average of one peso. On a positive note however, the Film Development Fund increased from an average of fifty million pesos of credit available to an average of 300 million during Parisier's time in office (Getino 2005: 121). Although very few films were produced in 1992, several national productions were box-office successes. From 1992 to 1993 films such as Adolfo Aristarain's *Un lugar en el mundo* (*A Place in the World*, 1992) and Eliseo Subiela's *El lado oscuro del corazón* (*Dark Side of the Heart*, 1992) were successful, with 492,033 and 556,378 viewers respectively. Marcelo Piñeyro's *Tango feroz* (*Wild Tango*, 1993) brought in 1.7 million spectators.

During Parisier's first two years in office he was able to create new cinematic laws with the help of his friend President Menem. In the area of film finance, two presidential decrees – 2736/91 and 949/92 – were mandated to assist the fiscal wing of the INC. Both ordered that free television, cable television channels and home video clubs pay a ten percent tax on the advertising monies gained when a national film was broadcast. Home video stores were required to pay a ten percent tax on video rentals. Unsurprisingly, the mandates were met with stinging criticism. Video club owners in particular began launching a series of lawsuits around the country, claiming the law was unconstitutional. One reason for the outcry was that the legislation was passed by executive decree and without debate. Sociologist Ronaldo Munck notes that 'executive decrees are legally reserved for exceptional circumstances, but Menem has routinised their use and thus reinforced Argentina's already strong presidentialism'. He also observes that Menem imposed hundreds of executive orders to 'avoid the inconvenience of parliamentary scrutiny', showing 'his disdain' for Congress (Munck 1997: 11). Home video rental owners (approximately 8,000) throughout the country and almost 300 cable and free television channels argued that these laws were an unfair form of taxation, and should be subject to review and approval by members of Congress (Batlle 1992: 20). Although the decrees were met with opposition, this situation actually ended up paving the way for new cinema legislation.

Parisier's stint in office, while making its mark in championing new cinema legislation, was regarded critically by many filmmakers. His leadership style, in particular, was criticised as being undemocratic and authoritarian. Part of this style stemmed from his 'chummy' relationship with the nation's president, a bond that enabled him to forego much consultation with Film Institute personnel or the film community. Because Parisier was not a recognised filmmaker, as earlier INC directors (such as Leopoldo Torre Nilsson, Mario Soffici, Manuel Antín, Réne Mugica and Octavio Getino) had been, he was regarded with suspicion for being part of the business world, an area often at odds with the art/cultural sector.

Parisier symbolised the new businessman-technocrat who increasingly occupied leadership positions in Menem's administration. Many filmmakers distrusted him and felt that his sole concern was to reap the benefits of a business venture, rather than to support national film production for its own sake. When Parisier did organise a group to further film production, such as a panel he assembled to review film projects for a competition, he did not invite any filmmakers, which rankled many.

This style of leadership – a somewhat autocratic style that did not allow for film community input or participation in Institute affairs – mirrored President Menem's style. Menem's tendency to pass executive decrees rather than passing bills through Congress earned him the name 'the last caudillo'. While Parisier's intentions were good and some of his initiatives were inventive, he was also self-serving. For example, he tried to apply state interventionist measures that coincided with his business interests, such as privatising the accounting wing of the INC and recommending only his favoured corporation for the contract. He also wanted to hire a private sector organisation to be in charge of collecting taxes and administering these accounts. This had been handled in-house, and Parisier wanted to privatise the system to make it more 'efficient'. Clearly, he faced a conflict of interest, and the situation resulted in a cloud of suspicion on the part of the majority of the film community. Parisier, they argued, was not working in the public interest. However, the director remained adamant about the privatisation proposal (one that would mean an annual payment of $2 million to the accounting firm), and most of the film community demanded Parisier's resignation during the signing of the new cinema legislation.

In fact, there was a rift among the film directors in the long-standing directors' organisation DAC (Directores Argentinos de Cinematografía). Eight to ten dissident members of the group defended Parisier, arguing that he should not be castigated for unethical practices. Some of these filmmakers, including Subiela, Favio and Raúl de la Torre, staunchly defended Parisier, with de la Torre even standing behind Parisier's drive to privatise accounting (Marchetti 1994: 31). The film directors who defended Parisier ultimately resigned from the DAC and formed a different association of directors in September 1994. This group called themselves the Asociación Argentina Directores de Cinematografía (AADC). Heading the organisation was Oscar Barney Finn, with María Luisa Bemberg as vice president. It split from the DAC due to differences in leadership styles.

Javier Torre, the AADC president (now shortened to Asociación de Directores Argentina – ADA) in 1999, described the differences between the two groups:

> The trouble also occurred when people [in the DAC] began to attack those films that were not smash hit successes; they felt that those directors should not be allowed to make those films anymore. People in the DAC said this because they cost 400,000 dollars and did not recoup the costs. I, personally, defend those that do this. For me, it doesn't matter how many people go to see a movie. I don't believe in a film's 'success'. A film has a value, just like a book of poems or a novel. Maybe 500 people have read a particular book. Imagine if one had to conform to a narrative formula to ensure a popular success. That is a cruel system, to have to depend on a smash hit ... So we [the AADC] defended this, that one couldn't judge a film according to its success at the box office. It depended on the creativity, but well, there were a lot of problems around this issue, and it continues today. There are directors who don't want those with minority views, or that are 'elitist'. They believe in films with popular appeal, with big 'show off' publicity campaigns, and television ads. (1998)

The key difference is that the AADC/ADA believes that cinema is an art and cultural form needing to be shielded by the state from the laws of the market, while the DAC believes that cinema is first and foremost an industry that needs to generate films that are successful at the box office. Thus, the AADC/ADA could be described as more 'elitist' while the DAC was more 'industrialist'. Both groups continue to struggle over the film industry's path of development, but the most contentious debates were over Parisier's leadership, as well as Ottone's in 1995 (discussed later in the chapter).

Although both groups agreed to work together on passing a new law, it was evident that the AADC/ADA was more 'in-line' and supportive towards the INC, while the DAC tended to be more confrontational with the administration (Santos 1997: 44). Parisier was accused of unethical business dealings in relation to his upscale night club Hippopotamus in the fashionable district of La Recoleta, and many filmmakers were suspicious of his motives to improve the well-being of the film industry. Ironically, there was a tension between the 'industrialist' filmmakers – who formed part of the largest directors' organisation, the DAC – and the director of the INC and his business cronies, including Menem, who were more 'commercial industrialists' and not as interested in film reflecting a kind of cultural identity.

The DAC was characterised as being '*progrés, combativo y modesto*' (progressive, combative and modest) (Batlle 1994b: 33). The president and vice president, Luis Puenzo and Adolfo Aristarain respectively, were both well-respected filmmakers who were instrumental in lobbying for an updated version of cinema legislation. The DAC had a membership of eighty and functioned as a mouthpiece for the directors in matters of film legislation and in dealings with state film officials. Founded in the mid-1950s, the organisation had a history of internal disputes, often along personal rather than ideological lines. This was the first time in the history of the organisation that an actual split occurred in the group. That this rift was symptomatic of how fragmented social relations were generally among Argentine film directors was demonstrated in more than one of my interviews with filmmakers. Director Bebe Kamin stated that this factionalism was indicative of how individual interests were undermining cohesion and unity among film directors. In an interview, he was asked whether both directors' associations have ideas that diverge from each other?

> No, the ideas are not different, but the interests are. The priorities are the issues of production over cinematic issues. I was able to travel quite a bit and have had contact with other directors' associations around the world. In Romania there is a cinema house where all of the directors get together, and the ones who have completed a project screen it for their peers. Everyone discusses the film, critiques it, they have a party, get drunk, and go home. This would be inconceivable here; it would be impossible that someone would reunite all of the directors and organise a screening. Why? ... There are very few directors that are friends. On some level we have adopted the idea that if I direct a picture, you do not. In reality, this is not so. If I film, you film, and if I don't, neither do you. To some degree this ideology pervades this culture in general, it isn't just relegated to the film industry. I believe that because of the history of this country, whether conscious or not we have an authoritarian 'strain'. We believe that things are resolved in an individual manner, it is a culture where 'I know the right answer, not you'. (1997)

Kamin, as well as other directors interviewed, felt that during the Antín administration, everyone in the film community interacted in a more closely knit and collaborative fashion. Although loans were small, there was a prevailing spirit of making films rather than an emphasis on individual achievement, opportunity and gaining a competitive edge on economic opportunities. Lito Espinoza, a screenwriter for more than twenty years, noted (1997) that in Antín's time as director, one could get a film loan regardless of one's income level. In the Parisier period and after, it became much harder to obtain film financing without a strong financial backer. In 1995, the Institute asked film producers/directors to back their loans '2 to 1': the producer/director should show that he or she had double the amount of money necessary in guarantees in order to ensure pay-ment back on the loan. Consequently, Espinoza stated, 'younger directors and those without money have a much harder time than before, therefore making the system less democratic than before' (1997). This loss of cohesion in the film community may have stemmed from the economic instability and uncertainty of the period. In addition, it may have arisen from the Film Institute's shift from a more artisanal, auteur-based appreciation for the cinema, to one directed by a businessperson's perspective, where administrators were more involved than members of the film industry in decision making, and where economic issues prevailed over cultural or artistic import.

Apart from the issue of privatising INC accounting, Parisier and a large sector of the film industry were able to join forces and lobby for improved film funding via legislation. It was clear from the outcome that privatisation was still not favoured by state legislators and the majority of the Argentine film industry. The task of handling the estimated $50 million fund was given to the DGI (Di-rección General Impositiva) rather than the private sector.

Hours after Congress passed cinema legislation in 1994, the majority of film directors turned against the Institute head, asking for his resignation. In addition to the conflict of interest related to his businesses, he was accused of utilising funds 'without transparency, rationality, frugality and representation' (Anon. 1994a: 42).

Some other accusations were that Parisier had initiated plans for a satellite channel on television with the private company Amexical S.A. Adolfo Aristarain (vice president of the DAC), one of Parisier's biggest foes, stated that the direc-tor was not an appropriate representative of filmmakers because he was looking out for his own interests, and did not support the push for basic rights for na-tional filmmakers, such as reinstating the screen quota. Parisier's response to this uproar was simply, '¿Renunciar? Ni loco. Soy un peón del Presidente Menem' ('Resign? You must be crazy. I am a servant for President Menem') (ibid.).

As the Argentine economic system shifted towards a more laissez-faire mar-ket-based approach, the cultural realm was significantly affected. Paradoxically, however, at a time when the state itself was being 'downsized', the system of state-subsidised film was not only left intact, but was actually strengthened dur-ing Menem's second term in office. The film industry under Menem was spared and even nurtured, as evidenced by the passing of the 1994 film legislation stip-ulating that new avenues of funding (taxes on home video rentals and television advertisements in addition to the original tax on box-office receipts) be directed towards the production of national cinema.

In 1990, a mere ten films were produced, the lowest figure since 1934. The film sector, in large part, was concerned over the fate of Argentine production, and pushed Congress to reform film legislation to infuse new sources of fund-ing into the film industry. In 1994, a law dubbed the 'New Cinema Law' was passed.

A precursor to the 1994 cinema legislation had occurred in 1969, when Congress voted to approve a Cinema Law (Ley del Cine 17.741) mandating that ten percent of all box-office receipts should go to the Fondo de Fomento de Cine (Film Development Fund). With the passing of the new law in 1994, additional revenue-producing mechanisms were developed to expand the funding base for national film production. In addition, the 'electronic media' subsidy was created. This gave financial compensation to film producers who were able to secure exhibition deals with television, cable and home video companies to show their films. In addition, a film loan committee and a film oversight committee were created to further 'democratise' such internal processes of the National Film Institute as selecting film projects and overseeing the budget. Finally, the Institute's administrative organisation was to decentralise and establish links with other audiovisual sectors, such as cable television, home video and 'free' television. To account for the Institute's integration with other audiovisual media, a new name was adopted: the Instituto Nacional de Cinematografía (INC) was now dubbed the Instituto Nacional de Cine y Artes Audiovisuales (National Institute for Film and Audiovisual Arts, or INCAA).

As far back as 1986, concerned film producers, directors, film union members and screenwriters knew that modifications in existing film policy were necessary to deal with changes in home entertainment technologies, the closure of movie theatres and the increased costs of film production. The greatest concern to the producers, directors and others was how to create new avenues of film funding. In 1993, director Luis Puenzo stated: 'Television has become the new space for viewing films, rather than the movie theatres. So, this ten percent law is no longer feasible. We want to compensate for this displacement of exhibition revenue' (quoted in Anon. 1993a: 20). In addition to this new ten percent law, a 25 percent surcharge on funds was diverted from the Comité Federal de Radiodifusión (COMFER), and allotted to national film production. Although COMFER initially protested the law, the organisation relented. Argentine advertising spending on television and radio had more than doubled since 1991, and was expected to reach $2 billion in 1994 (Paxman 1994). On average, COMFER was expected to raise around $100 million annually. The $25 million allocation was to comprise a significant proportion of funding for the INCAA, thereby making television an important contributor to the film industry, albeit via a government regulation body. The bill also proposed a new ten percent tax on every videocassette rented, whether a national or a foreign title, to support the national film production fund. Video rental businesses fought to repeal the legislation, but without success. They, along with Diego Lerner, the Argentine representative of the Motion Picture Association of America (MPAA), claimed that the video tax for film production was unconstitutional.[3] They also resented the new law's stipulation that feature films could not be exhibited by television or home video until six months after their theatrical release.[4]

This new film proposal was intended to revive the ailing film industry. The development fund was expected to grow from $10 million to almost $50 million annually. This would mean that instead of an average of 15 films per year, the number funded would be closer to 25 or 30 films annually. In terms of film accounting, Congress voted to house the funds in the state accounting mechanism called the Dirección General Impositiva (DGI).

The proposed legislation was pushed forward by Deputy Irma Roy and was approved in the Chamber of Deputies before it was passed into law in the Senate. Roy's project was realised with the bipartisan assistance of some key supporters, such as Deputy Patricia Bullrich (PJ), Deputy Martha Mercader (UCR), Deputy Enrique Llopis (Socialist Party) and Deputy Fernando Solanas (Frente del Sur). On 28 September 1994 members of the Senate passed the Nueva Ley de Fomento Cinematográfico (New Law for Film Development), otherwise known as the Nueva Ley de Cine (New Cinema Law).

This bipartisan undertaking was unusual; typically, cultural policies broke down along party lines. However, an examination of the discourses of the Chamber of Deputy debates over the New Cinema Law shows that both parties believed that state involvement was necessary to guarantee the survival of the Argentine film industry.

The debates in Congress over the New Cinema Law are illustrative of how the two main parties approach questions of national culture. On this issue, both major parties wanted to revamp existing legislation to make up for the lack of revenues the film industry was receiving from the decline in cinema attendance. That the Radical Party and the Peronists both voted in support of the new measure is surprising, given the varying perspectives they have traditionally taken towards cultural policy. Through an examination of the transcripts of debates in both the Chamber of Deputies and the Senate over approval of the New Cinema Law, it is possible to understand the vantage points of the Peronists and the Radicals.

In the Chamber of Deputies, the Radicals tended to see the state's role in supporting the film industry as one of upholding and confirming national identity; the Radicals also tended to believe that this national identity should be exported. Deputy Marta Mercader (UCR, Buenos Aires) stated:

> With images and words we constantly re-elaborate our identity. Never could a country lose its identity by getting subjected to other models if it is sure of its own identity. This identity is constructed when it recognises its own image, this Argentine image that no one can produce for us ... I'd like to mention an example that has truly made history: it is in France when General De Gaulle founds the Fourth Republic in 1957. The first thing he does, as an important cultural policy measure, is to appoint André Malraux as the Minister of Culture. De Gaulle and Malraux, in that moment, sowed the seed that grew ... and with [the help of] President Mitterand it blossomed into a

marvellous tree that enlightened not just France but Europe and the rest of the world as well ... This political vision to support culture in France has cost little money, and yet has reaped enormous prestige. The end result has been a massive influx of financial gain due to this international recognition.[5]

Thus, the Radicals compare their cultural legacy to that of the French; they envision the state as operating in a similar manner as the social democratic traditions most commonly found in European countries, one statist model being France.[6] In addition, the Radicals employ the rhetoric of national culture as a tool for international recognition, similar to that which Manuel Antín strove for during President Alfonsín's presidency.

Senator Antonio Cafiero (Province of Buenos Aires), a staunch Peronist and well-respected member of the party, supported the New Cinema Law for these reasons:

> The emergence of cinema in the lives of people has signified the democratisation of culture and the massification of entertainment ... This is an important consideration to make in deciding upon legislation such as this ... In addition, our *sainete criollo* [national popular theatre skits] was an expression of a mass cultural theatre. The cinema, in a sense, picks up on these antecedents and continues to expand them and transmit them to a larger society. For this reason, it is the responsibility of an industry, or more than an industry, of an art, that doesn't simply forge a path for culture, but in fact plays an important role in constructing a national culture through images.[7]

The Peronist view of culture, while not discounting the value of international recognition, stressed the importance of creating and preserving national (popular) culture for a broad sector of the population. This more populist ideal for cultural policy is in line with General Juan Perón's agenda of elevating folk and popular culture into the mainstream public sphere, an arena traditionally dominated by elites.

Another amendment, instituted on 9 June 1994, proposed that private television and cable channels commission eight films each year that would be released as television movies, or telefilms. This agreement satisfied both groups because films would be funded and exhibited, and television companies would have new content to promote. This style of film financing is modelled after what is called the 'European method', where broadcasters play a greater role in film production (Paxman 1995). This method has been utilised in other Latin American countries as well, such as Brazil. Television stars were also to begin acting for these films in order to lend their 'star power' to the films and publicise them further.

Beginning in 1985, cable television companies were penetrating both urban and rural markets in Argentina. By 1994 the level of home subscriptions reached thirty percent of total homes with television in the city of Buenos Aires. In the provinces, the percentage was significantly higher, with the average subscription rate at eighty percent of families with television. The country's average – 33 percent – was the highest of cable subscriptions per capita of homes in Latin America (Tijman 1994). One outcome of this cable channel explosion was that more material for television was necessary, and cable channel programmers were willing to work with the film industry to purchase films and commission telefilms for cable and open channel television. One cable channel, Volver, now in its tenth year of broadcasting, is owned by Artear (Grupo Clarín). It is dedicated to showing classic Argentine cinema, in addition to producing a few in-house programmes. This channel is similar to Turner Classic Movies in the sense that it mainly screens work from its Argentine film and television library (the largest in Argentina) rather than commissioning contemporary national cinema. Patricia Moro, then-head of the INCAA film school (the CERC) noted that eighty percent of material shown on Volver is old Argentine cinema owned by Artear. They also screen the films that Channel 13 has invested in as a result of the New Cinema Law. Moreover, other cable channels such as VCC and Amèrica have also invested in national cinema production to air on their channels post-New Cinema Law. By 1996, the percentage of national films screened in open-air television stations (that is, Channels 13, 11 and 4) had grown to 18 percent, compared to 78 percent of films shown from the United States (source: *Boletín de industrials culturales*, 1996).

Although these changes to film legislation were criticised by filmmakers and others wary of increased state intervention, many state deputies thought that more regulation was one way to rejuvenate the film industry. Some saw these changes as a positive move towards the decentralisation of the industry, and others viewed the changes as a cumbersome expansion of a bureaucratic entity. Some opponents of the changes, such as Manuel Antín, past director of the Film Institute, labelled the move 'corporatist' and 'excessively bureaucratic' (Anon. 1994b: 2).

Since the passage of the law, there have been problems with the new video tax, as well as with the administration of the Film Institute, which had four chief executives from 1994 to 1995, amidst political upheaval and controversy. In 1993, the Institute was able to collect from only around thirty percent – about 1,200 – of video rental outlets (Besas 1993: 66). A report written by the film union, DEISICA, indicates that the funds and subsequent number of productions for 1994–95 were not as high as expected. The problems that impeded the new changes included some of the political upheavals that took place in the INCAA in 1994. Filmmaker Antonio Ottone succeeded Parisier on 4 July 1994 after Menem replaced the minister of culture with novelist Jorge Asis. Almost immediately, Ottone was verbally attacked and forced out because filmmakers such as Luis Puenzo, Carlos Galettini, Marcelo Piñyero and others were angry about his funding decisions. Ottone was a proponent of the 'cine pobre' (poor cinema) philosophy whereby many low-budget films, rather than a few glossy, high-budget feature films, were funded. The idea was that younger talent and lesser-known filmmakers should have the opportunity to shoot national productions. Ottone believed that Argentina, as a Latin American country, needed to conceive of film production not as a commercial industry, but instead as a cultural form that could be produced on a small scale and still be noteworthy.

Ottone resigned under pressure from the 'cine rico' (wealthy cinema) proponents, and was replaced by the presiding secretary of culture, Mario 'Pacho' O'Donnell. O'Donnell was firmly in accordance with the proponents of 'un cine rico' and promised to promote national films as an export product. He stated, 'I believe that in speaking of culture, one doesn't have to subscribe to the sex themes of Los Angeles, but to form the foundation for the execution of an aggressive export culture; in that sense the cinema is emblematic' (Monteagudo & Schettini 1995: 7). Instead of the proposed twenty to 25 low-budget films slated for annual production, O'Donnell advocated for only ten higher quality films that could compete in the world film market. Cinema for 'cine rico' advocates was defined as an industry that could be preserved only if high production values were maintained. However, O'Donnell and Vice Director Bernardo Zupnik proved to be untrustworthy administrators, participating in alleged nepotistic hiring practices and other means of misappropriating film funds.

When O'Donnell stepped down in 1995 after his brief stint, tensions within the INCAA worsened when President Menem intervened to appoint one of his close friends, Julio Mahárbiz, to the post of INCAA head. As the presiding head of National Radio, he had little experience in film production, as well as a history of dubious financial dealings (Anon. 1995a: 6). However, like Parisier, Mahárbiz had the support of the president and was able to maintain a tight organisational grip on the Institute. Despite periods of rampant criticism from the film community, Mahárbiz was the administrator to stay longest in office during the Menem administration, serving between 1995 and 1999.

Octavio Getino (1998) notes that with the passage of the New Cinema Law in 1994, 'Argentina had the most protective film policy in Latin America, and most probably the world'.[8] However, funds for film loans and subsidies were not given out as freely as they had been during previous eras, such as under Antín's administration. Film producers now were required to present proof that they could pay back the loans. Consequently, many independent producers for whom the legislation was originally intended had a more difficult time securing film loans. Instead of catering to that constituency, the INCAA forged a relationship with the private television sector (operated by multimedia conglomerates) to invest in film production. In exchange for co-production agreements, the television companies could reap state subsidies ('industrial recuperation')according to a film's success at the box office.

In an age of neoliberal reform characterised by a shrinkage of the state, what becomes of cultural industries such as national cinema, which would be doomed without state support? In the case of Brazil under President Collor de Mello (1990–92), state support to the film industry was cut, bringing Brazilian film to the verge of collapse. In Argentina during the same era, similar neoliberal austerity measures were implemented, but the film industry was not as seriously threatened. Menem's government was characterised by the neoliberal impulse to privatise state enterprises, which involved a downsizing of blue- and white-collar employment and a liberalisation of the market for imported goods with low or no import tariffs for selected trading partners.

Two Argentine sociologists address the effects of neoliberalism in the economic, political and cultural realms:

> The application of neoliberalism is concretised in the economic realm with the adoption of politics of structural adjustment and rationalisation, the non-intervention of the state in the economic realm, and the privileging of competition and the free market. In the political realm the system of representative democracy is instituted; at the same time, the cultural realm takes on characteristics of globalised 'Western' values. (Menant & Siddig 1996: 12)

These high subsidy returns to multimedia groups demonstrate one of the key features of globalisation – that the power of the nation-state becomes more accommodating to the presence and influence of global capital, which takes the form of national and multinational corporations. This public/private sector alliance is not a novel development in neoliberal economic policy. Comparatively speaking, President Menem dealt with the film industry in much the same way that British Prime Minister Margaret Thatcher, in the 1980s, approached the relationship of private satellite networks to the English state. Private satellite companies such as Rupert Murdoch's Sky TV were given state subsidies (what is deemed 'corporate welfare') as an incentive to investment. Like Thatcher, Menem 'espoused the intervention of the strong state in order to protect the (free) market' (King 1998: 279). In Argentina, state intervention was utilised in the private interest while it purported to be acting solely in the public interest. It would be too extreme to assert that the state was helping the private sector at the *expense* of the public interest, because the alliance had beneficial consequences for both sectors. The maintenance of the film industry is greatly aided when large numbers of spectators buy movie tickets to blockbuster movies, thereby contributing to the taxes earmarked for national film production. In addition, the film exhibition sector is boosted, and employment in the production sector remains at a healthy level.

The policy goals at stake are whether the state is responsible for nurturing a film industry solely on the basis of employment levels, or whether it needs to make a commitment in assisting national film projects, promoting national culture in an effort to preserve the cultural patrimony of the nation. Ideally, of course, the state fosters both – assisting projects that do not necessarily conform to the laws of the marketplace, and at the same time encouraging commercial products that do attract a sizable home audience. In the current shift towards nurturing ties with television, the INCAA has helped the 'industrial' side of the film industry, but has done so at the expense of the smaller, less market-oriented filmmakers. While many times the latter have failed to attract many filmgoers, there have been a few low-budget successes, such as Alejandro Agresti's *Buenos Aires, vice versa* (1996). Agresti is considered the 'grandfather' or first generation of a younger group of alternative filmmakers who are not labelled 'auteurs'. Most are under thirty years old, and have not made more than one or two films.[9]

Most Argentine films have had a difficult time penetrating export markets. The INCAA has reestablished an international film festival in Mar del Plata (after a 26-year hiatus) with the intention of promoting Argentine cinema abroad. In addition to the festival, it showcases a film market featuring Argentine cinema; but thus far, the sales have proved to be less than satisfactory. Argentina's film industry, somewhat resuscitated after many years of financial crisis (due to general economic malaise and the rise in cable television and other home entertainment technologies) is currently healthy in an economic sense, but now struggles with content issues. The film industry is trying to establish equilibrium between producing commercially appealing, popular films and expressing some of the attributes unique to Argentine culture, thereby differentiating its products from standard Hollywood fare.

The INCAA preferred to give loans and subsidies to multi-media conglomerates (which are presumed to be more likely to return the loans and produce blockbuster hits) over the traditional independent directors and producers. This preference coincided with the more 'economistic' turn the INCAA has taken, in accordance with President Menem's interest in the bottom line and other neoliberal ideals that privileged the market over social spending and producing media for the 'public interest'. The blockbuster movie phenomenon arose in part from an alliance of large multimedia conglomerates that teamed up with film production companies to produce glossy films to be marketed across media owned by these companies.

In 1997, a remarkable year for the Argentine film industry, there was a surge in the popularity of films produced nationally, marked by a large increase in audience viewership figures. Carlos Olivieri and Alejandro Stoessel's animated film *Dibu, la película* (*Dibu, the Movie*), a television spinoff depicting the life of a cartoon character living with a live family, actually surpassed the Disney animated feature *Hercules*, drawing 1,162,905 spectators, versus 927,644 for the latter film (Scholz 1997b). This event was a major achievement for a national film industry such as Argentina's. In a country of 39 million people, where eighty percent of films shown are Hollywood movies, and where close to thirty films on average were produced annually (but where only a few attract a sizable audience), beating *Hercules* was no small feat.

At the end of 1997, three of the four highest box-office hits were Argentine: *Comodines* (*Cops*), directed by Jorge Nisco, drew 8.31 million pesos (at the time, one peso equalled one dollar), just a little less than Steven Spielberg's *The Lost World: Jurassic Park*. *Dibu, la película* brought in 6.98 million pesos, and *La furia* (*The Fury*), directed by Juan Batista Stagnaro, grossed 6.28 million pesos. Marcelo Piñeyro's *Cenizas del paraíso* (*Ashes from Paradise*), did well, being placed in the top eight box-office hits for that year. Ultimately, Argentine cinema outperformed Hollywood and others, grossing 25.9 million pesos, compared to 23.3 million pesos for US and other imported fare (Di Núbila 1998).

To outperform Hollywood in the contemporary era was an astounding achievement. These extraordinary successes had critics remarking that Argentina's film industry was witnessing a 'renaissance'. There was speculation that the era of 'cultural imperialism' was over, now that Argentine cinema had found its public. Communication theorists such as Livia Antola and Everett Rogers (1984) and Michael Tracey (1988) stated that the once media-weak Third World producers had now strengthened their national industries to compete successfully against dominant US and European media. In some cases (such as Rede Globo in Brazil and Televisa in Mexico), national industries had reversed media flows by exporting television programmes around the world. The theorists that point to these developments were proponents of a 'reverse cultural imperialism' thesis, arguing that cultural pluralism had arrived, whereby national cultures could now defend their ways of life and in some respects even share their images with the rest of the world.

While it is true that Argentine films were at last gaining market share over their foreign counterparts, it is important to identify who it was that was investing in these film productions – and reaping the profits – in the name of the 'national interest', and what it was that these groups were producing. How different was it from standard Hollywood product?

This new blockbuster movie genre contrasted with the post-dictatorship 1980s boom era of Argentine filmmaking, when films were testaments of national concerns and expressions of national identity. These 1980s films, such as Puenzo's *La historia oficial* and Bemberg's *Camila*, were lauded internationally, gaining prestige for Argentina's cultural sector. These more middle-class art films were not well received at the box office within Argentina initially (with some notable exceptions), but only later, after they received recognition abroad.

In 1997, the blockbuster films *Comodines*, *La furia*, *Dibu, la película* and *Cenizas del paraíso* were financed in similar ways. All four movies received co-production financing from private television stations, the majority of which are multimedia conglomerates (Channels 13, 11, 9 and 2) that also own print media sources and radio. That is, these film productions were all produced with private television support in addition to state Film Institute financing, rather than the traditional model of state film support to small independent film producers.

The state provides low-interest loans to film producers, and in addition pays subsidies to projects depending upon the number of spectators that attend the film. Film productions are rewarded with higher subsidies for obtaining high attendance figures at the box office. For the high-grossing action film *Comodines* subsidies amounted to 2.2 million pesos. In this way, large national multimedia conglomerates are helping and are helped by the state, and have become a higher priority for the INCAA than the smaller director and producer operations.

Film producer Patagonik and television station Artear (Channel 13) were given 875,000 pesos for *Cenizas del paraiso*. In addition, Patagonik received 600,000 pesos for *Dibu, la película* (in association with another television channel, Telefé, Channel 11).

Billed as the 'first Hollywood-style movie spoken in Spanish', *Comodines* beat the all-time record for first-week box-office receipts and amassed an unprecedented 433,763 spectators in 11 days. *Comodines* is a standard action movie that uses popular television actors from a successful cops-and-robbers show called *Poliládron* (*Thieves*), which previously aired on Channel 13.

In terms of form and content, *Comodines* is a hybrid film in that the form is a global genre – that is, a television serial spin-off action film. The content however, while formulaic, utilises local language, actors and other local colour within a Hollywood narrative structure. By using a typical 'action film' template, it was universally palatable to audiences. For example, the film is about two policemen who are forced to work together, but who initially cannot stand to be in each other's company. However, towards the end of the film, they help one another, and grow to be friends. While the film is essentially formulaic, it makes good use of local actors who are familiar faces on television, and thus have star power in Argentina. Another local aspect of the film is the use of typical Argentine Spanish (that is, the use of slang, or *lunfardo*), humour and a soundtrack consisting of Argentine rock bands that has special appeal to the youth market. Thus, the film takes pains to present itself as comparable to a Hollywood movie, but different enough that national audiences could identify with it and be proud to call it their own.

In what could be called a 'global aesthetic', one striking aspect of the film is its choice of locations. Although the plot is set in Buenos Aires, most of the action takes place in city spaces that are generally unrecognisable from any other large metropolis. Scenes shown throughout the film are set in generic locations such as supermarkets, office buildings, the freeway and a cemetery. There is another sign of urbanity and modern living in the film's opening sequence. It begins with a close-up shot of a gun battle video game whereby a machine gun, shown in play as a point-of-view shot of the film's characters, shoots and kills the various intruders and enemies in the game. These computerised images set the tone for an action film with special effects, explosions and fierce gun battles. In short, *Comodines*, while purporting to be distinctly national, is set in what David Harvey calls 'globalised spaces' – Western, industrialised and urban locations such as airports, supermarkets and elevators – that are not specific to any one locale (1990: 295). However, for actor and co-producer Adrián Suar, the success of the film was based on feelings of pride that Argentina could successfully compete in making action films with what he considers a different twist:

> We created something dignified. *Comodines* is a cop movie with an American rhythm. Action movies have been shown here for fifty years, but they were never made in Argentina. It isn't the same when you see two dudes like myself and Calvo running down Florida street. (Scholz 1997a: 3)

Suar mentions how the film takes an 'American rhythm' but then reflects how the two protagonists run down a pedestrian shopping street in the downtown area of Buenos Aires. So, for Suar, despite having a US appeal, this film utilises a distinctly Argentine space (that is, Florida street) that he thinks gives the film a local feel. While I would disagree with this characterisation, mainly because the street scene is filmed at night and thus could pass for any other street, it is true that use of local language, star power and music did give the film a local flavour.

In other interviews with Suar, he states that he and others hoped to (re)insert Argentina within the commercial film world on the same footing with Hollywood, thus reminiscent of the heyday of the studio system era in Argentina. Clearly, Suar was interested in bringing audiences action films that have never characterised Argentine cinema.

Moreover, *Comodines* is for many Argentines a source of national pride; in the eyes of many it is 'Argentine'. Given its Hollywood style and its generic urbanity, how can this be? Firstly, according to one viewer (the author, interviewed outside a movie theatre), *Comodines* is 'the first Argentine film in which there is a real helicopter explosion'. Thus, the level of technological innovation is to a large extent what has made this film such a success. If we take the new Argentine blockbuster genre as a model, 'national culture' could be defined in terms of national actors and popular entertainment content rather than simply seeing the 'national' as social content that grapples with national or local issues. The film could be considered an achievement for national cinema in the sense that it had attained a comparable status of special effects proficiency with Hollywood. Although advocates for Argentine art cinema have complained about the new blockbuster phenomenon, this new presence has helped to expand the somewhat reified notion of what is defined as 'Argentine cinema'. This has helped draw in audiences who ordinarily would have dismissed national cinema as inferior to US filmed entertainment.

In an interview with the director of *Comodines*, Jorge Nisco, he admitted his fear in creating a film that was long a part of US turf that was not to be touched by smaller, developing countries such as Argentina. He notes:

Comodines (1997): a blockbuster movie with an Argentine accent

> I felt a great risk in directing this film because the public is used to the large scale action pictures from abroad. For that reason we know that the expectations would be high, including the critics ... our goal was to make a similar looking film that could stand alongside the rest of the action movies. (Urien 1997:5)

In order to create complex and true-to-life action scenes, a helicopter explosion and other special effects, there had to be an investment in state-of-the-art film equipment. On Pol-Ka's web site, it states that the director of photography, Ricardo de Angelis, 'worked with a new camera that was brought to the country from the US company Film Factory'. De Angelis was responsible for all of the technical material and worked with seventy people in this sector. In their own words, 'the camera, an 'Arri[flex] 535' was the only one in Argentina and worked to capture the action scenes never before filmed'. Further, in terms of sound, Oscar Jadur and David Mantecom worked with Dolby Stereo and all of the sound effects were processed in a studio in the US (see www.pol-ka.com.ar). These statements allude to uses of cutting-edge technology, and its links with the United States demonstrates how Pol-Ka worked to distance itself from the 'typical' Argentine film. Part of the longstanding stigma associated with national cinema in Argentina has been the perception that these films could not compete with the high production values, sound quality and acting ability of the US and other more developed film industries. Therefore, when producers began making films with special effects, there had to be a consideration of technological capacity. In a continuation of the interview with Jorge Nisco he discusses technological issues associated with the film:

Q: Are there big differences in the way special effects are created here compared with the US?

A: Perhaps there they work more in computer effects. For cost reasons, we could not access that technology. For example, perhaps the helicopter explosion seen in the film would have been done via the superimposition of images by computer in the US That is impossible for us. We decided to do this with a model and it worked perfectly.

Q: This idea of two cops that hate each other but later become friends is typical of the movies...

A: And the explosions and everything else, yes, it isn't anything new. However, I adhere to what Adrián [Suar] says: 'we didn't invent gunpowder, but we know we can manufacture it'. (Urien 1997: 5)

The abovementioned discussion signals a recognition that until that point in time, Argentina could not compete fully with the more developed countries in terms of high quality special effects. However, he describes this contribution to Argentine cinema by noting that while they were derivative of Hollywood, they gained respect from Argentine audiences in that they were able to master the technology from the developed world and thus were now 'modern' and technologically 'cutting-edge' albeit with some economic limitations. In various articles the creators of *Comodines* touted their technological prowess of the genre more than any other facet of filmmaking. This, to them, along with the large numbers of box-office returns, signified their contribution to the Argentine national film tradition.

A further development in filmmaking during this period was the introduction of product placement advertising in Argentine cinema. Although this was a staple form of revenue production in the television industry, it had never been attempted on the silver screen until 1997. Traditionally, in the Argentine audiovisual industries there has been a separation between the television, film and advertising sectors. For one, many filmmakers did not like to work with television actors due to an elitist view that television was not sophisticated enough to commingle with the cinema. By the same token, the issue of product placement within the cinema never intersected, mainly due to the 'non-commercial' and artistic nature of national cinema; advertisers had never envisioned the national cinema as a large audience vehicle to advertise their products. With *Comodines*, product placement had its debut within a feature-length film. This was a natural convergence because a film such as this was based on a television series. In fact, the producers of television series *Poliládron* (1994) approached their advertisers to see whether they would be interested in 'larger format' adverts on film. According to *Comodines* co-producer Fernando Blanco, in Argentina, product placement is called 'non-traditional advertising' or 'advertising inside the *mise-en-scéne* of the programme' and is a beneficial way to minimise costs for Argentine television producers. From his perspective, it was 'long overdue for films to utilise product placement as they do in US and some European films' (1998). Moreover, in *Comodines*, the level of product visibility reached new heights. In addition to seeing products throughout the film such as an advert for Topline chewing gum on a television set, or a billboard for Crush soda in the subway, there was a series of television adverts as the trailer for the home video edition. There were adverts for products such as Burger King, Coca Cola, the cellular phone company Movicom and the gasoline company Esso. They were featured with an explanatory intertitle at the beginning that stated: 'The following companies sponsored the marketing of *Comodines*.'

This linkage of advertising with film has created a series of debates in the US regarding the nature of product placement, product tie-ins and corporate sponsorship. Some critics contend that product placement helps to link the spectator to the movie through the adverts shown on the screen to the adverts they experience everyday. In this way it works to incorporate the viewer on multiple levels of engagement while watching a movie. Others charge that product placement is gratuitous and excessive. From the positive perspective, film scholars have noted that on some level, placement such as product tie-ins and the like can work to 'democratise the narrative process by opening up the narrative to audience participation' (Schatz 1993: 34). Thomas Schatz points out that film as a multimarket 'intertext' offers myriad spaces for audience engagement such as video games and other multimedia reiterations (ibid.). For example, in the case of *Comodines*, this was the first time there was a shift to an 'interactive' mode for consumers of product tie-ins. Scratch-off games found in packages of Bimbo white bread (comparable to Wonder bread in the US) worked to engage viewers with this movie in daily life. From a different, more critical vantage point, film scholar Janet Wasko (1994) asserts that product placement has no positive effects: the commercialisation of products within the *mise-en-scéne* of films compromises the integrity of the narrative of the film itself. In Argentina, many critics complained that viewers of *Comodines* were bombarded with advertising and that it was untenable. Claudio España, esteemed film critic of the newspaper *La Nación*, writes:

> In terms of subliminal material, despite the obviousness of the advertising, it becomes unbearable the amount of product placement that taints the image: placards on ambulances, billboards on the main freeway, branding on television, gasoline ads, advertising in restaurants ... it becomes interminable. (1997:10)

Regardless of one's position on the pros and cons of commercial devices placed within films, it is evident that a film such as *Comodines* broke the mould of national cinema and took the unorthodox position of making a commercial film replete with product placement a viable practice within the realm of national cinema. While it might have been viewed as 'crass', 'commercial' or 'vulgar' (as art-house filmmaker Javier Torre and others deem it [1998]), the reality was that the film was made on a budget of $2.5 million (low for Hollywood but a large sum by Argentine standards) and it had high production values. This may have given others, such as potential investors, the idea that Argentine cinema could be a worthwhile venture and thus build up a more consistent industry.

Comodines was produced by Pol-Ka Productions, in affiliation with Flehner Films and Patagonik Film Group, all companies that produce television as well as advertising. Patagonik (which also produced *Dibu, la película* and *Cenizas del paraíso*) is partly owned by Channel 13 or Artear (Grupo Clarín) and partly owned by Buena Vista International, or Walt Disney. In describing the making of Marcelo Piñeyro's *Cenizas del paraíso*, Diego Lerner, the vice president of Buena Vista, notes:

> This is the first picture that Buena Vista releases with Artear and Patagonik where in addition, we are producers. Believe me that we won't be hush-hush with all of this. Patagonik holds stock in movie theatres, Artear has mass communication resources and Buena Vista has distribution all over the world ... There are few resources that we don't already have. If I had to pay for all of the media sources we've obtained through our co-producers associated with the film, it'd be impossible to do this financially. And I'm from Disney. (Quoted in Belaunzarán 1997: 16–17)

Buena Vista International owned 33 percent of Patagonik productions. (source: *Informe*, Universidad del Cine 1996). Many of these films (such as those made by Piñeyro) are co-productions with Buena Vista. Fabian Zamboni (1998), a producer at Patagonik, attributed Disney's interest in collaboration to the recent trends in foreign film success in the United States, as exemplified by such hits as *Como agua para chocolate* (*Like Water for Chocolate*, 1993) and *Il Postino* (*The*

Postman, 1995). Ricardo Wullricher, one of the co-founders of Patagonik, noted that it was the professionalism of the Argentine crew during the making of the American film version of *Evita* (1996), co-produced with Buena Vista, that drew them to Argentina in particular (source: *Informe*, Universidad del Cine 1996: 107).

Distributor Bernardo Zupnik, from the national distribution company Filmarte (now called Distribution Company) noted that the only way Argentine cinema could compete against Hollywood would be to include the financial strength and resources of television companies and other large multimedia groups (cited in D'Esposito 1997). Movie promotion, television advertising and the use of famous actors are only possible (for the most part) with the inclusion of companies that have access to cross-promotion of media content and that have the means to exhibit and/or distribute the film.

The television advertising campaign for *Comodines* played extensively on Channel 13, a co-producer of the film. Television adverts, which normally cost between 150,000 and 200,000 pesos a spot, are prohibitively expensive for most small Argentine film producers. Grupo Clarín owns two large radio stations, Radio Mitre and FM100, on which Artear/Grupo Clarín could presumably place advertisments. In addition to owning *Clarín*, the most widely circulated newspaper in Argentina, Grupo Clarín owns the largest cable television system, Multicanal, which is also used in marketing in-house products (Blanco 1993).

With the number of cable television households increasing yearly, the number of cable television channels grew to more than seventy in 1996. In that year, Argentina continued to be the country with the highest level of cable penetration in Latin America, and the third in the Americas, after the United States and Canada. The estimated number of homes with cable television was 4.7 million, a figure that represents 43.8 percent of total households, and 50.7 percent of urban households (Anon. 1996a). By 1998, that number had grown to 5.4 million homes (Paxman 1998b).

In 1996, Grupo Clarín was in the top fifty multimedia conglomerates in the world for the first time. Clarín occupied the 41st spot in terms of annual income, with 1.14 million pesos annually (Anon. 1996a).[10] The presence of these huge multimedia conglomerates in the world of cinema is a relatively new phenomenon. This new configuration has become a reality due in part to President Menem's push for media liberalisation in 1989, which paved the path for an eventual television/film partnership.

When Menem entered office in 1989, he announced that four television channels (two in Buenos Aires and two in the provinces) were to be sold within sixty days, along with ten radio stations. The television stations Channel 11 and Channel 13 were offered to bidders from print media conglomerates. During the military dictatorship, a law had been passed outlawing the ownership of audio-visual media by a print medium. However, Menem urged the Senate to overturn this law, promoting the liberalisation of media ownership (Morgan & Shanahan

1995). One of the main transactions in media business that year was the sale of Channel 13 to the newspaper giant Grupo Clarín.

When the state, under pressure from the film sector, decided to revise existing film legislation in 1994 to secure the industry's financial survival, it also changed its film policy to include television channels as new viable players on the national cinema stage. Some critics speculate that television stations influenced this legislation – trying to recoup the tax monies they contribute that are earmarked for film development and production by themselves entering the film production realm. Many have accused the state of favouring big industry in supporting purely commercial works, in what has been dubbed 'corporate welfare', that is, a policy that once transcended the market in its commitment to helping film projects now privileged commercial film producers, and ones that could probably have survived without state assistance. Victor Tomaselli, former head of the Film Development Fund, defended the practice of providing loans to television companies (which are more financially solvent compared to the small producer): 'Television stations contribute to the production of Argentine film by contributing taxes paid to the COMFER. Therefore, they should be allowed to access these funds if they so choose' (1998).

Film producers reap greater financial gains from television partnerships in other nations, such as Spain and France, where television stations contribute to national film production. Film critics Pablo Udenio and Hernan Guerschuny, editors of the film magazine *Haciendo cine*, note that television channels in these European countries are obligated to participate in film production with three percent of their gross income. This form of co-production includes the 'right of antenna' or the right to release the film on television. However, this is the only right given to television companies; they do not receive any money from the box office (1997: 20). So, comparatively speaking, the Argentine film/television relationship provides additional funding in the film industry, but does not provide as much financial help as in some European countries. However, it is important not to underestimate the gains made by integrating private television channels into the IN-CAA funding schema: 25 percent of the new funding made available to the film industry (the 1996 figure was $35 million) came from the tax paid by television stations (Anon: 1997a).

These Argentine television channels, notably Channels 13 and 11, and to some extent Channels 9 and 2, contributed to producing both mainstream films and art-house fare. Many of these film/television co-productions were cast with well-known television actors to try to attract large numbers of Argentines into the cinemas. By encouraging the participation of large television stations as film producers, Menem's vision (as administered by INCAA director Julio Mahárbiz) favoured a film culture predicated on television, in what could be characterised as a 1990s version of Peronist mass popular culture, or escapist, non-intellectual entertainment. One of Argentina's hottest young producers and actors, Adrián Suar, states:

Argentine cinema is trying to become an industry. For a long time they made films that no one understood. Now perhaps the scales have tipped the other way towards only one kind of movie, it is true. Lots of action and adrenaline. But it will soon be balanced [with quality fare]. A good example of a film I like would be *The Bridges of Madison County* [1995], which combines quality with a popular edge to it. (Quoted in del Mazo 1997: 10)

While it is debatable whether the artistic nature of Argentine films has been compromised by mirroring the products on television, it is important to bear in mind that, ultimately, this surge in film viewership helped to strengthen the film industry itself. Estimates show that in 1996 the film industry increased employment in the film sector for the second consecutive year. In 1997, employment in the feature-length film sector increased to 84.2 percent (source: DESICA 1997). Clearly, in terms of thematic content, the INCAA was distancing itself from the traditional European model of national film industries and moving towards the Hollywood commercial model of cinema.

Because these films are entertainment-oriented and use television actors from popular sitcoms and police dramas, they are products that have performed well for domestic audiences, but do not translate well across borders. On an aesthetic level, these films are made with high production values and are arguably 'globalised' in terms of special effects. However, in terms of casting and content, they exhibit local features. That is, they use local slang, humour and intertextual references that come from the television shows. This combination of local content enveloped by a glossy 'globalised' aesthetic is illustrative of what Roland Robertson calls 'glocalisation'. He states that the 'idea of glocalisation in its business sense is called ... micromarketing: the tailoring and advertising of goods and services on a global or near-global basis to increasingly differentiated local and particular markets' (1995: 28). Films such as *Dibu, la película*, *Comodines* and *La furia* are illustrative of this phenomenon. These films are financed by national multimedia conglomerates and US entertainment companies such as Buena Vista, and are intended to draw local and national audiences into the theatres rather than for export. Domingo Di Núbila states that television spinoffs are unlikely to gain critical acclaim overseas. He notes that just two films were at the Berlin Film Festival in 1997 (including *Cenizas del paraíso*), and they received only lukewarm reviews (1998: 48). Fernando Blanco (1998), co-founder of Pol-Ka Productions, stated that their intention was to dub the film into English and then sell it abroad as a globalised generic action film, but it has not attracted many buyers. Thus, these television-produced blockbuster movies are relatively high-end, Spanish-language, popular entertainment vehicles for television actors in the home market. They are fostering a renaissance for the national film industry on the domestic level, but have not been successful abroad.

This lack of international success may stem in part from the combination of a globalised form with localised content: the product appeals to a wide sector of the population at home and abroad (hence the term 'globalised'), but it exhibits localised content that appeals to mainstream audiences (youth, working-class people, some middle-class viewers) rather than to global film markets, international film festival venues or to intellectual enclaves in Argentina and worldwide. This formula for creating an accessible, commercially viable national cinema responsible for bringing people back to movie theatres has to do in part with the production strategies fostered by the INCAA administration leadership from 1995 to 1999.

Julio Mahárbiz, as previously mentioned, had been the head of a state radio station, Radio Nacional, and was a close friend of the president. A shrewd businessman, Mahárbiz appointed accountants and lawyers to the vice directorship and other key positions. Many personnel had worked with him previously at Radio Nacional.[11]

This leadership style contrasts sharply with that of Manuel Antín. Antín and many working under him had previous experience in film production and this affected the artistic direction of the Film Institute. During Antín's administration, film projects were judged from a cultural point of view as media of expression, as opposed to commercial products. In Menem's administration, film projects were judged in terms of whether the filmmaker had enough credit to insure the loan, rather than in terms of the quality of the proposed film itself. In an interview with filmmaker and producer Javier Torre, he states it more bluntly:

> When I enter the Film Institute, why do I need to speak with an accountant? I am a film director; then they ask me for my tax returns, proof of income, if I am in good financial standing. No one looks at the script and film project and says if it is good or bad, but no one. The overriding theme is if I have money or not, if I am all paid up on electricity bills – things that reach the point of absurdity. (1998)

In interviews, Torre and others who have made films under Antín's leadership commented that film production was less of a business and more of a creative form under him. However, because many films produced under Antín were chosen due to their public relations potential abroad, they were geared less by market considerations and more by the state's aim to make a good impression internationally. In other words, film production during the democratic *apertura* could be characterised as being constrained not by strict ideological measures, as imposed by the past military government, or geared towards competing commercially with Hollywood. Rather, film production at that particular historical juncture was produced for an international film festival audience, rather than a domestic one. This worked well for creating a cinema that served as a forum to discuss recent historical events, but it was limited to an elite audience. Film production under Menem allowed for a popular national cinema to reach a wider constituency, but the issues of national concern have been sidelined in favour of pure entertainment.

During the first and second Menem administrations, rhetoric embracing the 'laws of the market' replaced the notion that the state protected culture from the market, which had been Raúl Alfonsín's approach during his administration. The films made during Alfonsín's term contrast with the recent box-office successes of Argentine films, which in the late 1990s were not middle-class art-house fare, but rather geared towards a popular television audience. The audiences of these recent successes were composed of young people and fans of those television programmes that inspired films such as *Dibu, la película* or *Comodines*. Thus, the integration of television with the film industry has not only assisted in the development of production financing, but also in the development of the film audience, because a percentage of traditional television viewers have now crossed over into the film market.

Edi Flehner, co-producer of *Comodines*, explains that '*Comodines* had a simple script that recuperates the idea of entertainment, something that the national cinema began rejecting … In the 1940s and 1950s, national cinema had the basic idea of entertainment, which it later lost' (quoted in Lerer 1997: 11). Commercial filmmakers like Flehner often compare their efforts to Argentina's 'golden age' films. Although these genre films – melodramas, historical epics, thrillers, tango movies and others – were popular forms of entertainment in Argentina and were exported throughout Latin America. In the late 1950s to early 1960s the Argentine studios began facing decline due in part to strong competition from the US film studios (Balio 1976).

From the late 1950s and continuing on throughout different government policies to the early 1990s, films were subsidised by the state because they were seen as part of the cultural patrimony of the nation. In addition, the film industry was considered an infant industry that needed protectionist policies to keep it afloat in the face of US competition. Argentine films had trouble competing with US product in large part because of the size of their respective home markets. Argentina's home market is almost eight times smaller, and therefore a riskier venture. This small market, coupled with a history of economic crises, has often made the film industry an uncertain venture. This is why the option of teaming up with larger multimedia conglomerates, both national and multinational, provided a larger financial cushion than the traditional small producer-director model.

With the new cinema law in place, production financing problems were debated and discussed, but equally crucial problems in exhibition and distribution were systematically ignored. In 1994, only 325 movie theatres were open, as opposed to 996 in 1980. In fact, the 1994 figure was the lowest since the 1950s. Until the mid-1990s, exhibition was dominated by two national chains, SAC and Coll-Saragusti. Historically, these chains have reached agreements with major US distribution companies to provide them packages of Hollywood films, some commercially viable, the rest less so, in what is called 'block booking'. This strategy of cooperating with Hollywood studios inevitably prevented national producers from screening their films. Therefore, national filmmakers might make a film but then find it impossible to distribute it widely. Very few independent circuits of distribution survived outside of these two powerful entities, which owned the majority of theatres throughout Argentina. The few remaining theatres became the sites for screenings of Argentine cinema. Independent theatres such as the Lorca and the Lorange showed national cinema, but were often stigmatised by directors as being a ghetto for national filmmakers and a cinematic dead end.

In 1995, after fielding complaints by film producers about the monopolisation of the national theatre circuits by the majors, the INCAA decided that rather than attempt to enforce the screen quota laws, they would themselves purchase a movie theatre dedicated to Argentine cinema. On 28 December 1995, the Complejo Tita Merello (Tita Merello Complex),[12] a movie triplex installed with state-of-the-art Dolby sound and a refurbished interior, was opened to the public.

Although it constituted a means for exhibition of national films, many film directors viewed it with scepticism. State film officials felt that the Tita Merello would assist film directors in recuperating their production costs by ensuring them exhibition space, but Argentine directors thought otherwise. Some directors felt the selection process used to determine which films would be screened at the Complejo Tita Merello was inadequate and thus made the theatre an unpopular venue because one could not trust the quality of the films screened. In addition, the cinema was located near the old shopping and theatre district called Lavalle Street, which had gone out of vogue in the 1980s. Since then, middle-class shoppers and moviegoers had been increasingly drawn to modern shopping malls with multiplex cinemas in the wealthy neighbourhoods of Buenos Aires such as Patio Bullrich, Alto Palermo, Puerto Madero and in suburbs such as Haedo, Pilar, Belgrano and others.

In 1998, the INCAA opened up another movie theatre in the Teatro de la Comedia (Comedy Theatre), located in the more fashionable district of Barrio Norte on Santa Fe Street. One of the positive outcomes of maintaining exhibition spaces solely for national cinema is that national films are generally given more playing time on the marquees than they would at first-run commercial theatres. Patricia Moro, who worked for the National Film Institute for 24 years, and who served as the director of the national film school, noted that Argentine film is marketed differently than Hollywood cinema, primarily in that Hollywood tends to spend more money on promotion and advertising for a film. The US marketing strategy is to promote a film and hope that it performs well at the box office the first weekend it is released. An Argentine low-budget film, in contrast, takes time to gather a sizable audience, as people must view it and tell others about it in order for it to become moderately successful.[13] Moro (1998) explained that both the Complejo Tita Merello and the Teatro de la Comedia let films run for months before they are replaced. This is what allowed a film like Alejandro Agresti's *Buenos Aires, vice versa* to reach an audience of 500,000.

In terms of multiplex cinema development, from 1995 to the present there has been a sharp rise in multinational corporate investment in multiplex cinemas. Argentina, as well as other Latin American countries, has witnessed the influx of foreign-owned theatre chains such as the US-based Cinemark theatres, ShowCase cinemas and Australia's Village Cinemas. Gemma Richardson, marketing vice president of Sony Cinema Products, reported in 1998 that Latin America now had the world's highest rate of theatre growth (cited in Paxman 1998a). These movie theatres, located in upscale shopping malls and wealthy neighbourhoods, mainly screen Hollywood films, but occasionally make room for 'independent' films from the United States (that is, films from studios like Miramax, which is owned by Disney) as well as Argentina. In 1997 and 1998 the Argentine box office grew by twenty percent, and thus had proven to be a lucrative business venture for theatre entrepreneurs. Harold Blank, the Buenos Aires vice president for Hoyts, an Australian-owned theatre chain that opened its first multiplex in 1998, stated that 'Argentina has the highest per-capita income in the region. With 33 million people, I don't see any difficulty with there being 1,000 new screens – and there are 450 already in the pipeline' (Paxman 1998a: 64). In 2002, US-owned AMC theatres joined forces with Australia's Consolidated Press Holdings, one of Australia's foremost publishing and broadcasting corporations, to form Hoyts General Cinema South America. It has 95 screens in ten multiplexes (seven in Greater Buenos Aires, two in Córdoba and one in Salta) and in 2005 retained the number one market share – 23 percent – in movie theatre admissions (Fuchs 2005).

Multiplex cinemas have arisen in response to changes in viewership patterns, whereby a segmentation of the market has allowed for particular subgroupings with disposable income to see films or buy products that are specifically tailored to their tastes, rather than 'lowest common denominator' films created for a wide cross-section of the population. By creating small theatres and supplying a variety of films for different populations (along lines of age, gender, race, ethnicity, class, religion and so on) the concept of multiplexing is in theory a more democratic means of access because it includes a diversity of offerings to different niche audiences. In the film community, there was a hope that with the opening of film screen spaces, there would be more opportunities to screen Argentine cinema. In reality, however, the popular blockbuster movie *Titanic* (1997), for example, was simultaneously shown on six screens in the multiplex rather than on one or two. Although the presence of these new screens has brought in more revenue to the country in the form of employment, and the INCAA's film development pool has increased in the form of box-office receipts, it is not clear thus far whether these multiplexes will consistently screen national films. Those multinationally-owned multiplexes had the potential to expand spaces of exhibition for national filmmakers.

Another development under Menem's tenure was the relaunching of the Mar del Plata International Film Festival after a 26 year hiatus. Julio Mahárbiz, with the cooperation of the nation's president, decided to reinstate the Mar del Plata festival, an international event that began in the 1950s under the Perón presidency, but which ceased under the succeeding military dictatorships with their attendant censorship and economic distress. The film festival, which held an international juried competition, was meant to lend prestige to the Menem administration. It was to be sponsored by Channel 13, that is, Grupo Clarín, along with Aerolineas Argentinas and other corporations.

When the twelfth annual Mar del Plata International Film Festival was held in 1996, many in the film industry were wary of the high costs involved in launching an annual event. They asked that Mahárbiz not use the Film Development Fund for the festival, and instead tap other funding sources. The director was able to gain corporate sponsors such as Grupo Clarín in exchange for exclusive television rights to the opening and closing of the film festival on Channel 13. In one newspaper advert for the festival, run in *Clarín*, there is a glossy two-page spread picturing *Comodines* star Adrián Suar, dressed in a 'bohemian-style'

Comodines (1997): when high and popular culture cross paths

black turtleneck and running, presumably towards the festival, parodying the way he fled a huge explosion in the trailer for the film.

This postmodern blurring of 'low', or commercial, art with 'high', or artistic, cinema grew out of the pairing of a massive television channel with a smaller, more exclusive film festival. Channel 13 worked with the Mar del Plata festival in order to elevate its own status by broadcasting the festival ceremonies. By the same token, the film festival reworked its image by aligning itself with a 'mass entertainment' medium, thereby giving the event more exposure to home audiences throughout the nation. This use of a popular action hero to advertise a cultural event demonstrates how the market can team up with the state to produce cultural events with a commercial edge.[14] In addition, by utilising popular television actors in its promotional literature, the festival worked to appeal to more mainstream audiences, rather than solely a niche market with a relatively high level of disposable income.

President Menem has been touted as a celebrity 'groupie' or someone who enjoys mixing with the *farándula* (celebrities). The notion of hosting an international film festival derives from the urge to participate as a global player in a prestigious cultural event with a plethora of world press, presumably elevating Argentina's status as a developed and cultured nation. The objective of this festival is to promote quality films in an international film festival arena. Bill Nichols, in his analysis of film festivals, states:

> Films [as viewed in the festival context], wherever produced, clearly belong to an industrial, if not postindustrial mode of production. Though some may be made according to a naïve or primitive aesthetic, they are far removed from the traffic in tribal art as such ... Though made locally, film production is always a site where the global penetrates the local, the traditional, the national. (1994: 69)

In addition, reopening the festival after so many years of abandonment created nostalgia for the past, when the country faced more prosperous times. Fading stars such as Gina Lollobrigida, Alain Delon and Raquel Welch were invited to it, as they had been in previous eras. The festival, while always touted as being the only 'Class A' festival in the Americas, in reality has only received minor coverage in the film trade magazines, as compared with other film festivals that emphasize Ibero-Latin American cinema (for example, Spain's San Sebastian Film Festival, or the Netherlands' International Film Festival Rotterdam).

Although film funding via the New Cinema Law highly improved opportunities for a diversity of filmmakers, it was still at the whim of the Argentine government, which intermittently has faced short-term monetary crises. Therefore, despite efforts to remain a stable and financially solvent industry, there are larger organisations the Film Institute must answer to within the government. In October 1998, Minister of the Economy Roque Fernández, in the midst of a financial crisis, ordered the appropriation of 28 million pesos from the INCAA. Julio Mahárbiz was steadily losing popularity and credibility because payments for subsidies and loans had ceased months before. With the threat of even less money at the film sector's disposal, a movement at the behest of one directors' association, the Directores Argentinos de Cinematografía (DAC), along with producers' associations, film unionists and film students, denounced Mahárbiz. In addition to protesting the unfair monetary appropriation, the film community vowed to boycott the Mar del Plata film festival in retaliation for the budget cuts. Film director Eliseo Subiela renounced his position on the jury of the festival and pledged to lead a boycott by the film sector because of the debts owed to filmmakers (Schettini 1998). In an open letter written by members of eight of the nine film associations, film community representatives blamed Mahárbiz for the crisis, asked for his resignation and stated their reason for not participating in the film festival: 'It does not recognise the main reason for its existence in the first place: that a solid film industry should exist' (cited in Batlle 1998: 6).

The Mahárbiz administration, despite instabilities in funding, and what has repeatedly been described as an authoritarian leadership style, has worked to strengthen the film industry by cultivating relations with financially solvent television channels. This strategy is in line with promoting the industry approach, and more similar to Hollywood protocol in terms of marketing and synergy, rather than the more auteur-based European approach. This emphasis on mass commercial entertainment has resulted in an increase of moviegoers to national cinema from 1.6 million in 1996 to 5.2 million in 1997 (source: DESICA 1997). Out of the total moviegoing populace for 1998, 19 percent were paying to see national films, as opposed to US and other foreign films.[15]

Mahárbiz's administration clearly gave breaks to large multimedia companies in an effort to integrate them into the national film industry. This shift towards increased influence of large corporations over the state's dealings illustrates one of the key features of globalisation. In this case, large national multimedia conglomerates are routinely helping and are helped by the state, while smaller producers have had to endure long bureaucratic meetings and periods of waiting for film loans to become available to them. This institutionalised preference alienated the group of established auteurs towards whom cinema legislation was at one time directed. Although they were slighted for more 'bottom line' economic policies, another emerging group, the young debutante filmmakers, gained access to a small pool of funds for first-time films (a point that will be discussed in the next chapter).

The year 1997 was a testament to Argentine cinema's breakthrough, when cinema found its audience. This more commercial boom, compared with the art cinema boom in the mid-1980s, produced such box-office successes as *Comodines* and *La furia* and helped to economically boost the industry. But the question of commercialisation irks those who visualise Argentine cinema as a medium that should be used to tell local stories – not to replicate the language of Hollywood. Some have described these films as television made for the big screen. The images found in these blockbuster films invite the question 'How national are these films?' That they are spoken in Spanish seems to be the sole marker of difference from the Hollywood action film. Clearly, the public interest aspects of developing a national community via the cinema were increasingly lost in the 1990s in favour of appealing to large sectors of the population with mainstream movies. Although this trend is in conflict with the state's cultural aims of furthering national development through education and preserving cultural traditions, it ultimately served as an incentive for investment in a national industry that has traditionally been seen as unprofitable.

In Brazil, a new film law introduced in 1993 encouraged private investment in national cinema by promoting tax write-offs to interested corporate investors. Since the enactment of the Lei do Audiovisual, a large number of productions have helped resurrect the cinema in Brazil. Although this tax incentive has proved lucrative for the private sector as in Argentina, the difference is that in Brazil these companies are not eligible for state subsidies after a film is released or is picked up for distribution. A deeper analysis comparing the two models has yet to be made, but it is most probable that corporate elites in Argentina benefit more from large subsidies than do Brazilian elites.[16]

While many Argentine blockbuster films have taken on what has been called 'glocalised' attributes – that is, a glossy, high-production value 'global aesthetic' fused with local attributes such as popular television actors speaking typically *criollo* Spanish – this type of film is by no means solely what was being produced at that time. The trouble lay in the fact that this blockbuster genre had many more vehicles for exhibition, distribution and promotion than the more alternative experiments in national filmmaking. To be sure, those alternative experiments, embodied by a young group of first-time directors, gained a foothold in the cinematic arena at the same time the blockbuster emerged, the subject of the next chapter.

CHAPTER 4

YOUNG FILMMAKERS AND THE NEW INDEPENDENT ARGENTINE CINEMA

The mid-1990s was a period when the INCAA gave preference to directors with higher-budget commercial films over the traditional independent film producer-director model. However, at the same time, the creation of a low-budget film fund was instituted by the INCAA. In 1995, a movement spearheaded by young, first-time filmmakers came onto the film scene, in part due to an institutionally sanctioned effort by the INCAA to provide them with funding opportunities. It did so through a small pool of funds for first-time directors via a variety of competitions: best television movie script, best short film and a university scholarship for the best students from the provinces to attend national film school in Buenos Aires. Therefore, while Hollywood-style blockbuster movies hit the screens with much media attention and box-office appeal, there was also a reverse tendency emerging – that of a new, gritty, urban style of filmmaking by young fresh talent.

This new group came primarily from a host of film schools that opened in Buenos Aires (in addition to the few established film programmes like Avellaneda in Greater Buenos Aires) in the early to mid-1990s. Without calling themselves a 'movement', these filmmakers made cinema in a language that contested the imitative style of Hollywood, and yet they often rejected the auteurist approach of the well-established Argentine film community. These new experiments performed moderately well at the box office,[1] and were given labels such as *el nuevo cine argentino* (New Argentine Cinema), *las películas argentinas jovenes de éxito* (Young Argentine Film Successes) and *el nuevo cine independiente argentino* (New Independent Argentine Cinema).

In 1994, the Comité de Credito (Film Loan Committee) of the National Film Institute met to select film projects for state funding. Martín Rejtman, a young director, was a first-time applicant for funds to make his debut, *Rapado* (*Skinhead*, 1995). The committee decided that the film merited the *sin interés especial* ('without special interest') classification. This in effect meant that no subsidies would be awarded. It was unclear why the film was rejected (Anon. 1996b).[2] Rejtman responded:

> It was a question of ignorance ... The committee members only have one way of thinking about national cinema, and ... any proposals that move away from their established models of what is national and popular, do not deserve to be taken seriously. (Source: *Informe*, Universidad del Cine 1996: 53)

Young filmmakers began to face obstacles in obtaining funding relative to established filmmakers, and yet the INCAA did little to equalise this disparity at that time. *Rapado* was produced because Rejtman, at the age of thirty, obtained funding from cultural agencies in France and the Netherlands. The film was well received in art film circles and was praised for its minimalist aesthetic (lack of dialogue, sparseness of *mise-en-scène* and so on). The director stated that it was his intention to produce a film that worked against such conventions as excessive dialogue and a moralising tone, often found in Argentine cinema. In an interview he stated that his creative processes 'started from zero ... within Argentine cinema, if there are elements that do not interest me ... then how can I achieve something within this chaos? So I pared everything down' (Ricagno & Quintín 1996: 14).

Sergio Wolf has noted that these filmmakers try to resist the stereotypes that negatively tinge Argentine cinema, such as how film dialogue 'dictates the limits of speech, by substituting how people speak with how people *should* speak' (1993a: 4). He argues that there is a new Argentine cinema that has chosen a particular poetic language and aesthetic, and these young filmmakers, he suggests, 'resist globalisation by choosing different parameters and affinities or affiliations that are less standardised and that appeal to a different kind of spectator' (ibid.). Rejtman, for example, labels his cinema as one of 'surfaces' (*cine es superficie*) because, as he puts it, 'there is really nothing beyond the screen' (quoted in Suarez 2002: n.p.). Film critic Claudio España observes that more generally there is a disenchantment that pervades most of these independent films, but rather than 'prescribe solutions, [they] just present the facts by inscribing them within personal narratives' (2000c: 14).

This new poetic, illustrated by the work of Rejtman, was at first rejected by the National Film Institute. However, as the film student population grew larger and their voices louder, spaces opened up for 'alternative cinema' in theatres and film festivals abroad. With these changes, coupled with the provisions made as part of the new cinema law for *óperas primas* (debut films), the INCAA slowly opened its doors to this new group of filmmakers.

At the same time that the INCAA instituted the new methods of allocating funds, film schools were beginning to open and expand in the 1990s. Many private schools opened in Buenos Aires, a few established by well-known film

Rapado (1995): minimalism within the frame

directors. Currently, most of the private schools are quite expensive to attend, but there are a few state schools that are free of charge. Two distinguished programmes are those of the University of Buenos Aires and a film school in the suburb of Avellaneda. The most prestigious schools in Buenos Aires are Manuel Antín's Universidad del Cine and the National Film Institute's film school, the Escuela Nacional de Experimentación y Realización Cinematográfica (ENERC) (School of Experimental Film Direction), called the CERC until 1999. Six or seven other schools have emerged in the capital, in addition to regional schools offering instruction in film production in the cities of Rosario, Córdoba, La Plata and elsewhere (Chatruc 1996).[3]

Patricia Moro, the director of the INCAA-run school under Mahárbiz estimated that in 1997 over ten thousand students were studying film production in Argentina. Others, such as film critic Fernando Martín Peña, estimated the figure at closer to four thousand. In either case, these numbers represent a large increase over previous years. These young filmmakers needed a way to integrate themselves into the structure of the film industry.

Since the 1970s, young filmmakers have had to compete for state funding alongside more experienced film directors and producers. While efforts by the established film community were made to democratise the process of obtaining film funding during debates in Congress over proposed cinematic legislation, young filmmakers and students voiced their complaints in the hope of change. Thanks to their efforts, a decree was passed following the 1994 New Cinema Law. This fund provided small grant opportunities for first-time filmmakers. The INCAA initiated a few competitions for debut filmmakers to make their *óperas primas*. An annual screenplay competition was established for debut film-makers that awarded $40,000 for the production of short films (*cortometrajes*) in 35mm format. In 1995 and 1997 17 grants were given, and the end results were two feature films comprised of the short films, known as *Historias breves* (*Short Stories*, 1995) and *Historias breves II* (*Short Stories II*, 1997). Both films have been shown throughout Argentina and at film festivals to sell-out crowds. Five awards are given annually for *tele-films*, or TV movies. Some of the winners from both competitions included Bruno Stagnaro (aged 25), from the Universidad del Cine, for *Guarisove* (*War is Over*); Adrián Caetano (aged 27), for *Cuesta abajo* (*Downward Slope*), who studied at a film school in Barcelona, Spain; and Lucrecia Martel for *Rey muerto* (*Dead King*). Those who won the *telefilms* competition in 1996 included Stagnaro and Caetano with *Pizza, birra, faso*; Fernando Díaz, who studied at the Universidad del Cine, with *Plaza de almas* (*Soul Plaza*); and Fernando Musa, with *Fuga de cerebros* (*Brain Drain*), who studied at the INCAA's film school, the CERC. Other award-winning students who trained at the CERC were 29-year-old Diego Kaplan, director of ¿*Sabés nadar?* (*Can You Swim?*) and Esteban Sapir, aged 31, who made *Picado fino* (*Finely Cut*).

The outcome of these competitions signalled a renewed interest in young talent. During the screening of *Historias breves*, many of the winners, who were young filmmakers from different schools and cities with varied experiences, met and discussed the possibilities of collaborating on future film projects. They have stated in various interviews that although the INCAA brought them together for the first time, as young directors they did not feel integrated into the larger film community, and thus have since collaborated with each other in planning scripts and film shoots (Rogue Pitt & Schaer 1998).

In 1991, two years after he had left his post as director of the National Film Institute, Manuel Antín founded what was then called the Fundación Universidad del Cine (Foundation for the University of Cinema). Although it has since received accreditation as a degree-granting institution, the school is still commonly referred to as the FUC. Considered the most prestigious institution (and also the most costly, with fees of $500 per month if the student does not receive scholarship funds), it has become the film school that produces the most student projects in South America. In addition, of all of the Argentine film schools, it has shown the most student films abroad in film festivals (Anon. 1995b). The first feature-length film produced by the FUC, *Moebius* (1995), was the result of an advanced production seminar of 45 students under the supervision of filmmaker Gerardo Mosquera. The film appeared at numerous film festivals in 1995, and won awards for cinematography and sound at the Havana Film Festival. It aroused the interest of international distributors, and provided an opportunity for Mosquera to obtain work in Hollywood (Moss 1997). *Mala época* (*Bad Times*, 1998) was the second feature-length film to be made entirely by students at Antín's school.

The CERC was founded in 1965 as part of the National Film Institute. Always free of charge, the school holds competitive entrance exams each year to allow the top students to attend. In 1995, eight students were admitted for each of five majors. Since then, there has been such an overwhelming demand that the number of places has increased dramatically. In 1997 the CERC admitted an additional eighty students, thus increasing the student body to 170 (Anon. 1998). Part of the expansion stemmed from the inclusion of students from the provinces who were guaranteed a percentage of places as a result of the new cinema legislation. This programme, while limited in terms of resources, has been successful in producing nationally recognised directors and producers. It is the oldest and only federal film institution in the country, and the only one responsible for providing training for students from all over the country.

Many recent film graduates have been successful in releasing feature-length films. Out of 28 films released in 1997, seven were from first-time filmmakers, the majority under thirty years old. All of these films exhibited a realism that exposed a side of Argentina that most medium-budget, middle-class dramas had not. These filmmakers look at problems in Argentine society with a quirky, youth-oriented perspective. With very low budgets, this type of cinema has enabled first-time directors to experiment with film in ways that are more daring and bold than the work of more established film directors. However, because of tight funding situations, many directors have used co-productions (such as the French group Fond Sud, known for helping 'developing countries' in cultural matters) and other methods (such as donated labour) to complete projects. For example, *Pizza, birra, faso* was made with $300,000 dollars – $187,500 given by the INCAA, and the remainder provided by a Dutch foundation.

Directors like Caetano and Stagnaro (*Pizza, birra, faso*) or Sapir (*Picado fino*) tell visual stories about a generation of youth who are not status-seeking, middle-class Argentines. They are either poor street youth who rob to make a living on the Buenos Aires streets, or they are Generation X-style youth who encounter problems in everyday life, but are realistically portrayed without the characteristic clichés (youth as 'slackers', drug addicts and so on). *Pizza, birra, faso* is about two young men in Buenos Aires, Córdoba (Héctor Anglada) and Pablo (Jorge Sesán), who commit robberies on the streets and in the bars of the city. It is also about human relationships, and how Córdoba and his pregnant girlfriend Sandra (Pamela Jordán) try to escape life on the streets.

Claudio España notes that the film demonstrates how 'the protagonists are overwhelmed by the city, but try to become a part of it at any cost, [and by doing so] they paradoxically regard its centre as an urban periphery' (2000c: 12). He and other critics have also recognised the trend whereby 'invisible' populations in Argentina – immigrants from Bolivia, Paraguay and Peru, among others – have begun to appear in some of these films. Typically occupying lower paying jobs and without much political voice, their 'existence had previously gone unacknowledged on Argentina's screens' (ibid).

Pizza, birra, faso (1996): Héctor Anglada and Jorge Sesán at Ugi's Pizzeria

Adrián Caetano, one of the co-directors of *Pizza, birra, faso*, went on to direct the hard-hitting black-and-white film *Bolivia* (2000). It depicts a day in the life of a Bolivian immigrant who works as a cook in a Buenos Aires café. In addition to portraying racism and xenophobia in the workplace and on the street, the film moves beyond his place of work to describe the typical immigrant's experience in inserting himself into a social milieu of other recently arrived workers. The film poignantly shows the protagonist learning to live in a society that does not allow much opportunity for or display of tolerance towards these newcomers.

Many of these films have been well received both by critics and young film audiences because they depart from the typical storylines and images found in Argentine cinema. *Clarín* film critics José Bellas and Pablo Schanton write of *Pizza, birra, faso* that it 'is not filled with *psicobolche* [slang for 'leftist psychobabble'] moralisms, nor forced dialogue by characters that know what happened during the military dictatorship of which the other characters are unaware' (1998: 4). In an interview, young filmmakers commented that contemporary Argentine cinema, from their vantage point, 'doesn't want to tell a story, rather, it wants to make a statement' (Quintín & Bernades 1995: 25). This is not to say that these younger filmmakers are not grappling with social issues that affect the Argentine public. The difference is that their stories are told from a different standpoint, and they are not necessarily openly polemic or ideological.

Plaza de almas, for example, depicts the life of two young people, Marcelo (Alejandro Gance) and his girlfriend (Vera Fogwill).[4] The main protagonist lives with his grandparents because his father has died and his mother lives in Spain. The plot centres on the disclosure of family secrets, such as spousal abuse, deception and other family problems. The main character's grandfather (Norman Briski), while seeming warm and caring, actually turns out to be a man with violent tendencies. Although not framed as a military torturer, he still demonstrates an authoritarian disposition because he spent years abusing his wife (Olga Zubarry) without any repercussions. The lead female character experiences her own trauma when she realises that she is pregnant and decides to have a termination. The scene in the abortion clinic is one of the most powerful and unsettling parts of the whole film due to its gritty, unrelenting realism. Films such as this are testaments to the 'new poetic style', as Sergio Wolf describes these emerging voices (1993a: 4).

Another such film to garner critical attention was by Pablo Trapero, aged 27, who graduated from Antín's Universidad del Cine. His film, *Mundo grúa* (*Crane World*, 1999) was shot entirely in black-and-white and took over one year to film. The main character, Rulo (Luis Margani), is an unemployed construction worker who would like to be a crane operator. He has a teenage son and lives in an older suburb of Buenos Aires. Trapero wanted to depict daily life in Greater Buenos Aires (a densely populated region of the country almost as large as Buenos Aires proper), a location where few films have been set.

Apart from Adriana Azemberg, a well-respected actress (who plays Rulo's love interest), and two other actors, most of the cast, including Luis Margani, were not professional actors. Trapero's hope was to create a mood evocative of Italian neorealism, or what has been dubbed the 'neo-neorealism' of filmmaking in Argentina. *Mundo grúa* reflects Trapero's philosophy that 'daily life in itself

Bolivia (2000): the immigrant experience heats up in the workplace

is absurd' (quoted in Lerer 2000: 6) by painting a realist portrait of a man in search of work and his identity in a globalised world. Rulo has never emotionally resolved the loss of his former status in his heyday as a musician in a semi-successful rock band during the 1970s. The prospects for work are daunting; the lack of opportunity forces him to leave his neighbourhood, family and girlfriend to look for work in the south of the country. It is a tale of limited possibilities in Argentina, a reality known too well by many.

Mundo grúa was Trapero's first feature film. His first short was an 18-minute piece entitled *Negocio* (*Store*), about a day in his father's auto parts store. This film won the short film prize at the Mar del Plata International Film Festival. Based on the success of that film he won a $20,000 grant from the Rotterdam Film Festival's Hubert Bals fund to make his first feature. In addition to this money, Trapero enlisted family and friends to donate money to the project. One of his benefactors was his grandmother, who also acted in this film (she played Rulo's mother). He did not receive any funding from the National Film Institute. *Mundo grúa* was filmed in 16mm, later blown up to 35mm. With reference to the shoestring budget and lack of resources on the set, Trapero quipped, 'Neither did we have the best lenses, so all of this discussion of the dirtiness of the image was something I liked' (quoted in Babino 1999: 26)

While some critics have taken note of this 'dirty realism' that helped create a strong documentary feel, writers Horacio Bernades, Diego Lerer and Sergio Wolf go on to point out that in 1995 the Danish digital video movement Dogme 95 was created in reaction to the excessive Hollywood glitter and special effects in films of that decade. Their clarion call was to revert back to a simpler, 'barebones' style of filmmaking that privileged the story over glossy aesthetics, special effects and highly-paid stars. While 1995 could also be considered the year that young Argentine filmmakers began showing their films in national theatres and other venues, theirs was an aesthetic born out of 'necessity and urgency' and not 'as a movement that sprung out of a "bourgeois experiment"' (2002: 10).

Mundo grúa, with its simple plotline that captured the sentiment of a population stung by the cruel realities of a neoliberal Argentina, garnered prizes at the Venice and Rotterdam film festivals, and Luis Margani won the prize for Best Actor at the first annual Buenos Aires International Festival of Independent Cinema in 1999. Margani, himself an auto mechanic and a friend of Trapero's father, could only act in the film on the weekends when his shop was closed. The film also blurs the line between fiction and documentary with the references to Rulo's past career as a successful rock musician in the 1970s: Margani was the bass player for the pop group Séptima Brigada, which had a modicum of fame referenced specifically in the film itself. Thus the film's narrative is constructed around the real life of the protagonist. Margani has gone on to star in other films directed by this young generation of filmmakers.

Perhaps the independent debut to gain the most attention worldwide is Lucrecia Martel's film *La ciénaga* (*The Swamp*, 2001). Richard Peña, director of

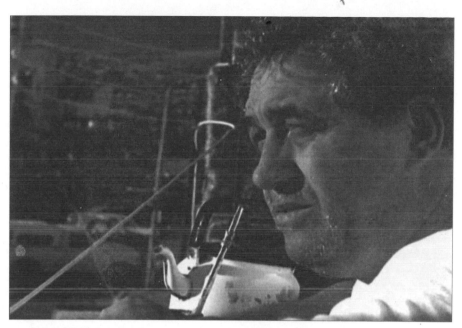

Mundo Grúa (1999): Rulo (Luis Margani) searches for work in Patagonia

the New York Film Festival, called it 'the most impressive debut feature yet from the ever-surprising new Argentina' (quoted in Rich 2001: 20). The film was produced in part by a prize awarded to Martel for Best Screenplay by the Sundance Film Institute and the powerhouse Japanese television channel NHK (Japan Broadcasting Corporation) as part of their annual International Film-makers Award. Other funding came from the National Film Institute,[5] Spanish producers and from well-known television host/producer Mario Pergolini's production company Cuatro Cabezas. Lita Stantic, best known as María Luisa Bemberg's producer, produced *La ciénaga*.

The film is unconventional in myriad ways. Firstly, it is a story set in the north of Argentina, in the province of Salta. It is an incredibly realistic film, partially because Martel herself grew up in Salta, and based some of the script on her experiences growing up there. It is important to note that most films set in other regions of Argentina typically are directed by *porteños* (residents of Buenos Aires), rather than the locals themselves. Thus, the '*porteño* gaze' leaves an indelible mark on films set in the north, south or interior of the country. These films are narrated from the point of view of a protagonist outsider (usually a *porteño*) who is passing through the region, or has moved there to escape the urban centre. Examples of such films are Adolfo Aristarain's *Un lugar en el mundo* (*A Place in the World*, 1991), his more recent *Lugares comunes* (*Common Ground*, 2002) and Eduardo Milewicz's *La vida según Muriel* (*Life According to Muriel*, 1997).

Although Lucrecia Martel left Salta to study film and animation in the capital, she based her script on conversations and events that she experienced

La ciénaga (2001): Isabel (Andrea López) pushes José (Juan Cruz Bordeu) in the dance hall

growing up in the north, and shot the film in its entirety in Salta. Using a combination of well-known actors and locals, she presents a bleak portrait of life for the provincial middle class, and one that is slowly sinking in the swamp of decadence and obsolescence. Martel has commented that 'there is a lack of philosophy, a lack of goals, and a lack of ideology in the middle class. It is as if some new vision is missing, some trust in the possibility of changing the world through your own will' (quoted in Macnab 2002: 11)

The film tells the story of two families living in sweltering heat, co-existing on a run-down estate, where time passes slowly. Another unusual facet to the film is the way in which the narrative is structured. It is presented in a polyvocal way, with no one character dominating the point of view of the narrative. As Viviana Rangil points out:

> In Martel's *La ciénaga*, it is difficult for the spectator to identify with any one character. The movie has a fragmented narrative structure that skips from one character to the next, providing multiple points of view for the same time and events, thus both disrupting and demanding the viewer's participation in the decoding of its layers of meaning. (2001: 8)

These families, one headed by Mecha (Graciela Borges) and the other represented mainly by her cousin Tali (Mercedes Moran) are trapped in the miasma of their own surroundings. Mecha is constantly consuming red wine and staggers around in a drunken stupour. She represents the decline of her upper-crust bourgeois family living in a crumbling estate. The swimming pool has not been cleaned in years. The atmosphere is suffocating; the characters lie about their bedrooms clad in bathing suits and trunks in the sweltering heat, and not much happens from scene to scene.

While the pacing is slow at times, it resonates with audiences who can relate to those quotidian experiences when things do not function correctly (people block the road, gates are locked, the power goes out). Adults and children lay around the pool, sometimes in utter silence. Throughout the story, characters often get bruises and cuts, and are affected by other mishaps, perhaps as a fore-shadowing of some larger fate that might befall them in what appears to be a life without any larger purpose.

The sequences of everyday events, such as boys shooting pellet guns in the forest, little girls entertaining themselves by singing into an electric fan so their voices vibrate, and an excursion to buy a shirt in the town, give the viewer a side of the minutiae of everyday life in an Argentine town that is not normally exposed in the national cinema. Similarly, this film contains elements that differ from conventional Holly-wood movies. On occasion, multiple people speak at the same time (such as the scene when Tali is talking on the phone and a group of little girls all speak at once). The cameras often frame characters in close-up while omitting part of the forehead. There are medium shots with only part of the character's body showing (although the person's identity has been established earlier in the scene), such as the film's opening shot, in which Mecha and her husband Gregorio (Martín Adjemián) drag chairs around the pool as they make clinking sounds with their chilled red wine.

The ugly side of Argentine social relations, racism and classism is touched upon when the power dynamics between Mecha and Isabel (Andrea López), her maid, are clearly oppressive to the latter, who is indigenous. Throughout the film, Mecha makes accusatory statements about how 'los indios' are always stealing towels.

However, there are also instances when indigenous people like Isabel fight back. In a dance hall scene, in the town, one of Mecha's sons, José (Juan Cruz Bordeu) tries to flirt with and tease Isabel. He then gets beaten up and his nose punched by Isabel's boyfriend and others. Near the end of the film, Isabel re-signs, much to the chagrin of Momi (Sofia Bertolotto), one of Mecha's daughters, who has a secret crush on the housekeeper.

La ciénaga is effective in exposing a retrograde conservatism and racism that is often assumed and unquestioned within the worldview of upper-crust white families in Argentina. It reveals this injustice, but also subtly shows the resistance that Isabel, her boyfriend and others summon up in the film. Rangil sums up the conflicts of the film succinctly by observing that in *La ciénaga*, 'the social oppression of belonging to a certain class, the decadence of imposed roles, the known lies and inability of religion to provide guidance are all powerful elements of criticism woven into the narrative' (2001: 9).

While Martel does have a critical edge to her story in the way in which certain characters are depicted, she, like many filmmakers of her generation, has expressed a tendency to move away from overtly denunciatory tones. B. Ruby Rich, in her interview with Martel, notes the following:

> Arguing that the Argentine middle class has yet to address its complicity during the years of dictatorship, [Martel] ruefully concluded that her generation had been raised with a distaste for politics. 'It's why we all avoid polemics and want to speak about that which is personal, local and even familial.' (2001: 20)

The film also evokes earlier films about the faltering and oppressive upper class, such as Leopoldo Torre Nilsson's *La casa del ángel* (*The Angel's House*, 1957) and *La mano en la trampa* (*The Hand in the Trap*, 1961).

La ciénaga's major accomplishment was that it won a top prize, the Bauer Award for the Best First Feature, at the Berlin Film Festival in 2001. It won four prizes at the Havana International Festival of New Latin American Film: the top prize, for Best Film (Gran Premio Coral); Best Director; Best Actress (Graciela Borges); and Best Sound. Among other prizes won that year was the Critic's Prize at Toulouse. The film found acclaim in Italy, where critic Tulio Kezich from the newspaper *Corriere della Sera* dubbed Martel a 'mini-Chekhov of the tropics' (quoted in Batlle 2001: 7).

Like other successful debut directors in Argentina, Martel started her career by making a short film before embarking on a feature. Her piece, *Rey muerto*, is a commentary on domestic violence that was screened as part of *Historias breves* in 1995. It was there that she met other young filmmakers such as Daniel Burman and Bruno Stagnaro. Out of this meeting came a writing group that encouraged each of them to write a feature-length screenplay. Martel's work is emblematic of a fresh, innovative aesthetic that aims to create a new film language for the Argentine cinema and explore themes that have traditionally not been depicted within the boundaries of what Argentine cinema has come to mean. Her 2004 film, *La niña santa* (*The Holy Girl*) was produced by Lita Stantic Productions, Pedro and Agustín Almodóvar's Deseo Productions and Italy's Teodora Films for US$1.4 million. HBO films distributed *La niña santa* in the United States (Newbery 2003: 26). Both of Martel's films have been described as 'an ability to make the ordinary seem bizarrely unsettling' (Rohter 2005: 16). This confirms what many directors of her generation deem as a move towards 'smaller stories and a smaller focus' (ibid.), including Lisandro Alonso, director of *La libertad* (*Freedom*, 2001) and *Los muertos* (*The Dead*, 2004), and María Victoria Menis, director of *El cielito* (*Little Sky*, 2004). Lisandro Alonso, in an interview, explains his rationale for selecting a narrative that involves the everyday, average life of a poor woodcutter in Argentina, the subject of *La libertad*:

> I chose not to show the extraordinary or spectacular accomplishments that occur every two or three or five years in somebody's life, such as to have a

El cielito (2004): a quiet film with many silences

child, a serious accident, or something out of the blue. One lives half of their life in a routine that no one pays attention to. I wanted to register these minimal moments so that when we see them, we'd rethink what we are doing with our lives ... In fact, more than the titles they have, like *La libertad* and *Los muertos*, I am telling the same story, I think it will be my pet issue throughout my life. For me, the dead man is him, a guy who stopped living. The same thing happens with Misael in *La libertad*. Freedom from what? (Quoted in Pernasetti 2005: 113)

While these filmmakers have a different, more critical vision of Argentine reality, they nonetheless apply to the INCAA for funding, and thus they are working within the film establishment to make their films. This contrasts with the earlier youth film movement, the 1960s generation or *Nueva ola*, which, as previously mentioned, rejected the studio system of the era and preferred to make both short and feature-length films based on literary works about middle-class urban alienation. At that point in time, the Film Institute refused to grant loans to the young directors, and thus the movement was marginalised by official film culture. It was only later, after the films were given international awards, that they were accepted into the official discourse of the Film Institute. Manuel Antín notes some differences between the film movement he had participated in thirty years earlier and this new breed of filmmakers: 'They [the new 1990s generation] are not alone the way we were in the search for a better world. The INCAA supports them, actors and film union workers understand them, and the film critics believe in them' (1998: 11).

This new style of filmmaking, although still not accepted in mainstream movie theatre circuits, is nonetheless supported by the Film Institute and is thus offered financial backing as well as opportunities to compete abroad in film festivals. For example, in 1997, for the first time in festival history, the Film Competition Selection Committee nominated three films by first-time filmmakers to represent Argentina: *La vida según Muriel, Plaza de almas* and *Pizza, birra, faso*. According to film critic Ricardo García Oliveri, these choices were unusual in an international forum, where typically films by seasoned directors with name recognition are chosen for their more 'formal' qualities. He applauded the INCAA for proposing such 'stimulating, refreshing and risk-taking films' (1997: 9).

Geoff Gilmore, head programmer for the Sundance Film Festival, stated that 'currently there are only two places – Japan and Argentina – where there is a resurgence of a new and interesting group of film directors' (quoted in Montesoro & Batlle 1999a: 9). Echoing that sentiment, articles by film critics state that young film directors are receiving a positive response abroad, and are now 'eclipsing the Subielas, Solanas and Aristarains, those consecrated figures that up to a few months ago were the only references that Argentine cinema had on an international level' (quoted in Montesoro & Batlle 1999a: 4). Fernando Díaz's *Plaza de almas* won two awards at the Mar del Plata film festival. One was for Best Ibero-American Film, and the other was the top prize awarded by the National Catholic Organisation (OCIC). *Pizza, birra, faso* won the award for Best Latin American Film from the International Federation of Film Critics (FIPRESCI) at the Mar del Plata film festival in 1998.

Film students and young directors are actively encouraged to attend the annual Mar del Plata film festival. Various schools give their film students scholarships to attend. Many are given transportation, accommodation and a discounted rate for movie tickets. Patricia Moro (1998) commented that at the CERC in 1997, seventy students were given scholarships to attend the film festival, along with five professors. In addition, during the same year, the Universidad del Cine, headed by Manuel Antín, organised the third International Festival of Film Schools, held within the Mar del Plata festival. The awards ceremony featured members of the film jury, such as famed Argentine documentary filmmaker Fernando Birri and Spanish actor Eusebio Poncela.

One consequence of the proliferation of film school graduates is a source of inexpensive labour. The global phenomenon that is called the 'flexibilisation' of labour has affected film production in Argentina. The traditionally strong power of the film union Sindicato de la Industria Cinematográfica Argentina (SICA) has weakened. In addition, the laws that made union work mandatory have also been weakened with the 'downsizing' of all industries, including film. New laws have stipulated that film student assistants must be paid for their work on production shoots. Thus, film students have embarked on making films on a shoestring budget with their fellow students. This has created a different atmosphere on the film set, according to Fernando Díaz:

> Evidently these people [film students] are entering the job market in a big wave. Everyday there are more film schools and this will create a change [in

film production crews]. I think that film work happens through personal contacts. For me, I'd prefer to have someone drive a truck that I can engage in a dialogue. (Quoted in Rogue Pitt & Schaer 1998: 50)

This form of interdependence that young filmmakers have come to rely on to initiate and complete film projects has given rise to other kinds of support services to assist young filmmakers, not only in joining an already existing film community but at the same time in creating a new one for themselves. Rather than depending on technicians in the SICA or on established film journals, they are creating new forms of cinema culture. For instance, in the early 1990s, at least five or six film magazines created by young filmmakers appeared on newsstands. Titles such as *Film*, *Sin cortes*, *Ossessione* and *Haciendo cine* supplemented film journals that had appeared only a few years before, such as *El amante*. Ironically billing themselves as *Los hijos de Menem* ('the sons of Menem'), the founders of the magazine *Film*, Fernando Martín Peña, Paula Felix-Didíer, Sergio Wolf and Diego Cabello, were critical of Menem's neoliberal project, but nevertheless applauded the stabilisation of the economy, which allowed for new journalistic endeavours.

These magazines provided communication about the new and pending legislation of the INCAA, reviews of new underground or alternative screenings (often organised and sponsored by the film magazines themselves), and articles focusing on young directors.

Although young filmmakers had applied for funding from the INCAA, they did not entirely endorse the Film Institute's position on the state of Argentine cinema during the late 1990s. Firstly, young filmmakers such as Diego Kaplan, who has directed over fifty music videos, vowed that for his first feature-length film, *¿Sabés nadar?* (released in 1998), he would not rely on Film Institute funding. In an interview, he stated:

It was a completely independent production. I didn't have official support, nor did I apply for it. I didn't want to enter into any kind of institutional delay, nor have an organisation that places judgement on whether what I filmed was considered up to par. (Quintans 1997 : 37)

Secondly, these emerging directors did not feel represented in the institutional structure of the governing body that incorporates one representative from each film directors' organisation (the DAC and the ADA)[6] into decision-making processes. Young directors who do not feel included by either organisation informally banded into the Group of 24 and hoped to create their own official body. Gregorio Cramer, one of the 24, states: 'We wish to defend a form of production that is different from the kind that already exists in Argentine cinema' (quoted in Montesoro & Batlle 1999a: 5). Many refer to themselves as 'independent' filmmakers, in the sense that they have no studio or production company backing. They also choose this term because it denotes a certain imperfect aesthetic, a rawness that is purposeful, as compared to the usually polished work of more established filmmakers in Argentina.[7]

French critic Edouard Waintrop has called these film directors 'the orphaned generation' in terms of their cinematic influences. In the Toulouse Film Festival catalogue he wrote: 'One cannot categorise this group as a school nor as a "new wave" of Argentine cinema in the strict sense of the term. Instead, it is more of the entrance of a new generation on the screen' (quoted in ibid.). Filmmaker Ana Poliak, director of *Parapalos* (*Pin Boy*, 2004) explains that 'there isn't a movement with defined tenets, but rather the sum of individual personalities' (quoted in Blejman 2004).

If any similarities can be found in the work produced by this new group, they include the fact that they generally choose marginalised figures in Argentine society, do not conform to the same classic styles of camera angles and cuts that earlier directors used, and they typically do not make genre films.

Film scholar Gonzalo Aguilar rightly observes some of the quirky characteristics of the narrative structure and personality traits of what he calls 'New Argentine Cinema' subjects:

> One of the issues in which the new cinema has moved away most radically from past cinema is in its relation with its audience. Open endings, an absence of emphasis and allegories, more ambiguous characters ... a somewhat erratic narrative trajectory, self-absorbed zombie characters, an omission of national issues that provide context, a rejection of identity and political demands: all of these decisions, that in a major or minor part, are detected in these films, make stories more opaque, that instead of directing us, open us to the game of interpretation. (2006: 27)

The only Argentine filmmaker mentioned as a possible influence is Leonardo Favio, who made moving portraits of solitary human beings, such as his *ópera prima, Crónica de un niño solo* (*Chronicle of a Boy Alone*, 1965) and *El dependiente* (*The Dependent*, 1967). Others cite influences from the filmmaker John Cassavetes, who is considered the father of American independent film. A characteristic of these films is a soundtrack that incorporates national rock bands (the least commercial ones); in the case of *Pizza, birra, faso*, the location and sounds of a working-class dance hall, a *bailanta*, are used. While these films do not show the bourgeois or 'acceptable' side of Argentine society, one can speculate that the INCAA is supporting these filmmakers because their films have come to satisfy a niche audience abroad for world independent film. From 1998 onwards, Argentine independent film has made waves in the independent film festival circuit abroad.

In addition, the inclusion of this generation of film students helped to level off mounting criticism in the film sector. Fernando Martín Peña, editor of the magazine *Film*, suggested that the support the INCAA has afforded young film directors was not altruistic. He suggests that this treatment was a form of co-optation in the traditional populist style of leadership found in Argentina. He states:

> It isn't capricious that Mahárbiz has announced a new competition for $300,000 for each winner [of debut films]. The mass of film students is sufficiently important to pay attention to, and it is the same logic that contributes to filling the movie theatres with young scholarship winners during the Mar del Plata film festival. Once again, the offer of a modest benefit (which still is more than previous administrations) works to placate complaints without having to give up any power. (1998: 57)

Marhárbiz continued to function in the face of increasing mistrust because he was able to please some sectors of the film industry by giving them opportunities to show their films at home and abroad, and in many cases they were allotted a small amount of funding. I would argue that even if this was a political manoeuvre to pacify a particular sector, it had positive results. Martin Rejtman, whose next film *Silvia Prieto* (1998) was picked up by Buena Vista (owned by Disney) for international distribution, stated in 1996:

> If the Institute, rather than putting one and a half million bucks into a feature-length film, invested it in ten national films by new people, I think there would be many more possibilities to have two or three successful films than in the present form. (Quoted in Ricagno & Quintín 1996: 14)

In 1997, Rejtman's line of thought was implemented. From the early 1990s to the present, young filmmakers have become more integrated into the film community and culture at large. This in part has to do with the level of state support granted to this sector from the INCAA and other organisations.

In 1999, the first-ever Buenos Aires International Festival of Independent Cinema (Buenos Aires Festival Internacional de Cine Independiente, Bafici) was funded in large part by the city of Buenos Aires. The main objective of the festival was to screen films by first- or second-time film directors from all over the world – no veterans were allowed (West 2001). In this forum, many new Argentine directors were seen by large audiences. This festival has steadily gained momentum and international recognition from its inception to the present by showcasing cutting-edge films not only from Argentina, but worldwide. Past invited guests and honorees have included Jim Jarmusch, Lourdes Portillo and critic and journalist Jonathan Rosenbaum. Rosenbaum was so impressed with the festival that he attended for two years in a row (2001 and 2002) and has given master classes and lectures as part of the scheduled events. Eduardo 'Quintín' Antín was its third director until he was fired in 2004 and replaced by Fernando Martín Peña, who currently heads the festival.

Despite the profound economic problems facing the country during 2002, Quintín and other festival organisers worked to finely execute an impressive lineup of the festival's programming at the Hoyts cinema, within one of the newer urban shopping malls, the Mercado del Abasto, in April. In general, this event has been a beacon of hope for independent filmmakers in Argentina and has given them a platform from which to exhibit their work, interact among themselves, view the latest international independent work and conduct seminars about the contemporary state of filmmaking in Argentina. The festival has continued to increase its offerings and its popularity annually. In 2006 there were 234,200 tickets sold, a 27 percent increase from 2004, and 79 Argentine films were screened (38 feature films; 41 were *cortometrajes*, less than 50 minutes long). This film festival, due to its extreme popularity and its financial support from the Ministry of Culture and the city of Buenos Aires, continued to host international filmmakers and organise screenings despite the horrific economic crisis to befall the whole of Argentine society in December of 2001.

In late 2001, the country plunged into massive economic and political difficulties. Protests erupted on 19–20 December when Fernando de la Rúa's government froze domestic savings accounts in an attempt to salvage the country's home and international banking interests. The government's repression of the rebellion resulted in the deaths of 32 demonstrators (Burbach 2002). The population joined in a massive protest, known as the *cacerolazo* ('the night of the banging casseroles'), whereby people of all social classes stormed the streets, banging pots and pans in objection to the government's failing economic policy and endemic corruption. President Fernando de la Rúa resigned and fled the country, and the nation devolved into chaos. The film industry, too, was stalled and in a state of uncertainty. Overriding the law created two years earlier to make the INCAA an autonomous, or autarkic, agency, the Economic Emergency Law was passed authorising the treasury department to confiscate all National Film Institute funds.

After the situation stabilised, Jorge Coscia was selected as the new head of the INCAA. By 2002 the INCAA's autarky was reinstated, and funding was restored to the extent that film production remained at a high level, with 43 films (Perelman & Seivach 2003). Despite the economic turmoil and rising unemployment, Argentine filmmakers continued to produce good-quality, low-budget films. As Marcela Valente explains: 'The success of cinema in the midst of the longest economic depression in Argentine history is explained in part by the fact that crisis tends to motivate artistic expression' (2002b). Manuel Antín described this high level of artistic expression under difficult economic circumstances in philosophical terms: 'This progress in the film world is proof that Argentina is experiencing a material crisis, not a spiritual crisis' (quoted in ibid.).

Although the country suffered tremendous economic blows, it became a time when citizens began to rethink the old system and make changes to help people cope with daily life. For example, in response to the devaluation of the currency, people began setting up swap meets where people could barter food, crafts and necessary items. Some workers who found their factories on the brink of closure took over the operations after their bosses had fled the companies, as at the ceramic tile factory Zanon in Ushuaia, Tierra del Fuego. In creative and ingenious ways, Argentines made the best of their situation, and in much the same way filmmakers tried to maintain a steady cycle of film production amidst the crisis. Fabián Bielinsky, a film director who debuted with the successful con-artist film *Nueve reinas* (*Nine Queens*, 2000) opined that 'today, as never before, people are gathering in neighbourhoods, looking for solutions, looking for ways to participate in our daily, social and political life. And that is quite a change' (quoted in Kaufman 2002).

In the realm of this cinema of crisis, one could argue that these new film-makers felt that they needed to see the world differently. They diverged from previous auteurs: many in this new generation embodied the aesthetics of *cine pobre* signification, but rather than create overtly polemical statements or march under the banner of a political movement, they are working to expand the no-tion of Argentine citizenship to include subjects and characters who have tra-ditionally been invisible or excluded from Argentine screens. Examples are the Bolivian immigrant in Caetano's *Bolivia*; the young girl protagonist in Martel's *La ciénaga*; lower middle-class Jewish characters such as Ariel's family in Daniel Burman's *El abrazo partido* (*Lost Embrace*, 2004); the Korean-Argentine charac-ters who speak Korean in practically the entire film in *Do U Cry 4 Me Argentina?* (2005) directed by Bae Youn-suk; Laura, a bisexual video editor who is Ariel's love interest in *Esperando al mesías* (*Waiting for the Messiah*, 2000); and Alber-tina Carri's *Los rubios* (*The Blonds*, 2003). Carri's film is, in the words of David Oubiña, 'a collage that combines both documentary and fiction modes layered on top of Carri's autobiography. The director appears as herself, a director, but there is also an actress who plays Albertina. The moments where Carri and her crew appear on the screen are the moments that they form a kind of documen-tary about the filmmaking process itself'(2006). It is an experimental narrative in which the actor who plays the role of Carri is challenging the mythos and memories of her disappeared parents during the Dirty War.

These filmmakers want to break with the notion of an Argentine excep-tionalism, whereby Argentina is viewed as different from other Latin American countries, because of its large immigration base from Italy and Spain. This 'ori-gin story' has helped forge a sense of European superiority from other nations, rather than Argentines embracing a *mestizo* (hybrid) or indigenous past. In other words, this younger generation of filmmakers in large part does not identify with a European-influenced and -inflected culture. Rather, they identify with ethnic minorities and working-class people and project a more varied and heterogene-ous face of national identity in Argentina. They show films from a grittier, work-ing-class perspective (especially after the economic crisis of 2001), as shown by such films as *Un oso rojo* (*A Red Bear*, 2002) by Caetano, *El bonaerense* (2002) by Trapero and Gabriela David's *Taxi, un encuentro* (*Taxi, an Encounter*, 2001). Additionally, there are films that work to deconstruct or disrupt the hegemony of the middle- or upper middle-class family, as in *La ciénaga* and *Cama adentro* (*Live-In Maid*, 2004).

Deeper explorations of specific minority groups, such as Argentina's Jewish community, is being considered from a generational perspective, an angle that has not been explored in previous Jewish-themed Argentine films. In decades past, the few films that represented what has been and continues to be the largest Jewish community in Latin America were titles such as Juan José Jusid's *Los gauchos judios* (*The Jewish Gauchos*, 1974), Beda Docampo Feijóo's *Debajo del mundo* (*Beneath the World*, 1987), Raúl de la Torre's *Pobre mariposa* (*Poor Butterfly*, 1986) and Eduardo Mignogna's *Sol de otoño* (*Autumn Sun*, 1996). The directors themselves, with the exception of Feijóo, were not of Jewish origin, but they have made what are arguably thoughtful films with wide-ranging and nuanced depictions of Jewish people in Argentina. Some films are set in traditionally Jewish neighbourhoods (in Buenos Aires' *barrios* such as El Once and Villa Crespo), or in the case of *Los gauchos judios*, it was based on the eponymous novel by Alberto Gerchunoff which explored the immigrant group who settled in the province of Entre Ríos as part of an agricultural colony, earning them the name 'gaucho'. The province of Entre Ríos later became known (perhaps as a curiosity) as the main area populated by a Jewish colony dating back from the 1880s. This Jewish-Argentine geographic space was invoked relatively recently on the silver screen when in *Nueve reinas*, one of the main characters poses as 'a cousin from Entre Ríos', which is coded as someone's 'Jewish cousin' despite the fact that it is not said in the film. Thus, even the invocation of 'Entre Ríos' in certain circles can identify one's religious/cultural background in unspoken ways.

In the twenty-first century, young director Daniel Burman made a documentary about the Jewish neighbourhood of Once, called *Siete días en Once* (*Seven Days in Once*, 2001) and is known as the director of a trilogy of films dealing with Jewish identity, *Esperando al mesías*, *El abrazo partido* and *Derecho de familia* (*Family Law*, 2006). His first feature, *Un cristantemo estalla en Cincoesquinas* (*A Chrysanthemum Bursts in Cincoesquinas*, 1998), featured an Orthodox Jewish character in a supporting role.

Gabriel Lichtmann's film *Judíos en el espacio o ¿Por qué es diferente esta noche a las demás noches?* (*Jews in Space or, Why is this Night Different from All Other Nights?*, 2005) and Ariel Winograd's *Cara de queso-mi primer ghetto* (*Cheeseface: Or My First Ghetto*, 2006), along with Burman's films, explore questions of Jewish identity within the context of a largely Catholic country. While these films treat the Argentine-Jewish experience in specific ways (from a typically bewildered, bumbling, youthful and naïve male perspective peppered with a lot of humour), they attempt to grapple with age-old questions that plague all minority communities: the concern about continuing the legacy of traditions from the past, questions of intermarriage, getting along with one's elders, ways to interact

Judíos en el espacio (2005): a humorous and poignant portrait of a dysfunctional Argentine-Jewish family

with members of the dominant culture versus their own communities, and various neuroses that plague them.

The films in Burman's 'Ariel' trilogy (so named because all three have a protagonist with the same first name, despite different surnames) are all semi-autobiographical, given that Burman draws on his experiences growing up in the *barrio* of El Once. In *El abrazo partido*, particularly, there was an emphasis on the daily goings-on in a galleria – a mall-like arcade – with all of the shopkeepers' daily lives keeping the frame abuzz with the various business transactions and interactions among themselves and their clientele. As Pablo Suárez rightly observes, Burman's preference for camera work has been characterised as 'frenetic handheld movement, jump cuts and maddening rhythms' (2006: 59), clearly influenced by the French New Wave. His main characters, such as Ariel Makaroff in *El abrazo partido* or Ariel Goldstein in *Esperando al mesías* are confused, inarticulate, neurotic and wish to escape their comfortable surroundings in pursuit of something 'out there', whether that be a better life in Poland, or another part of Europe, or in having a relationship with a non-Jewish woman and working in an environment outside of the neighbourhood. On some level, in *Esperando al mesías*, Ariel has the profound desire to assimilate into the dominant culture, and to do so he must leave what he deems his comfortable 'bubble'. In the author's interview with Daniel Burman in March 2006, he comments on the Jewish themes of his films:

Q: Were *Waiting for the Messiah* and *Lost Embrace* reactions to stereotypes or lack thereof in Argentine cinema?

A: I felt like making these films and I continue to make them as a way to reflect upon my search for identity; however, it's not limited to Jews only. It has to do with a person whose identity is part of a smaller group, and at the same time one that is part of a larger society. It is about those tensions.

Q: How did the Jewish community react to these films compared to the mainstream press?

A: My films have been well-received by the mainstream community, some better than others. The Jewish community had differing opinions with respect to my latest film [*Lost Embrace*]. It was strange since it was very popular in many countries around the world, and here it took a long time for the Jewish community to accept it.

Q: Why?

A: I am not sure, but I heard this from one source in the established Jewish press: 'How sad that the Jews see ourselves reflected in such a decadent manner.' This is something I heard time and time again; it's very sad to hear this from sectors of the official community – not to admit that we can be as decadent as those Argentines who have nothing – we are as decadent or as wonderful depending on the day, depending on who you are talking about. It is flawed to think that we do not have any faults or contradictions, that those faults belong to the Other.

Q: In *Waiting for the Messiah*, there is a certain pressure from the Jewish community on Ariel [Daniel Hendler], the main character. Ariel has to choose between his girlfriend and moving away from the Jewish community as he knew it.

A: That pressure comes from the community, not from society. I think it's a destructive pressure because you cannot force anybody to fall in love with any person, for example. That creates hate, rejection, resentment, yes, yes. The worst thing that can happen to someone is to resent who he/she is, to resent his/her origins. One has to be careful not to create the pressure of becoming what is expected of them. Every person has to become what he/she believes during the time when he/she believes so, and not according to a calendar. There is no such thing as a 'Jewishometer', a marker that shows you when you are a good Jew or when you are not.

While Burman points out that there are some outmoded strains of thought within the Jewish community, there are also allusions within his films to contemporary issues that are an aspect of daily life in El Once: that of orange pylons outside synagogues and Jewish community centres. These refer to a horrific at-

Esperando al mesías (2000): Estela (Melina Petriella) lights candles during Chanukah

tack on the Jewish community (and the community at large) on 18 July 1994, when a bomb exploded at the Argentine Israeli Mutual Association (AIMA) building and left 85 people dead and 300 wounded. It was the biggest attack on Argentine soil since World War Two. To commemorate it, ten filmmakers – Jewish and non-Jewish – created an omnibus film, *18-J* (2004), in which each made a ten-minute short that illustrated what might have happened to people in Buenos Aires (and in Jujuy, in one piece by Alberto Lecchi) on the day of the attack. These stories are poignant and show the repercussions that the bombing had on families, communities, individuals and their loved ones. There are many sombre parts, some linking the instability of violence to what life might be like in a country such as Israel (in the piece by Lucía Cedrón, who grew up in Paris due to her father, Jorge Cedrón's exile during the Dirty War). One extract, a dance performance directed by Mauricio Wainrot, links the symbol of rumpled clothes and shoes to images of a not-so distant past: to an iconography of the *Proceso*.

In general, we might dub this new independent cinema one of 'crisis': both of economics (in relation to the financial difficulties that had been mounting for some time) and identity. With a change in economic stature in Latin America (and possibly the world), Argentina now had to acknowledge that it was no longer different from its Latin American neighbours, and that it had to change its outlook and attitude. The young directors have sprung on this window of opportunity to present a new, more nuanced and varied image of the nation. Along with social activists who have staged protests and other acts in the hopes of gaining greater participation in the public sphere (for example, the *piqueteros* (the unemployed worker movement), members of the Bolivian community creating art and cultural exhibits, the gay and lesbian community being active and visible, and the activist performance pieces and protests of the next generation of those affected by the Dirty War, the H.I.J.Os (the sons and daughters of the disappeared)), so too have these new directors pushed forth an agenda of difference and change, and in many cases a simple, stripped-down aesthetic. With a commitment to realism, a wider panorama of faces and places throughout the country are now, slowly, being registered more visibly through myriad representations. In addition to changes in representations of subject matter, there were alterations to be made in the exhibition and distribution realms.

In 2002 film exhibitors – in an effort to reach filmgoers – reduced the price of movie tickets. While this lowered the amount of tax money earmarked for national film production, it helped make the cinema the only cultural industry that did not experience a drop in the level of activity for that year (Perelman & Seivach 2003). In 2003, the same strategy was employed by the movie chain Sociedad Anonima Cinematografica (SAC), which announced that it would reduce the cost of movie tickets for shows between Monday and Wednesday to 4.5 pesos from the approximately 7 peso admission fee (Martínez 2003).

Exhibition issues were addressed to some extent beginning in the mid-1990s when the INCAA invested in some urban movie theatres to create a dedicated space for Argentine cinema. In addition to the Sala Tita Merello complex on Calle Suipacha (now dubbed Espacios INCAA Km 2), in August of 2003 they inaugurated a theatre called Espacio INCAA Km0, the site of the Gaumont movie theatre. The idea behind these theatres is not to have to be beholden to the whims of exhibitors, who by and large consider national films to be more risky and less profitable than Hollywood's. Since 2003 there has been an initiative to open these state theatres both on a national and international scale. By the end of 2003 the INCAA had opened more than ten theatres in the provinces of Argentina, such as Córdoba, Chubut, Formosa and Santa Fe, along with creating the southernmost theatre in the world, in Antarctica (which opened in 2005). In Coscia's words these theatres would return to the Argentines 'their own image, their reflection, their histories' (Anon. 2003). On 30 April 2004 a movie theatre was inaugurated across the Atlantic, in Madrid. The Espacio INCAA Km10,000 was designated as such to reflect the distance from its sister theatre in Buenos Aires. This theatre, which holds 120 seats and is in the Colegio Mayor, an institution of Argentina's ministry of education in Spain, was the first of its kind on the European continent. Soon thereafter, one opened in Rome at the Casa Argentina (Espacio Km11,100), a third in Paris at the Argentine Embassy and a fourth in New York City at the Argentine Consulate. Two more, Km12,200 (Tel Aviv) and Km13, 450 Moscow, demonstrate the distance the INCAA is willing to travel to potentially gain access to worldwide audiences. Victor Bassuk, INCAA international affairs director, explained that the project seeks to 'train the public' to get out to see more Argentine films, and is complemented by another programme to 'promote consumption' of films from abroad. 'Admission is free because we want our film industry to be known amongst critics, the curious and students, who in the future can help disseminate Argentine films abroad – and conquer new markets' (quoted in Valente 2004: n.p.).

In September 2004 Jorge Coscia stated that the INCAA theatres recouped one percent of the film market in Argentina at the level of admissions, but that they were trying to improve this. He mentioned that ticket prices were lower in some theatres so as to potentially reach a sector with no means to pay regular ticket prices. The effort behind bolstering exhibition is to combat what could be dubbed the 'occupied screen' phenomenon (by Hollywood) and which Randal Johnson describes as an 'occupied market' effect which plagues Latin American film industries without exception (1996: 131). Coscia's pragmatic approach to this 'David and Goliath' dynamic is the following:

> With the recent regulatory measures we don't want to (and can't) eliminate Hollywood from our screens. We had simply taken the necessary steps to pre-vent Hollywood from eliminating us. We are not planning to have an 80% share of the Argentine market (when actually Hollywood has 85%), neither are we banning nor limiting American cinema's access, like China does. What we attempt to do is to achieve a market share which we understand is ap-propriate considering the quantity and quality of our film production: 20% growing up to 30%, as the new regulations consolidate. (2004)

Although the notion of creating state-run theatres to circumscribe a space dedi-cated to Argentine cinema is a noble one, the reality is that these movie theatres, by and large, are in parts of town where people no longer go to see films. In critic Ezequiel Luka's words, 'the risk that the 'Espacios INCAA' runs today is that they'll repeat the Tita Merello complex's fate, which in the 1990s turned into a sort of Argentine film graveyard' (2004). If they were able to open a theatre on Corrientes Street, where other movie theatres are, or even make a deal with an exhibitor to rent a space within a popular multiplex in a wealthy neighbourhood like Recoleta or in the suburbs, then perhaps more people would see homegrown films.

Another way to improve one's chances at exhibition abroad is for directors to seek co-production funding, thus gaining an avenue into screening the film in that co-producing country. For example, Daniel Burman, who had some success with his debut film, was able to get financing from Spain and Italy to produce his feature film *Esperando al mesías*. A mainstay for funding in recent years has been the Hubert Bals Fund, under the auspices of the International Film Fes-tival Rotterdam. In 2005, the fund had an annual budget of $1.3 million and provided development, post-production and distribution support for approxi-mately sixty features per year (Hofmann 2005: A4). Burman received $20,000 in post-production funds from Hubert Bals to complete *Esperando al mesías*. He observed that 'this fund played an important role in encouraging the new wave of Argentinean cinema. It's not just the money – receiving their support is a sign of quality for distributors. It makes people take notice of your film' (quoted in ibid.).

Pablo Trapero was able to shoot his second feature, *El bonaerense* (2002) with help from France's Fond Sud. Adrián Caetano's next film following *Bolivia* was *Un oso rojo* (*The Red Bear*, 2002), which was funded by a grant from the Ibermedia fund (Kaufman 2002). Another important source of support has been the mentoring provided by experienced producers such as Lita Stantic, who has taken some filmmakers under her wing (Lucrecia Martel, Adrián Caetano, Pablo Trapero and others) and helped to fund and secure distribution for these new directors (see Guerschuny & Udenio 2002). Other award-winning low- to no-budget films include Lisandro Alonso's *La libertad*, *Sólo por hoy* (*Just for Today*, 2000) by Ariel Rotter, *Vagón fumador* (*Smokers Only*, 2001) by Verónica Chen, Alejandro Chomski's *Hoy y mañana* (*Today and Tomorrow*, 2003) and Celina Murga's *Ana y los otros* (*Ana and the Others*, 2003) to name just a few.[8]

A novel co-production treaty between Argentina and two autonomous regions in Spain was announced in January 2005 between the INCAA and various cultural entities of Galicia and Catalonia. Named the Fondo Raices de cine, or the Roots of Cinema fund, it was the brainchild of the head of the INCAA, Jorge Coscia. In an interview, he stated that the project arose 'out of necessity that our country and the autonomous regions create alliances to confront a film industry such as the United States, which floods the movie screens of the world' (2005b). But as if to answer to any critics who might accuse him of setting up possibly problematic barriers to Hollywood (such as the ill-fated import quota set by Perón, which effectively shut down the exhibition sector due to a lack of screen product to show) he noted this: 'But let us clarify that no one wants to expulse Hollywood, but rather, Hollywood has expulsed us' (ibid.). The fund totals US$600,000 that each partner contributes to equally. There are a maximum of four grants to be given out annually, and each grantee is awarded funding according to the needs of their film project. One of the criteria is that the projects have the potential to be commercially viable and successful in their respective markets. Thus far, two films have come out of the Raices de cine fund, *No sos vos, soy yo* (*It's Not You, It's Me*, 2005), an Argentine-Catalan co-production directed by Juan Taratuto, and *Cama adentro* by Jorge Gaggero. Both films performed well at the box office, but *No sos vos, soy yo* defied expectations by playing to packed houses in Madrid for two months, thus earning the status of one of the top-ten films most seen in Spain in 2005, with almost 350,000 spectators and box-office receipts totalling two million euros. It won the distinction of being the first Argentine film to be in the top-ten most-seen films for seven straight weeks (Anon. 2005a).

Coscia has stated that the impetus to initiate the Argentine/Spanish regional agreement was two-fold: (i) the economic situation has made production in the

No sos vos soy yo (2004): Javier (Diego Peretti, left) laments his love life, with his analyst (Marcos Mundstock)

country more favourable to those companies from abroad, and (ii) he compares the box office to a cut of Argentine beef that is 'less juicy' (*menos jugosa*) than in previous years and thus 'we have to find outside business that will compensate for this' (2005a).

This film is the closest phenomenon to the 2001/02 success of Juan José Campanella's *El hijo de la novia* (*Son of the Bride*) which brought in an astonishing 1.5 million people in Spain. A recent book published on the transnational network of Argentine actors to Spain is called *Che, qué bueno que vinisteis: El cine argentino que cruzó el charco* ('How Great of You to Come: Argentine Cinema that Crossed the Atlantic') by Juan Carlos González Acevedo. The author argues that there is a natural affinity between Argentina and Spain. He posits that, beginning in 2000, there was a strong desire by both film sectors to collaborate on film co-production by the two countries. For one, Argentina has the largest diaspora from Galicia, with one million *gallegos* in Argentina. He interviews Argentine actors such as Ricardo Darín, Federico Luppi, Cecilia Roth, Miguel Angel Solá and Héctor Alterio, many of whom had lived in exile in Spain during the *Proceso*. Alterio is a transnational figure not only due to his popularity as an actor, but also because his Argentine-born children, themselves actors, now reside in Spain (2005: 18).

Diego Batlle, film reporter for the newspaper *La Nación*, notes that with this success in Spain, the positive response in France of *Whiskey Romeo Zulu* (2004) by Enrique Piñyero, and a positive run in some US art houses of Martel's *La niña santa* and Burman's *El abrazo partido*, 'the good financial repercussion and the critical acclaim signals how well Argentine cinema is faring abroad' (Batlle 2005). One issue is clear: the New Independent Argentine Cinema is winning international accolades, witnessed by recent awards at Cannes, Berlin and San

Sebastian. Daniel Burman's *El abrazo partido* won the Silver Bear for Best Actor (Daniel Hendler) and the Grand Jury prize for Best Film at the Berlin Film Festival in 2004; María Victoria Menis' *El cielito* won multiple critics' awards at San Sebastian the same year; and Paz Encina's Paraguayan-Argentine co-production *Hamaca paraguaya* (*Paraguayan Hammock*, 2006) won a critics' prize in the *Un Certain Regard* category at the Cannes Film Festival. All of these films, made by newer directors (many of them women, the number of which is unprecedented), captured the international scene.

A current debate that has polarised the film community post-economic crisis is the question surrounding what kind of cinema should be supported during this belt-tightening era. Proponents of the New Independent Argentine Cinema have complained that while these innovative filmmakers are producing work that is winning international film festival awards, it has not translated into domestic box office returns. Film critic Quintín lamented that Argentine independent cinema has not even succeeded in its own country: of all the films screened, each box office hit reached no more than a quarter of a million tickets sold – and this was outnumbered many times by commercial films like *Nueve reinas* or *El hijo de la novia* (Quintín 2003).

Even more troubling to critic Luciano Monteagudo is that film exhibitors have been losing patience with the lack of audiences for Argentine independent cinema. He quotes the numbers for some independent films that gained fame on an international level:

> In the 2001 season Martel's *La ciénaga* reached 120,000 spectators; and last year Adrián Caetano's *Un oso rojo* received 190,000 and Pablo Trapero's *El Bonarense* achieved 220,000. None of these numbers seem possible today [2003] for Argentine independent cinema, for the exhibition business – which has never been generous with local films – chooses, as everywhere else, to focus on a few highly profitable releases, such as Hollywood productions or 'industrial' Argentine cinema, rather than taking any risk with non success-guaranteeing pictures. (2003)

The discourse of the 'industrial auteurs' (characterised by directors such as Piñeyro, Campanella and Bielinsky) versus the new independent cinema (Martel, Caetano, Trapero, Rejtman) has created tension in the film industry because the economic situation is so terrible that filmmakers have to fight to receive any sort of state film financing. Héctor Olivera, considered to be a veteran industrial auteur, wrote a critique in the French film journal *Cahiers du cinema* (2003). According to Monteagudo, he said, the official support for Argentine new cinema is generous enough, but 'for an industrial film producer, standard practice means investing hundreds of thousands of pesos only to pay the actors, technicians, musicians and extras. Then it is obvious that artisan filmmakers have not fulfilled, are not fulfilling and will not fulfill the current working agreements'

Nueve reinas (2000): the heist film as a treatise on Argentine corruption and greed

(2003). This has been taken to mean that 'artisan' cinema has not been able to cover its costs, and thus not pay back the INCAA for its loans, which, in turn, has forced the 'entertainment' or mainstream cinema to bear an unfair burden towards the maintenance of Argentine national cinema. Ultimately, however, these industrial filmmakers are funded by companies like Patagonik and Pol-ka, which are, as has been discussed earlier, owned by various multimedia conglomerates with access to vast resources.

Thus, there have been some ripe opportunities for the industrial auteurs to recruit first-time filmmakers to make higher-budget, more commercial projects. For example, debut filmmaker Fábian Bielinsky was able to direct his screenplay *Nueve reinas* after he won a competition organised by the film production company Patagonik. This competition was open to first-time screenwriters to submit scripts, in a fashion similar to actors Ben Affleck and Matt Damon's Project Greenlight in the United States. Bielinsky had a US$1.5 million budget, and had incredible success with the film in 2000. The film garnered seven Condor Awards (the Argentine equivalent to the Academy Awards) and amassed 1,235,000 spectators. Also, the film was received well in Spain, Brazil, Chile and Mexico (Iglesias 2001).

Bielinsky is considered an industrial auteur and has been compared to Adolfo Aristarain for working within a genre in a studio system setting. Yet he has been labelled a new innovator in that he has employed a David Mamet-esque narrative style, whereby the viewer, by the plot's end, cannot discern between reality and fiction. His latest, and last film (before his premature death in 2006), *El aura* (*The Aura,* 2005) is slower and darker, with a film noir visual style.

Over the second weekend of October 2005, three national films – a police comedy, *Tiempo de valientes* (*Time of the Braves*), directed by Damian Szifron, a

Falklands Islands award-winning drama by Tristan Bauer, called *Iluminados por el fuego* (*Blessed by Fire*) and the age-old romantic comedy *Elsa and Fred*, directed by Marcos Carnevale – took in nearly 45 percent of the 370,000 total admissions, up from an average ten to 15 percent share of the market from the same time period of the previous year (Newbery 2005c). All three directors fall into the industrial auteur camp.

Juan José Campanella's *El hijo de la novia* was also a tremendous hit at the Argentine box office, with 1,263,000 viewers. It featured iconic actors Norma Aleandro and Héctor Alterio (their first pairing since *La historia oficial*) and starred Ricardo Darín (also a main actor in *Nueve reinas*). Darín has been characterised as the darling of the industrial auteur cinema.

It is not surprising that *Nueve reinas* and *El hijo de la novia* were the only Argentine films to be picked up by Sony Pictures Classics for US theatrical release in 2002. Both films performed well at the box office and caught the attention of Hollywood film actors/entrepreneurs. Adam Sandler has purportedly signed up for an American remake of *El hijo de la novia*, for Sony Columbia Pictures, planning to play Ricardo Darín's leading role, and *Nueve reinas* was remade into the mediocre *Criminal* (2004) directed by Gregory Jacobs for Warner Independent Pictures and starring John C. Reilly and Diego Luna.

New technologies, such as the rise of digital formats to produce high-quality broadcast images, have been another low-cost option taken by some filmmakers. Working within the digital realm facilitates the need for less people on a crew, which has aided the rise of the young independent filmmaker (Felix-Didier *et al.* 2002). The use of video for feature filmmaking in Argentina is not new. A director who is considered the most revered video pioneer and who has inspired this new generation is Raúl Perrone.

Perrone began in the early 1990s by shooting video pieces in his birthplace of Ituzaingó, a neighbourhood in the province of Buenos Aires, and has continued making work to the present day. He has chosen to work in video not only to cut costs, but to experiment with its aesthetic. He describes his work as a kind of *naturalismo sucio* ('dirty realism') and antithetical to Hollywood television shows. In an interview with Fernando Martín Peña he describes his trilogy *Labios de churrasco* (1994), *Graciadió* (1997) and *5 pal peso* (1998) in these terms:

> One day I was watching *Beverly Hills 90210* and I told myself 'How horrible is this! Why couldn't there be a programme in Argentina that tells a story from a different place? Those teens never do anything real, they never go to the bathroom … So I got a group together and I proposed that we do something … I thought, 'How great would it be if I could make a trilogy about a group of people that live in a neighbourhood and things happen to them?' (2003: 143)

At the 2002 Buenos Aires International Festival of Independent Cinema there was a Perrone retrospective and a screening of his latest work, *Late un corazón*

(*A Heart Beats*, 2002). This film was shot using a digital, handheld camera. As Daniela Espejo (2002) points out, Perrone's films are very difficult to find, as they are not released commercially or available on video. This has made Perrone something of a cult figure in independent film circles. *Late un corazón* was awarded an Honorable Mention by the jury of Lo Nuevo de Lo Nuevo (The Newest of the New), a new Argentine cinema competition within the festival. Perrone's film was described by Espejo in this manner:

> By simply placing his camera before his subject, Perrone unobtrusively reveals the main characteristics of this neighbourhood: the lack of money, constant violence and theft, and codes of social exchange. And there is a feeling of nothing to do, that time will never lead to any kind of success. (2002)

Younger directors identified with the New Independent Argentine Cinema such as Santiago Loza (*Extraño, Strange*, 2003) and Ana Katz (*El juego de la silla, Musical Chairs*, 2002) also shot and produced their films digitally (Aguilar 2006: 15).

A director whose work, like Perrone's, is not shown in commercial settings is Mariano Llinás, director of the documentary *Balnearios* (*Beach Resort*, 2002). This film blends oral history, photographic stills, historic footage and recreations of melancholic days gone by with apocryphal stories (Bernades 2002). Critic Horacio Bernades has extolled the film: '*Balnearios* is, without a doubt, one of the most fascinating movies to emerge from the unpredictable and strange concoction labelled the New Argentine Cinema' (ibid.). It was shot on 16mm which made it prohibitive to screen in regular movie theatres unless it was blown up to 35mm. The director opted to forgo that mainstream film circuit route because, in his words:

> ...and all this, for what? To compete in a disadvantaged way against *Signs* [2002], *Scooby Doo* [2002] or *K-19: The Widowmaker* [2002]. A theatre like the Malba [The Latin American Art Museum of Buenos Aires] gives me the opportunity to not have to subject my film to this 'cookie cutter mold' [horma fija], and it will give me a month to screen it and to give people a chance to see it ... I think it is the time that certain films find alternative circuits, so that the public see them as such, so they come in knowing that it won't be the same film that they find in the shopping malls. Not better, not worse: simply different'. (Ibid.)

The film screened to 10,000 people at the Malba venue, which in many cases surpassed Argentine films which played on the traditional circuit (Luka 2004).

Another veteran filmmaker who has not been left behind in the shift to technology is Eliseo Subiela. He is the first of the older, more established generation of filmmakers to shoot a feature film entirely in the digital format. Entitled *Las adventuras de Dios* (*God's Adventures*, 2000) the film is a testament to the new avenues that Argentine filmmakers are taking in an increasingly cost-conscious era. Subiela states in an interview that the shift to the digital medium was one born out of necessity, and not only an aesthetic choice; it was a survival mechanism for him as he would have had to leave the country in search of film financing (Internet Surf 2003). This film is also unconventional in that the film crew consisted of film students and faculty at Subiela's film school, La escuela profesional de cine (The Professional Film School).

Other notable veterans such as Fernando 'Pino' Solanas have adopted digital video technology to return to a style of filmmaking which is more televisual, direct and immediate in feel. His latest films which are documentaries, *Memoria del saqueo* (*Social Genocide*, 2004), *La dignidad de los nadies* (*The Dignity of Nobodies*, 2005) and two more scheduled to form a quartet – *Argentina Latente*, (*Latent Argentina*) in post-production and funded in part by Programa Ibermedia, and *La tierra sublevada* (*The Roused Land*) which will serve as a conclusion – are in a style reminiscent of the New Latin American Cinema movement that Solanas was integral to. These four films are stand-alone pieces, but are united under the following theme: 'Argentina: from the devastation and plunder to the intent at reconstruction and the alternatives to a new project' (Anon. 2006).

Solanas is unapologetic about the two-hour long *Memoria del saqueo*, used to denounce three decades of corruption, greed and mismanagement which he argues has amounted to a social genocide on the people of Argentina. Solanas has implied in interviews that these documentaries are a continuation of where he left off in the late 1960s with *La hora de los hornos* (made with Octavio Getino). As with the aforementioned film, he displays images of destitute, humble people, but more often than in previous works he employs the contrast editing technique whereby a roving camera with a wide-angle lens spans corridors of power (such as the marbled floors and chandeliers of various state office buildings, including the Presidential Casa Rosada) and then there are cuts to poor *villas miserias* (shantytowns) in Matanzas, an area outside of Buenos Aires city limits. These shots of *el pueblo* marching in the streets and surviving at home were shot using a compact mini-DV camera. He states unequivocally, 'I want to show how life is, to show these people whose wealth was sold out from under them, whose votes were betrayed, whose jobs were taken along with their savings' (quoted in Valente 2002a). His aim is to give this large group of dispossessed people some visibility (which they have already achieved on their own with the *piquetero* movement, the workers who took over their factories post-2001), and some of the commentaries by these anonymous, ordinary people are more incisively critical and astute than many of the professionals interviewed who work with this population (such as school teachers, labour lawyers, a school principal).

Aesthetically and narratively speaking, the film also invokes *La hora de los hornos* in the sense that Solanas structures the film into ten 'chapters' with intertitle cards with titles such as *Crónica de la traicion* (*Chronicle of a Betrayal*) and *La mafiocracia* (*The Mafiaocracy*). Moreover, there are graphic slogans which

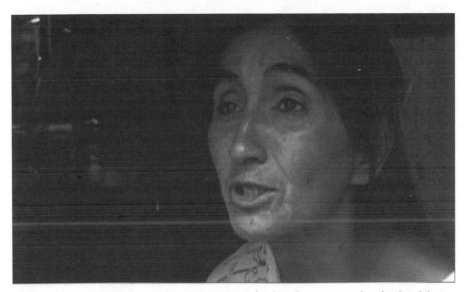

Memoria del saqueo (2004): poor residents in Argentina explain how the government has abandoned them

punctuate the film and recall the other work, except that there are no quotes from famous revolutionaries. Rather, they are ironic commentaries in lower case letters, such as '*lo privado: modernidad y eficiencia*' (private ownership is modern and efficient) or direct agit prop like '*impunidad*' (impunity) framed as an Eisensteinian call to action; to rouse the viewer to feel outrage, just as audiences weremade to feel almost forty years earlier. While most of the shots are traditional and not as innovative as his previous work, he does have a few animation sequences with extreme close ups of the 'bad guys' in different shades of rich colour, with loud jazz accompaniment providing a dizzying effect. Most of the time, however, there is an alternating orchestral score which is either weepy or ominous, depending on the tone he tries to achieve. The soundtrack and music is not overlaid as masterfully as in *La hora de los hornos*, but there is one segment, such as near the end of the film, where an Argentine woman chanteuse is rapping a protest song over images of rebelling citizens in the street, confronting the police during the popular unrest of 19–20 December 2001. This image and sound reflects a more recent vision of youthful protesters 'fighting the power' to the beat of African-American-inspired hip-hop in *español*.

In one of the remaining chapters, Solanas narrates on the voiceover track that 'when our country can produce enough commodities to feed 300 million people, the level of poverty denounced in *The Hour of the Furnaces* in the 1960s never foresaw the incredible neoliberal genocide of the 1990s'. The director, who is often shown in the frame, conducted exhaustive research on the political and economic machinations of the Argentine government and society beginning with the *Proceso* until the breaking point of the crisis in 2001. Utilising historical footage, direct cinema techniques, didactic historical commentary, testimonials and a voiceover track of a detailed political analysis, Solanas' work displays a no-holds-barred approach to social criticism and uses the film as a vehicle to explain why the Argentine people have descended so low (as one politician puts it, 'We are all in Dante's inferno').

Compared to his work from the 1960s–70s, made under clandestine conditions under threat of death, here the film was made in 2004 during the current left-of-centre Kirchner government and was even officially sanctioned by it. On the back of the DVD cover the film was described by the Ministry of Education as being 'of educational interest'. What this meant was that it was shown, free of charge, to all of the high schools in the country (Gemunden 2004: 52)

Another trend to appear within the video and digital filmmaking communities are young Patagonians (residents of the provinces in the South of the country) who are creating images of the South that, like Lucrecia Martel's project, differ from the traditional 'porteño gaze' of the region. One video collective known as ARAN (Asociación de Realizadores Audiovisuales de Neuquén) organised an annual film festival called 'Imágenes de Patagonia' as an outlet expressly for those who have created work in or about the region. The festival has travelled throughout the country and has helped push for a decentralisation of cultural production in the provinces, albeit a modest effort at the time of writing.

Other, more politicised forms of media production have arisen as a response to the economic crisis, including TV-piquetera, a low power, pirated television signal broadcast on a local channel created by the piqueteros, the unemployed worker movement, as a way to counter the mass media's criminalisation of the piqueteros' political protests in the area (Trigona 2004). The piqueteros have become a more visible urban movement on the Argentine landscape, vis-à-vis political demonstrations, their involvement in the recuperated factory movement, with popular neighbourhood assemblies and in the dissemination of alternative forms of media such as television shows and a prolific number of videotapes distributed free of charge for community activists. Their ability to produce hundreds of low-budget documentary videos, used to record the movement, for screenings at assembly halls harken back to the use of the newsreel, whereby films used to educate audiences could be shown on a regular basis to keep members of the movement informed of the piqueteros' actions. A sense of denunciation and militancy replete with a serious voiceover track has formed part of a recent group of films now dubbed the 'New-New Latin American Cinema' to demonstrate how desperate times have called for urgent cinematic styles to be revived (Cine piquetero (piquetero cinema), the radical workers' film collective Cine ojo obrero (Workers' Cinema Eye), and Uruguayan Mario Handler's documentary film, Aparte (Aside, 2002), would fall under this rubric).

A further recent phenomenon of filmmaking has occurred in the city of Saladillo (located 112 miles south of Buenos Aires), where two young aspiring directors, Julio Midu and Fabio Junco, have directed 17 films and several television mini-series involving 200 citizens in their town of 30,000 residents. Their 'neighbourhood cinema' makes 'telenovelas' in addition to films. One of Midu's television serials has over 100 episodes, and they are broadcast on two Argentine television networks (Channel 5 and TV Centro). All the neighbourhood actors volunteer their time, and each film costs roughly 500 pesos (US$174). The films receive some support from the Saladillo city government (Anon. 2005b). Their 'neighbourhood films' festival (*cine de vecinos*) was a big hit, screening films featuring amateur actors from all over Argentina. With over ten percent of the town's population attending, the festival was deemed a grand success: Junco explains that 'the neighbours were happy to see that in remote parts of the country, like Jujuy or Rio Gallegos they also make films with ordinary people and they tell stories that are close to the heart of their residents' (quoted in Sabat 2005). This trend of filmmaking demonstrates that there is a need to reposition production away from the nation's capital and create a local cinema which embraces the 'small stories' approach.

As the situation stabilised under President Néstor Kirchner's administration, normalcy slowly returned to the country. Cultural life has continued, witnessed by the continuation of the Buenos Aires International Festival of Independent Cinema despite economic woes. However, changes did occur that bore witness to the ever increasing divide between the 'haves' and 'have-nots'. Within the sprawling metropolis of Buenos Aires, there were those with access to resources that helped it progress and grow compared to the very difficult situation in the provinces. A flash point which brought these contradictions of 'progress' and 'improvement' to more rural places in the country occurred in May 2005, when arsonists in the province of San Luis, an area known for video editing and production, burned down a production set of the telenovela *Salvame María*. This was one of a number of violent protests that occurred against the province's film and television industry that week. San Luis, a province that *Variety* characterises as having 'pretensions to become the Hollywood of Argentina' (Newbery 2005a) was under fire because the provincial legislature approved a ten million dollar allocation towards film sector development to governor Alberto Rodriguez Saa and his brother, Adolfo, better known as one of the short-lived presidents during the 2001 crisis (ibid). Here is an example of a province attempting to tap its potential as a national and possibly global industry, yet confronting the local reality of poverty and resource scarcity.

The province, dubbed 'Hollyluis', has granted credits, co-production money, tax and technical assistance to 14 films. Another six are in production, including a project by actress Faye Dunaway (ibid). While business was booming for the film industry in San Luis, and the main impetus was to create jobs, many opponents accused Rodriguez Saa of masking a poor administration under the guise of a new economic development project. Many dissenters wished the money to go instead to education, public health and infrastructure and to increasing salaries for teachers and state workers (Newbery 2005b). Other provincial cities such as Mendoza and Río Negro claim to be revamping their film commissions to attract film pesos from the capital as well as currency from abroad but the results have yet to be seen (Minghetti 2005).

Film critic Quintín, founder of both the film journal *El amante* and the Bafici, summarises the New Independent Argentine Cinema by stating:

> Considered as a consequence of Argentina's deep economical and social crisis, this new cinema has made out a path among the ruins of a country torn by ferocious dictatorships, anaemic democracies and neoliberal experiments. They have found an answer by staring at their reality, without shouting out its calamities but rather including them in a rich and sophisticated poetics, without lying or using a demagogic and forced optimism. (2003)

This surge in young independent filmmaking since 1995 has revived the film community in Argentina, even though there are debates about the importance of their apparent lack of commercial success. Regardless, it has resonated with the concerns of a younger, more cynical and disillusioned generation in Argentina, and it is one that is willing to confront the various problems related to the neoliberal crisis affecting the country. The strength of this new movement is an aesthetic that is more daring, experimental and challenging than that which characterised the previous two decades.

CONCLUSION

Throughout the roughly one hundred years of its existence, Argentine cinema has had to compete against the Hollywood behemoth to garner an audience. Sadly, it was largely successful in only two periods of its film history: during the 1930s–50s, when the studio system produced high-quality, popular genre films, and once again in the early 1990s, when multimedia conglomerates began investing in blockbuster films that brought back audiences in droves.

Clearly, the Argentine film industry must contend with many factors in order to ensure that it is on a healthy footing. Aside from the decades beginning in the 1930s, the Argentine film industry has had to depend on state support. Since the founding of the National Film Institute in 1957, state cultural policies in different eras have helped shape national culture in the cinema in various ways.

During the post-dictatorship period, when President Alfonsín was democratically elected to office, national cinema was utilised by the state as a public relations tool abroad. The majority of films produced presented tales of the recent horrible past, and provided testimony to the openness and renewal of Argentine culture in a time free of political censorship and violent repression. The Radical Party considered the cinema a bastion of high culture, and films were exported to scores of international film festivals. During this time films were mainly shown in art-houses and were made in a similar vein to the European art-house aesthetic. Although the films were successes in middle- to upper-middle-class film festival crowds, they were not large financial successes at the box office, and many working-class Argentines did not pay to see them.

Although Alfonsín's government looked to the European model for cinema aesthetics, for President Menem the model was the US Hollywood film industry – higher-budget movies with special effects and blockbuster marketing techniques. Menem, taking a more Peronist view of mass popular culture, considered films to be fashioned for a domestic audience. His two administrations were marked not by an interest in promoting Argentina's image at prestigious film festivals as much as by an active attempt to cultivate the national cinema's industrial capabilities. He took an 'economistic' perspe...ctive, whereby the commercial potential for film production superceded other considerations. Under Menem, films were made with a glossy, globalised aesthetic and appealed to a wide general audience, thus boosting the economic viability of the industry. However, state support for a national culture used to inspire, educate and cultivate a national sense of community was compromised.

Beginning in the mid-1990s, young directors, the majority of whom had graduated from one of many film schools in Argentina, began producing low-budget, independent films in a style that earned this group the classification of the New Independent Argentine Cinema.

Quintín, in an essay comparing the new generation of filmmakers with the 'dinosaurs', describes how issues of class are played out in this new cinema:

> Poverty is not a horror outside the frame or postcard of a shantytown but is the material from which these films have been made. The extreme economic decline of recent years, the appearance of new social groups and new forms of language and relationships, found no answer in the old Argentine cinema, confined to its own blindness, immune to what was happening beyond the front-page newspaper headlines. By contrast, the new directors have not found solutions to the ills of the country, although they are not afraid of examining them. (2002: 114)

It is these filmmakers who will continue to push the boundaries of Argentine national identity through a low-budget cinema. Since their auspicious debut in the mid-1990s, however, some of these first-time directors, such as Pablo Trapero and Adrián Caetano, are now so esteemed and well recognised that each were recently funded by larger production companies for their next projects. Trapero, in addition to starting his own production company, Matanza cine, collaborated with the producers of *Comodines*, Pol-Ka (who partner with Disney) on his feature, *Familia Rodante* (*Rolling Family*, 2004). Adrián Caetano worked with celebrity television host Marcelo Tinelli's company to produce an 11 part television series, *Disputas* (*Catfight*) before going to direct and co-write *Crónica de una fuga* which received production funds and distribution rights through 20th Century Fox Argentina. Although some filmmakers are moving up the ranks and gaining more commercial exposure – as witnessed by long time low-budget auteur Alejandro Agresti's film *Valentín* (2002) which was distributed in the US by Miramax, and his first Hollywood film for Warner Brothers, *The Lake House* (2006) starring Keanu Reeves and Sandra Bullock – these are the exceptions rather than the rule. This handful of 'crossover' directors calls the term 'independent' into question, and this was hotly debated at the Buenos Aires International Festival of Independent Cinema in April 2004. Despite the fact that there was no resolution, it debates the idea that Argentina has a fully-fledged film industry. The larger studios would claim that there is not, thus affording themselves state subsidies; and other, smaller director-producers would say that there is.

Labelling debates aside, the feasibility of exhibition and distribution access for lesser-known filmmakers in Argentina and abroad still has not been resolved despite worldwide recognition of this new wave of directors. Another discussion to emerge at the independent film festival was during a roundtable with Bernardo Zupnik (head of Argentine film distributor Distribution Company), Manuel Antín, Juan Villegas (young director of *Sábado*) and David Blaustein (a documentary filmmaker). The issue of implementing a screen quota was raised, and interestingly enough the majority of filmmakers in the room felt that this was one way to ensure better access to exhibition for national films and to fight the 'occupied screen' effect. Of course, Zupnik, the lone distributor's voice, was adamantly opposed to the idea, stating that 'one cannot force exhibitors to screen films that are not good'. He frames this debate as a quality issue, rather than a power dynamic or economic issue between Hollywood and the Argentine film industry. From a distributor's perspective, at least, a quota would hurt the industry as a whole.

In June 2004, the INCAA spearheaded the passage of a new screen quota law, whereby each movie theatre is obligated to show one national film per quarter. Therefore, a 16-screen multiplex must screen 64 Argentine films per year. Another law stipulated a 'continuity average', which obligates film exhibitors to continue screening national films if they fall between six and 25 percent capacity that week. In this way exhibitors could not arbitrarily drop national films or change screening times mid-week (Newbery 2004).

Because by and large Argentine film producers do not have the funds to market their films, they rely on word of mouth to get people to the movie theatres. In contrast to the producers of a Hollywood blockbuster, who invest in high priced 'blitz' campaigns (to rake in significant box-office revenue the first weekend), an Argentine film will gain momentum through favourable word of mouth reviews. Jorge Coscia argued that exhibitors often did not give Argentine films time on the marquee for the film to attract audiences, but instead discriminated against it in favour of the Hollywood import, no matter the quality of the film. Therefore, he argued, having the screen quota would ensure some continuity of the film in the movie theatre. Coscia, in his explanation of the two pronged approach (both the screen quota and the 'continuity average'), gives an example of how and why this system could preserve Argentine cinema:

> For example, *Luna de Avellaneda* [at the time of writing] is complying with the screen quota at its exhibiting movie theatres. Nevertheless, had we not enforced this legislation, and based on the exhibitors' and foreign distributors' needs, the film could have easily been withdrawn from the screens to give way to new imported programming. Now, we have two benefits: the

film stays, and exhibitors do not lose money, since the film is having good box-office results. (2004)

If one looks at the admissions for the abovementioned film, it opened with 85,000 people on 25 May 2004, and by the end of a three month run, it had been seen by 1.2 million people, one of the highest attendance rates for an Argentine film that year. It is notable that Coscia chooses a film directed by a very well-respected and financially sound 'industrial auteur' as his example. While it is possible that an exhibitor might drop this film in favour of a Hollywood one, it is less likely than in other scenarios where a first-time director might be cut. As a point of comparison, Campanella's previous film, *El hijo de la novia,* was released at the end of August 2001 (before the screen quota was enacted), with 314,000 admissions. By 13 November it had 1.26 million spectators, a sum that was somewhat larger than his most recent work. While this cannot definitively say anything in favour or against the effectiveness of the screen quota (since it is overdetermined, with variables including but not limited to: the time of year, competition from abroad, how many prints are available and so on) it demonstrates that this particular director, even in times of crisis (*El hijo de la novia* played on the eve of the devaluation of the peso), can perform well at the box-office. What needs to be examined is whether lesser-known or first-time directors were in fact more successful in their theatrical run by being allowed to stay on the marquee for longer. To counter opinions exemplified by distributor Zupnik that bad films are protected against consumer preferences, Coscia counters that the INCAA has no interest in forcing a film to be shown if there is little audience. The logic is that this would contradict the spirit of the cinema law ('La Nueva Ley del Cine') which depends on high box-office returns to subsidise Argentine film. Therefore they would 'destroy the cinema they are trying to protect' by forcing unpopular films to be shown (Coscia 2004).

At stake is whether the state has the license to regulate culture by adopting protectionist measures, a term that has become pejorative and stigmatised. Because of this, a new term has been embraced by those who support a screen quota –the 'exceptionists'. These exceptionists are appropriating the term from the rhetoric of 'cultural exceptionalism' that was successfully championed by France and Canada during the 1993 GATT agreement against the US. While the term has given way to the concept of 'cultural diversity' (see Moisés, 2002; Frau-Meigs, 2003), currently even organisations greatly influenced by the United States such as the Organisation of American States (OAS) have supported UNESCO's declaration to protect the diversity of cultures against globalising forces. In his essay 'The Screen Quota, A Fundamental Step Forward', Jorge Coscia concludes with the following statement:

> The screen quota is not a flag by itself; the real flag is the defence of our interests, our culture, our jobs and our cinema, constantly cornered in our

own market ... Hence policies are tools, they are not the ends but the means. The screen quota is a fundamental issue, because culture is essential to a country's project. But it is also relevant because debates and discussions continue to establish new means of development, sovereignty and growth. (2004)

While the screen quota may function to the best of its ability in this juncture, it may soon be ineffective according to Harvey Feigenbaum, who argues that cultural policy tools may be undercut by changes in technology to the point where direct satellite broadcasting, data-casting, near video-on-demand, digital compression video-on-demand and distribution via internet streaming may create more porous borders and allow the floodgates of Hollywood's film and television in to 'undermine the state's effort to protect national culture' (2004: 256). Feigenbaum recommends different kinds of subsidies in addition to individual subventions in production, an emphasis on distribution and marketing and in infrastructure, such as production facilities and training as the antidote for preserving the health of a small national film industry (2004: 260–1). While this may not serve the production sector in the long run, it is clear that most directors welcome this move by lawmakers.

However, the biggest national commercial hit for 2006 was not serious art-house fare, but rather the beach comedy franchise *Bañeros 3, todospoderosos* (*Bathers III, Superpowers*, 2006), directed by Rodolfo Ledo: a crude comedy vehicle designed to show off scantily-clad beach babes with protagonists who cracked sarcastic jokes that sadly descended into racist and xenophobic comments against minorities, but especially against Asians (the 'bad guys' were Hong Kong mafiosos) – characterisations that were offensive to at least one critic (Blejman 2006). Critic Pablo Sirvén notes how ironic it is when a film such as this one, which amassed over 500,000 spectators in two weeks, in essence served as a 'lifejacket' to 'save Argentine film' from what he considers to be an 'excessive offering of silent, dark and indecipherable debut films' (Sirvén 2006: 3).

Other issues at stake in 2006 are the problems that arise when there is 'too much of a good thing': out of 71 Argentine films screened in 2005, only seven had more than 100,000 spectators; 51 did not draw more than 10,000 viewers and 22 barely attained 100 admissions (ibid.). José Miguel Onaindia, who served as INCAA head under the De la Rúa government, felt that 'films have less spectators when there is an excess of offerings' (quoted in ibid.). In addition, issues of inflation, low ticket prices for movie theatre admissions, and escalating costs of advertising and prints have hurt distributors (Newbery 2006b). Some film producers, such as Oscar Kramer's company, co-producer of Caetano's *Crónica de una fuga* (*Chronicle of an Escape*, 2006), are dependent on international sales to cover costs. On the domestic front, Kramer's company, Shok films, has teamed up with 20th Century Fox Argentina for a cash advance for the costs of release, marketing and prints so that a film like *Tiempo de valientes*

(2005) could be released on fifty screens as opposed to ten to twenty screens without temporary assistance (Newbery 2006a). This is significant, because on average Argentine films are released with roughly ten prints of a film, compared to Hollywood studios, that typically 'bombard' exhibitors with 140 prints for area theatres (Coscia 2005c: 109). Carlos Mentasti, general manager of Telefe Cine, whose company produced Juan José Jusid's *Apasionados* (*Passionate People*) during the crisis of 2002, took a relaxed approach to the threat of impending inflation. In an interview he stated that 'this country has been hit by so many crises that if I was scared I wouldn't have ever made a film ... we are used to it' (Newbery 2006b).

One issue that reached consensus at the round table was how the Buenos Aires International Festival of Independent Cinema proved to be an ideal space for Argentine cinema to be exhibited, alongside other independent films from around the world. What was needed, according to one audience member, was space for this cinema all year round. If Argentine cinema is to continue forging new territory, it will be in the hands of the following groups: young filmmakers, film critics and enthusiasts who have helped create new venues in which to showcase this work; veterans (such as Lita Stantic, distributor Pascual Condito, film school director Manuel Antín and others) who are working as executive producers; and, of course, the INCAA.

Concurrently, the industrial auteur production companies must continue to forge ties with television companies in order to compete with the Hollywood behemoth. All of these segments of the Argentine film sector have been able to weather the financial chaos that has recently plagued Argentina (which will no doubt rear its ugly head again in subsequent decades). This resilience has helped to shore up a recent interest in Argentine cinema, but more institutionalised or commercial efforts on a larger scale must be made to promote greater exhibition and distribution of both low-budget independent and 'industrial auteur' films so that the larger, global market can ensure larger audiences.

NOTES

INTRODUCTION

1 This in part stems from Argentina's large European immigrant population, who arrived between the 1880s and the 1920s. Argentina also has a history of systematic genocide of the indigenous population during the process of 'nation building' in the 1880s by the founding fathers.

CHAPTER 1

1 The *sainete* of the popular theatre, tangos and later the cinema, were truly popular art forms that attracted working-class talents who performed for the working classes, often crossing genres and media (*sainete* actors like Pepe Arias worked in films, *sainetes* were adapted to and inspired films, tangos and their performers were popularised by the cinema and so on). Shunned by elites, the working class were free to enjoy their *sainetes*, tangos and especially films without knowing of or heeding the criticisms of the wealthy.

2 For more information on what studios, both large and independent, were operating during this period, see España 2000a.

3 Octavio Getino adds that 'there was no previous instance of an industrial, technical, or commercial entity, although limited, in Latin America' (2005: 28).

4 For example, a riot ensued after a screening of the Hollywood film *Argentine Nights*. In the *Detroit Free Press* article 'Get the Facts Straight' (21 May 1941) the author quotes a film critic of the Argentine newspaper *La Nación*: 'As long as Hollywood insists on seeing Argentina as an incredibly ridiculous tropical country, no Pan-American understanding is possible no matter how many good-will travellers are sent here.'

5 I am grateful to Daniel 'Paraná' Sendros for pointing this out.

6   It is important to point out that the United States was never seriously threat-
     ened by Argentina's domination of the market; rather, its market share may
     have been compromised to a certain degree by the success of Argentina's
     films. As noted by Schnitman, 'Even when the Argentine film industry
     reached a high point of 49 films in 1940, three of the large North American
     companies (in this case, Paramount, Metro and Warner) could each release
     as many as that or more' (1978: 73).

7   Juan Carlos Garate, longtime accountant of Argentina Sono Film, recounts
     how the company dealt with the lack of film stock: 'One business tactic …
     was to work with film stock as contraband from Brazil and Chile. I flew
     many times with rolls of film from Santiago, and I've walked many nights
     on the port of Rio de Janeiro trying to put five to ten rolls of film on a ship
     [bound for Buenos Aires]' (quoted in España 1984: 272).

8   Short films such as David José Kohon's *Buenos Aires* (1958) and features
     such as Lautaro Murúa's *Alias gardelito* (*Alias Big Shot*, 1960), amongst oth-
     ers, were banned on the grounds of being 'obscene'. These films provided
     social testimony to the impoverished areas surrounding Buenos Aires. State
     officials did not approve of showing these films publicly – especially on the
     international circuit; they were seen as 'airing dirty laundry'. A film like
     Fernando Birri's *Los inundados* (*Flooded Out*, 1961) was not banned, but
     when European film festivals requested a print, the reactionary INC officials
     ignored requests for screenings at Locarno and at Cannes (Feldman 1990:
     69–84).

9   Leopoldo Torre Nilsson may be Argentina's most internationally recognised
     auteur. His critically acclaimed film *La mano en la trampa* (*The Hand in the
     Trap*, 1961) won the top prize at the Cannes Film Festival that year.

10   I would like to thank Fernando Martín Peña for his insights on this issue.

11   My thanks to David Oubiña for pointing this out to me.

12   It was difficult to find box-office numbers for these more commercially
     popular yet politically populist films. See Schettini 1997 for a discussion
     of Argentine films that produced large box-office successes without the fi-
     nancial help of private television channels. What the author fails to address,
     however, is to what degree television actors helped to draw crowds to these
     commercial films.

13   The term *desaparecido* ('disappeared') refers to the way in which people were
     kidnapped by government goons or military officers, often in the middle of
     the night. Concerned families or loved ones would often not be given any
     information by the authorities regarding the victim's whereabouts.

14   In regard to the anecdote concerning the scene where a mother robs to aid
     her son, see statements by Armando Bo (in Avellaneda 1987). Regarding the
     objections to scenes in a film about gauchos, see Juan José Jusid's statements
     in July 1983 when filming *Los gauchos judios* (*The Jewish Gauchos*, 1975),
     cited in Avellaneda 1987.

15 The request to extradite Getino was denied (see AIDA 1981: 147).

16 In 1991, Ramón Ortega was elected governor of the Tucumán province. A close friend of President Menem, he served as a cabinet minister, and in 1999 made an unsuccessful run for vice president of the country.

17 Sergio Renán later recanted his involvement with the regime. He became very active in the Radical Party and was later appointed to head the famous opera house, the Teatro Colón from 1989–96 and later in 2000. He continued to direct films, one entitled *El sueño de los heroes* (*The Dream of Heroes*, 1997), based on a novel by Adolfo Bioy Casares, which cost $3 million to produce and ultimately failed at the box office, and *La soledad era esto* (*This Was Solitude*, 2002).

18 For excellent analyses of this film and its political implications, see Reati 1989 and Newman 1992.

CHAPTER 2

1 Domingo Di Núbila (1986) points out that while box-office numbers declined for Argentine films, this could not be attributed to economic decline, because film attendance figures for foreign (read: US) films increased that year.

2 This is an extraordinary success in a home market that comprised 34 million people at the time.

3 There were films made that catered to a mass and mainly male audience however. With the lifting of censorship the highest grossing adult films were sexploitation films such as *Atrapadas* (*Condemned to Hell*, 1984) directed by Aníbal di Salvo, *Sucedió en el internado* (*It Happened in Boarding School*, 1985) by Emilio Vieyra and *Los gatos* (*Prostitución de alto nivel*) (*The Cats: High Class Prostitutes*, 1985) by Carlos Borocosque Jr, which brought in 992,600, 697,700 and 579,900 spectators respectively (Sapere 2003).

4 *Variety* notes that 'Argentine films predominantly find their market among Anglo audiences, with only 25 percent coming from US Hispanic sectors' (Anon. 1987a: 94).

5 See Raul Beycero's essay on Luis Puenzo's aesthetics and filmmaking technique in the film *La historia oficial* (1997: 15–23).

6 The literal translation is 'friendship-ness'; idiomatically, it means 'cronyism'.

7 Out of a pool of 59 filmmakers receiving 'special interest' loans (a term that will be discussed later in the chapter) 37 were known to have partisan ties or political leanings. Out of that group, 19 were Radicals, nine were Peronists and nine were independent.

8 Corman founded the production and distribution company New World Pictures in 1970 and sold it in 1983. He then founded Concorde-New Horizons, which was solely a production company. In 1995 he opened the film studio Concorde Anois near Galway, Ireland, to produce US-Irish co-

productions.

9   For more on Corman's co-productions, see Falicov 2004.

10 The film *La muerte blanca*, a thriller, received a 'special interest' designation from the INC.

11 As *Variety* never failed to point out (especially between 1981 and 1986), video piracy was the unstated norm. The MPAA exerted pressure on the government to end this activity.

12 See 'New Strategies for Film Production' and 'The Broadcasters and Film Production' in Lange & Renaud 1989: 88–91 and 266–69.

13 As Patricia Moro points out (1988), in European countries such as Spain pre-sales to Spanish television would often account for around 25 percent of a film's budget.

14 For INC data, see Getino 2005: 365.

15 The Grandmothers of the Plaza de Mayo formed in October 1977 after a group of mothers began meeting there in April of the same year. While both organisations work together, there are various branches of each group. In 2002, the Grandmothers estimated that around five hundred children were still missing, and that they have been able to identify 71; see Arditti 2002.

16 For example, during the dictatorship a placard placed under the Obelisk (a national landmark near a busy intersection) stated *Silencio es salud* ('silence is healthy'). It referred to preventing street noise such as car horns and other noise but clearly had other implications.

17 Contrary to the belief that it was the majority of young, radicalised, middle-class university students who were victims, it has been shown that although 21 percent of the disappeared were students, the largest population of those murdered (thirty percent) was from the working class; see Carabello 1986: 88.

CHAPTER 3

1   Edward L. Gibson notes that the association between a Peronist president and representatives of a multinational corporation (especially one that historically was the biggest corporate adversary of Perón) 'marked a shift in the institutional forms of linkage between the state and business, displacing traditional links in favour of direct interaction between state policymakers and large business firms' (1997: 357).

2   Data from the Ministry of Culture and Education (cited in Blanco & Marchetti 1992: 2).

3   The video sector has been asked by the INCAA to officially register with them in order to keep track of the ten percent tax levy. The last figures reported that 1,300 stores had registered. Julio Raffo, a film lawyer who drafted the new film law, stated in a 1997 interview that the law would probably go unheeded by the home video sector.

4 Diego Lerner, senior vice president for Disney in Latin America, felt that the new law would contribute to the 'already massive' video piracy. He stated in *Variety*: 'Some movies don't need a six-month window, and depend on subsequent media to break even. You need to jump on video before pirates get there first' (quoted in Paxman 1994: 47). Lerner was the main lawyer for the MPAA before taking up his new position.

5 Transcripts from the Chamber of Deputies, 11 May 1994, 478–79. These portions of Sra. Mercader's speech are translated by the author.

6 Of the social democratic nations, France probably has the strongest state policy, or *dirigiste*, stance regarding both culture and industry. It was also at the helm of the 'cultural exemption' movement during the 1993 Uruguay round of GATT talks with the United States regarding trade in cultural goods.

7 Transcripts from Senator Antonio Cafiero, Senate Chamber, 28 September 1994, 3054. These portions of Senator Cafiero's speech are translated by the author.

8 While this may be true for Latin America (except for the Cuban film industry, which is entirely state-supported), it is debatable that other policies such as France's are more protectionist (unlike Argentina, France has a system of screen quotas for film and television imports).

9 Alejandro Agresti could be called the 'grandfather' of young Argentine independent filmmakers. He has made 25 films, the majority produced in the Netherlands. Only eight of his films have been exhibited commercially. While considered an auteur in his own right, he has spearheaded a young cinema movement to produce very low-budget films geared towards young urban sensibilities. One theatrical release, *La cruz* (*The Cross*, 1997), was made for under $200,000.

10 Of other Latin American multimedia groups, Mexico's Televisa was ranked one spot higher, while Brazil's Globo was ranked at number 27 ($2.2 million annually).

11 An article in *La Nación* from 22 June 1995 profiled Mahárbiz as having a dubious financial past.

12 Named after a famous actress from the 1930s and 1940s. Other theatres were named for other 'golden age' actresses Mirtha Legrand, Amelia Bence and Delia Garcés. The allusion to this prime period for Argentine cinema is not uncommon in describing the film industry's legacy.

13 Argentine blockbuster films such as *Comodines* were also released at the Complejo Tita Merello but had television advertising and full-page adverts in newspapers in the same way that Hollywood films market their films. Thus, they were released in shopping mall multiplexes in addition to the art cinema complex reserved for national cinema.

14 While clearly the dichotomy between the commercial market and the cultural state (that is, the notion that there is no commercial appeal in state-spon-

sored events, or that the market lacks quality) is false, this bridge between the realm of commercial television and a traditionally elite film festival is also a result of the reconfiguration of state-supported cultural industries in Argentina.

15 This was the highest figure in decades. The percentage going to see US films was 71 percent. From 6 July 1998, the top grossing national films were those made by the production companies that had teamed up with television stations: *Un argentino en New York* (Juan José Jusid, 1998, produced by Argentina Sono Film), with 1,634,702 spectators; *Cohen vs. Rossi* (Daniel Barone, 1998, produced by Pol-Ka), with 734,211 viewers; and *Manuelita* (Manuel Garcia Ferré), the animated film based on a famous children's story by María Elena Walsh, which drew in record crowds (2,043,945) in 1999 and was nominated for Argentina's selection at the Academy Awards. This film was financed in part by Telefé, or Channel 11 (Anon. 1998: 7).

16 My thanks to Randal Johnson for clarifying the Brazilian Lei do Audiovisual.

CHAPTER 4

1 For example, when it was screened in 1997, Alejandro Agresti's *Buenos Aires, vice versa* (1996) drew in 90,000 spectators. In 1998, *Pizza, birra, faso* drew in more than 100,000 people.

2 Producer and Film Loan Committee member Claudio Pustelnik stated in an interview that he did not agree with the rejection decision and suggested that Rejtman appeal. He also emphasised that because this was a new system, inevitably there were going to be discrepancies and disagreements. Furthermore, he acknowledged that these committee decisions were subjective; see Anon. 1996b.

3 Four of these schools are la Escuela de Cine del Instituto de Arte Cinematográfico de Avellaneda, la Escuela Provincial de Cine y Televisión de Rosario, la Universidad de Córdoba and la Universidad de la Plata.

4 Vera Fogwill, daughter of bohemian writer Rodolfo Fogwill, became the darling of young independent cinema for a time. She has starred in numerous films by Agresti, including *Buenos Aires, vice versa*, *La cruz* and *El viento se llevó lo qué* (*Wind with the Gone*, 1998), among others. She has gone on to co-direct and star in an excellent film, *Las mantenidas sin sueños* (*Kept and Dreamless*, 2005), which was Argentina's nomination for the foreign film category in the 2006 Golden Globe awards, held in Los Angeles.

5 Although the INCAA did give a film loan to this project, it was not given the 'special interest' designation. In an interview, Martel stated that they felt the film did not have enough 'star' actors to make it commercially viable. It is unclear whether the INCAA changed the designation after Graciela Borges and Mercedes Moran and others signed on to the project or not.

6   These are professional associations that have differing perspectives with respect to how Argentine cinema should be produced. Their philosophies are discussed in chapter three.

7   The proper use of the term 'independent' has been debated because the reality is that practically all of the films produced in Argentina (with the exception of those produced by the few studios that remain and a handful of private production companies) are independently made and financed. Other descriptions of the term include a film's 'independence' from state funding.

8   The finest filmography of the most recognised films from the New Independent Argentine Cinema can be found in the bilingual book edited by Horacio Bernardes, Diego Lerer and Sergio Wolf and published in 2002: *Nuevo cine argentino: Temas, autores y estilos de una renovación/New Argentine Cinema: Themes, Auteurs and Trends of Innovation*. Buenos Aires: FIPRESCI/ Ediciones Tatanka.

BIBLIOGRAPHY

Abel Martín, Jorge (1977) *Cine Argentino '76*. Buenos Aires: Metrocorp.

___ (1978) *Cine Argentino '77*. Buenos Aires: Metrocorp.

___ (1979) *Cine Argentino '78*. Buenos Aires: Cero Seis.

___ (1980) *Cine Argentino '79*. Buenos Aires: Corregidor.

___ (1981) *Cine Argentino '80*. Buenos Aires: Corregidor.

___ (1983) *Cine Argentino '81*. Buenos Aires: Corregidor.

___ (1984) *Cine Argentino '82*. Buenos Aires: Corregidor.

___ (1987) *Cine Argentino: Diccionario de realizadores contemporáneos*. Buenos Aires: Instituto Nacional de Cine.

Acheson, Dean (1944) Letter to Norman Armour, 7 March 1944, National Archives, Washington D.C. College Park.

Achugar, Walter (1986) 'Using Movies to Make Movies' in Julianne Burton (ed.) *Cinema and Social Change in Latin America: Conversations with Filmmakers*. Austin: University of Texas Press, 221–36.

Adelman, Jeremy (1994) 'Post-Populist Argentina', *New Left Review*, 203, 65–91.

Aguilar, Gonzalo (2006) *Otros mundos: un ensayo sobre el nuevo cine argentino*. Buenos Aires: Santiago Arcos Editor.

Aguinis, Marcos (1987) 'Evolution of a Democratic Argentine Culture', in David William Foster (ed.) *The Redemocratization of Argentine Culture, 1983 and Beyond: An International Research Symposium at Arizona State University, February 16–17*. Tempe, AZ: Center for Latin American Studies, Arizona State University, 7–10.

AIDA – Asociación Internacional para la Defensa de los Artistas victimas de la represión en el mundo (1981) *Argentina: Como matar a la cultura: Testimonios 1976–81*. Madrid: Editorial Revolución.

Aksoy, Asa and Kevin Robins (1992) 'Hollywood for the 21st Century: Global Competition for Critical Mass in Image Markets', *Cambridge Journal of Economics*, 16, 1, 1–22.

Anderson, Benedict (1991) *Imagined Communities: Reflections on the Origins and Spread of Nationalism* (revised edition). London: Verso.

Anon. (1941a) *Heraldo de Cine*, 12, 495, 8 January, 1.

_____ (1941b) *Heraldo de Cine*, 9, 520, 30 July, 3.

_____ (1941c) Memorandum to Foreign Committee from Motion Picture Society for the Americas, 19 August. Beverly Hills, CA: Academy of Motion Picture Arts and Sciences, Margaret Herrick Library, 1–2.

_____ (1941/42) Motion Picture Society for the Americas Subcommittee Minutes, Record Group 229, memo no. 31, 14 October. Beverly Hills, CA: Academy of Motion Picture Arts and Sciences, Margaret Herrick Library.

_____ (1942a) 'Bum Rumor of Nazi Tie-up Almost Bulls US Relations', *The Hollywood Reporter*, 18 February.

_____ (1942b) *Heraldo de Cine*, 12, 556, 15 April, 5.

_____ (1942c) 'B.A. vs. 42nd St', *Variety*, 28 July, 15.

_____ (1942d) 'Argentina Bans 20th Pic at Jap Request', *Hollywood Reporter*, 12 August.

_____ (1942e) 'The Invaders Banned by Argentina After 10 Days', *Hollywood Reporter*, 13 August.

_____ (1942f) 'Pro-Nazi Campaign Against US Pix for Argentine', *Variety*, 26 October.

_____ (1942g) 'Argentina Top Producer of Spanish Pictures', *Motion Picture Herald*, 7 November, 12.

_____ (1942h) 'Resume of Activities Directed to the Argentine in the Field of Motion Pictures', OCIAA collection, Motion Picture Division Folder, Rockefeller Archive Center, Sleepy Hollow, New York.

_____ (1943a) 'Argentine Pic Biz Faces 50% Raw Film Stock Snip', *Variety*, 23 April.

_____ (1943b) 'US Ups Mex Films, Cuts Argentina for Axis Stand', *Variety*, 17 May, 1, 15.

_____ (1943c) 'List of Blacklist in Argentine', *Variety*, 30 June, 25.

_____ (1943d) 'Argentine Pic Business Thrives: Homemade Product Taking Trade Away from Our Films', *Hollywood Reporter*, 19 October.

_____ (1943e) 'US Has 65 to 1 Ratio over Nazi Pix in Argentine', *Hollywood Reporter*, 29 October, 1–2.

_____ (1943f) 'US Cos. Reported Exit from Argentina', *Variety*, 12 August, 18.

_____ (1943/44) 'Progress Report', OCIAA collection, Series O, Washington, D.C. Files – Presidential Appointments, in the Nelson A. Rockefeller Personal Papers, Record Group 4 of the Rockefeller Family Archives at the Rockefeller Archive Center, Sleepy Hollow, New York.

_____ (1944) 'Argentine Notes', *Hollywood Reporter*, 24 November 24.

_____ (1984) 'La democracia llegó al Instituto', *Heraldo del Cine*, 13 January, 1.

_____ (1986a) 'Viewers Flock to Argentine TV; Reprivatised Station Is Big Draw', *Variety*, 12 March, 114.

_____ (1986b) 'Cine debate: Mesa redonda de "Cine en la cultura" acerca de *El exilio de Gardel*', *Cine en la cultura argentina y latinoamericana*, 9 June, 25–7.

_____ (1987a) 'Argentine Pictures Rack Up $6–7 Mil In Yankee Market', *Variety*, 25 March, 94.

_____ (1987b) 'Crisis a la Argentina', *Heraldo del cine*, 23 October, 1.

_____ (1988a) 'Manotón de ahogado: La TV sin cine', *Página 12*, 11 October.

_____ (1988b) 'El "Día del Cine" fue un éxito', *Crónica*, 31 October, 25.

_____ (1993a) 'Luis Puenzo habla', *La Maga*, 6 January, 20.

_____ (1993b) 'Buenos Aires' High Prices Take Box Office Up', *Variety*, 29 March, 66.

_____ (1994a) 'Entidades del cine piden la renuncia de Guido Parisier', *Clarín*, 14 May, 42.

_____ (1994b) 'Muy duro Antín con la inminente Ley del Cine', *Ámbito financiero*, 11 August, 2–3.

_____ (1995a) 'Marhárbiz el nuevo Jefe', *La Nación*, 22 June, 6.

_____ (1995b) 'Donde se estudia cine: Hoy. La Universidad del Cine', *El amante*, 4, 5, 44.

_____ (1996a) 'El grupo Clarín entre las mayores empresas de la comunicación', *Boletín de industrias culturales*, Fundación CICCUS publicación no. 2, September, 2.

_____ (1996b) 'Entrevista con Claudio Pustelnik: Se reúnen diez tipos una mañana, ven la película y opinan', *Haciendo Cine*, 2, 5, 37–8.

_____ (1997a) 'Recaudaciones del I.N.C.A.A en 1996', *Boletín de industrias culturales*, Fundación CICCUS publication no. 3, 3 June, 7.

_____ (1998) 'Nueva sede para la Escuela y la Cinemateca Nacional', *Cine argentino: Boletín informativo*, 1, 1. Buenos Aires: Instituto Nacional de Cine y Artes Audiovisuales.

_____ (2003) 'Pantallas argentinas en todas las latitudes', *Raíces del cine*, no. 6, November; http://www.raicesdelcine.com.ar/numero_6/notas_06/espacios_06.htp [accessed 12 December 2006].

_____ (2005a) 'No sos vos, soy sigue batiendo records', *Cómo hacer cine*, 13 July; http://www.comohacercine.com/actualidad_detalle.php?ide+3695&c+Taquillas [accessed 7 August 2005].

_____ (2005b) 'Volunteers Make Argentine Town Filmmaking Hub', *Agence France Presse*, 27 July.

_____ (2006) 'Solanas llegó a Montevideo para presentar su nueva película', El País de Uruguay, 9 October; http://www.findgalegroup.com.www2.lib.ku.edu:2048/itx/infomark.do?&contentSet=IAC [accessed 21 December 2006].

Antín, Manuel (1995) Personal interview with the author, 13 July.

_____ (1998) 'Opinión por Manuel Antín: por suerte ellos no están solos', *Clarín*, 11 January, 9.

Antola, Livia and Everett Rogers (1984) 'Television Flows in Latin America', *Communication Research*, 11, 2, 183–202.

Arditti, Rita (2002) 'The Grandmothers of the Plaza de Mayo and the Struggle against Impunity in Argentina', *Meridians: Feminism, Race, Transnationalism*, 3, 1, 19–41.

Armes, Roy (1987) *Third World Filmmaking and the West*. Berkeley: University of California Press.

Armour, Norman (1944) Memo to State Department, 16 May, National Archives, Washington D.C.

Aufderheide, Patricia (1986) 'Awake Argentina!', *Film Comment*, 22, 2, 51–5.

Avellaneda, Andrés (1986) *Censura, autoritarismo, y cultura: Argentina 1960–1983*, vol. 1, Buenos Aires: Centro editor de América Latina.

_____ (1987) 'The Process of Censorship and the Censorship of the *Proceso*: Argentina 1976–1983', in David William Foster (ed.) 'The Redemocratization of Argentine Culture, 1983 and Beyond: An International Research Symposium at Arizona State University, 16–17 February'.

Babino, Ernesto (1999) 'Pablo Trapero (Interview)', *Sin cortes*, July, 26m, 24–6.

Baker, Jr., Houston, Manthia Diawara and Ruth Lindeborg (eds) (1996) *Black British Cultural Studies: A Reader*. Chicago and London: University of Chicago Press.

Balio, Tino (1976) *The American Film Industry*. Madison: University of Wisconsin Press.

Barber, Benjamin (1995) *Jihad vs. McWorld*. New York: Times Books.

Barnard, Tim (ed.) (1986) *Argentine Cinema*. Toronto, Canada: Nightwood Editions.

Barnard, Tim and Peter Rist (eds) (1996) *South American Cinema: A Critical Filmography 1915–1994*. New York: Garland Publishing.

Barone, Luis (1997) Personal interview with the author, 5 November.

Batlle, Diego (1992) 'Varios fallos de la justicia complican el impuesto del INC', *La Maga*, 12 August, 20.

_____ (1994a) 'Estamos cansados de lavar siempre la ropa sucia en casa'. *La Maga*, 16 February, 30–2.

_____ (1994b) 'Los realizadores se dividieron en dos asociaciónes que pelean por lo mismo', *La Maga*, 21 September, 33.

_____ (1997) 'En busca del credito perdido', *La Maga*, 8 October, 36.

_____ (1998) 'Mahárbiz debe renunciar: Asi pidieron las entidades de cine, que boicotearan el festival marplatense', *La Nación*, 7 November, 6.

_____ (2001) 'Producción nacional de exportación', *La Nación*, 3 August, 7.

_____ (2005) 'Argentinos taquilleros: Interés por *No sos vos, soy yo* y *Whisky Romeo Zulu*', *La Nación*, 16 July; http://www.lanacion.ar/721715 [accessed 16 July 2005].

Belaunzarán, Jorge (1997) 'El cine argentino es negocio (de la TV)', *La Maga*, 23 July, 16–17.

Belaunzarán, Jorge and Eduardo Blanco (1993) 'El gobierno necesita que en cultura no pase nada', *La Maga*, 12 May, 6.

Bellas, José and Pablo Schanton (1998) 'Palo y la bolsa', *Clarín*, 16 January, 4

Bermúdez, Julia, Ana Alberro, Andrea Carlino, Celeste Egea, Ezequiel Fernández, Caroline González, Lelia González, Anastasia Macagni, Pablo Piedras, Silvia Spadaccini and Romina Spinsanti (2003) 'Revistas de cine en la Argentina', in *Otrocampo: Estudios sobre cine*; http://www.otrocampo.com/7/revistasargentinas.html [accessed 23 December 2004].

Bernades, Horacio (2002) 'Hombre al agua: Balnearios', FIPRESCI Argentina; http://www.fipresciargentina.com.ar [accessed 13 December 2006].

Bernades, Horacio, Diego Lerer and Sergio Wolf (2002) 'Introduction', in Horacio Bernades, Diego Lerer and Sergio Wolf (eds) *Nuevo cine argentino: Temas, autores, y estilos de una renovación/New Argentine Cinema: Themes, Auteurs and Trends of Innovation*. Buenos Aires: FIPRESCI/Ediciones Tanaka, 9–16.

Besas, Peter (1993) 'Tax Windfall Sprouts Argentine Pix', *Variety*, 29 March, 66.

Bethell, Leslie (ed.) (1993) *Argentina Since Independence*. Cambridge: Cambridge University Press.

Beycero, Raúl (1997) *Cine y política: Ensayos sobre cine argentino*. Santa Fe, Argentina: Universidad Nacional del Litoral.

Bhaba, Homi (ed.) (1990) *Nation and Narration*. London: Routledge.

Birri, Fernando (1986) 'For a Nationalist, Realist, Critical, and Popular Cinema', in Tim Barnard (ed.) *Argentine Cinema*. Toronto: Nightwood Editions, 79–82.

_____ (1987) *Pionero y peregrino*. Buenos Aires: Editorial Contrapunto.

Blanco, Eduardo (1993) 'El Grupo Clarín controla o tiene participación en casi 30 empresas', *La Maga*, 24 November, 2.

Blanco, Eduardo and Pablo Marchetti (1992) 'El gobierno menemista bajó el presupuesto de cultura', *La Maga*, 8 July, 2–3.

Blanco, Fernando (1998) Personal interview with the author, 28 July.

Blejman, Mariano (2004) 'Todos vienen a buscar al cine argentino' (Interview with Ana Poliak, Mariano Llinás and Daniel Rosenfeld), *Página 12*, 13 April; http://www.pagina12.com.ar/diario/suplementos/espectaculos/6-34019-2004-04-13.html [accessed 19 December 2006].

_____ (2006) 'El 'humor' de Bañeros 3', *Página 12*, 13 July; http://www.pagina12.com.ar/diario/suplementos/espectaculos/5-3098-2006-07-13.html [accessed 18 December 2006].

Bohan, Merwin L. (1942) 'Reasons Why American Industry Should Give Enthusiastic, Strong Support for Plan', 26 May, OCIAA collection, Motion Picture Division Folder, Rockefeller Archive Center, Sleepy Hollow, New York.

Bruski, Natalio (1942) 'Argentina Top Producer of Spanish Pictures', *Motion Picture Herald*, 7 November.

Burbach, Roger (2002) '"Throw Them All Out": Argentina's Grassroots Rebellion', *NACLA: Report on the Americas*, 36, 1; http://www.nacla.org/art_display.php?art=2098 [accessed 4 January 2003].

Burton, Julianne (1978) 'The Camera as a "Gun": Two Decades of Culture and Resistance in Latin America', *Latin American Perspectives*, 5, 1, 49–78.

_____ (ed.) (1986) *Cinema and Social Change in Latin America: Conversations with Filmmakers*. Austin: University of Texas Press.

_____ (1990) *The Social Documentary in Latin America*. Pittsburgh: University of Pittsburgh Press.

Caistor, Nick (1988) 'Argentina: 1976–1983', in John King and Nissa Torrents (eds) *The Garden of the Forking Paths: Argentine Cinema*. London: British Film Institute, 80–92.

Calistro, Mariano (1992) 'Aspectos del nuevo cine, 1957–1968', in Jorge Miguel Couselo, Mariano Calistro and Claudio España (eds) *Historia del cine argentino*. Buenos Aires: Centro Editor de América Latina, 109–38.

Cantor Magnani, José, and Heriberto Muraro (1978) 'La influencia transnacional en el cine argentino', *Comunicación y cultura* 5, March, 19–69.

Carabello, Charlier and Garulli (1986) *La dictadura 1976–1983: Testimonios y documentos*. Buenos Aires: Universidad de Buenos Aires.

Castagna, Gustavo J. (1993) 'La generación del 60: Paradojas de un mito', in Sergio Wolf (ed.) *Cine argentino: La otra historia*. Buenos Aires: Ediciones Letra Buena, 243–64.

Catálogo del nuevo cine argentino, 1984–1986 (1987) Buenos Aires: Instituto Nacional de Cinematografía.

Catálogo del nuevo cine argentino, 1987–1988 (1989) Buenos Aires: Instituto Nacional de Cinematografía.

Catálogo del nuevo cine argentino, 1989–1991 (1993) Buenos Aires: Instituto Nacional de Cinematografía.

Centro Argentino para la cooperación internacional y el desarollo (CACID) (1996) *Reflexiones del fin del siglo: Un propuesta desde los jóvenes*. Buenos Aires.

Chatruc, Celina (1996) 'The teaching of cinema in Argentina', *Cultura: Special Report: Argentine Cinema Today*, 57/58, 20–1.

Cine por la Red, 'El cine argentino abre un espacio en Madrid con la inauguración de la Sala', INCAA Km. 10.000. 5 June 2004; www.porlared.com/cinered/noticias/e_act04050501.html [accessed 26 July 2005].

Ciria, Alberto (1995) 'Historia, sexo, clase, y poder en los filmes de María Luisa Bemberg', *Más allá de la pantalla*. Buenos Aires: Ediciones de la Flor, 153–70.

_____ (1995) *Más allá de la pantalla*. Buenos Aires: Ediciones de la Flor.

Colas, Santiago (1994) *Postmodernity in Latin America: The Argentine Paradigm*. Durham, NC: Duke University Press.

Corradi, Juan E. (1995) 'Menem's Argentina, Act II', *Current History*, 94, 589, 76–80.

Corti, Captain Carlos Alberto (1977) Memo by Director of press for the presidency, May 1976, in *Guia de Heraldo*, Buenos Aires.

Coscia, Jorge (2004) 'The Screen Quota, A Fundamental Step Forward', *Raíces de cine*, 9; http://www.raicesdelcine.com.ar [accessed 24 May 2005].

_____ (2005a) 'El presidente' *Raíces de cine*, 11 Feb; http://www.raicesdelcine.com.ar [accessed 10 July 2005].

_____ (2005b) 'Crear des de la diversidad', *Raices de cine*, 12 May; http://www.raicesdelcine.com.ar [accessed 10 July 2005].

_____ (2005c) *Del estallido a la esperanza: Reflexiones sobre cine, cultura y Peronismo*. Buenos Aires: Corregidor.

Council of Europe (1979) *El cine y el estado*. Madrid, Spain: Ministry of Culture.

Couselo, Jorge Miguel, Mariano Calistro and Claudio España (eds) (1992) *Historia del cine argentino*. Buenos Aires: Centro Editor de América Latina.

Cowie, Peter (ed.) (1994) *Variety International Film Guide*. Hollywood, CA: Samuel French.

Crofts, Stephen (1993) 'Reconceptualising National Cinema/s', *Quarterly Review of Film and Video*, 14, 3, 49–67.

Curubeto, Diego (1998) Personal interview with the author, 9 October.

Dagron, Alfonso Gamucio (1986) 'Argentina: A Huge Case of Censorship', in Tim Barnard (ed.) *Argentine Cinema*. Toronto: Nightwood Editions, 84–98.

DeCardona, Elizabeth (1977) 'American Television in Latin America', in George Gerbner (ed.) *Mass Media Policies in Changing Cultures*. New York: Wiley, 22–45.

DEISICA: Informe sobre los aspectos económicos-culturales de la industria cinematográfica, 7 vols. Buenos Aires: Film Workers' Union, 1991–97.

De las Carreras, María Elena (1995) 'Contemporary Politics in Argentine Cinema: 1981–1991', unpublished Ph.D dissertation, University of California, Los Angeles.

De Pascal, Vincent (1941) 'Argentina', *Hollywood Reporter*, 21 February.

_____ (1942) 'Argentine Films Need Help; Asks Vital US Materials', *Hollywood Reporter*, 15 September.

del Mazo, Mariano (1997) 'Lo unico que me interesa es el producto: Adrián Suar habla de su mejor año', *Clarín*, 14 December, 10.

del Tronco, José (1996) 'Populismo, Peronismo, y Menemismo', in *Reflexiones del fin del siglo: Un propuesta desde los jóvenes*. Buenos Aires: Centro Argentino para la cooperación internacional y el desarollo (CACID).

D'Esposito, Leonardo (1997) 'Así se construye un éxito argentino', *La Maga*, 2 July, 27.

Di Núbila, Domingo (1959) *Historia del cine argentino I/II*. Buenos Aires: Editor Cruz de Malta.

_____ (1986) 'Production Up While B.O. Off', *Variety*, 12 March.

_____ (1998) 'Argentine Pix Heat Up at Home', *Variety*, 23–29 March, 48.

D'Lugo, Marvin (2003) 'Authorship, globalization, and the new identity of Latin American cinema: from the Mexican "ranchera" to Argentinian "exile"', in Anthony R. Guneratne and Wimal Dissanayake (eds) *Rethinking Third Cinema*. New York and London: Routledge, 103–25.

Dreher, Burckhard (1976) *Filmforderung in der Bundesrepublik* (third edition). Berlin: Deutsches Institut fur Wirtschaftsforschung.

Dyer, Richard and Ginette Vincendeau (eds) (1992) *Popular European Cinema*. London and New York: Routledge.

Elena, Alberto and Marina Díaz López (eds) (2003) *The Cinema of Latin America*. London and New York: Wallflower Press.

España, Claudio (1984) *Argentina Sono Film*. Buenos Aires: Editorial Abril.

_____ (ed.) (1994a) *Cine argentino en democracia, 1983–1993*. Buenos Aires: Fondo Nacional de las Artes.

_____ (1994b) 'Diez años de cine en democracia', in Claudio España (ed.) *Cine argentino en democracia: 1983–1993*. Buenos Aires: Fondo Nacional de las Artes, 12–53.

_____ (1997) 'Un artefacto demasiado controlado', *La Nación*, 19 June, 10.

_____ (ed.) (2000a) *Cine argentino: Industria y clasicismo, 1933–1956*, vols. 1 and 2. Buenos Aires: Fondo Nacional de las Artes.

_____ (2000b) 'El modelo institucional: formas de representación en la edad de oro', in Claudio España (ed.) *Cine argentino: Industria y clasicismo, 1933–1956*, vol. 1. Buenos Aires: Fondo Nacional de las Artes, 22–157.

_____ (2000c) 'Keeping Tabs on the Latest Hot Spots', *Film Comment*, 6, 4, 12–15.

Espejo, Daniela (2002) 'Spotlights in the dark – Argentine films at the Buenos Aires IV International Festival of Independent Cinema Hit by the Crisis', *Senses of Cinema*, 20, May–June; http://www.sensesofcinema.com/contents/02/20/argentine.html [accessed 22 December 2003].

Espinoza, Lito (1997) Personal interview with the author, 3 October.

Fabbro, Gabriela (1994) 'Las cooperativas de trabajo', in Claudio España (ed.) *Cine argentino en democracia: 1983–1993*. Buenos Aires: Fondo Nacional de las Artes, 288–9.

Fagg, John E. (1963) *Latin America: A General History*. New York: McMillian.

Falcoff, Mark and Ronald H. Dolkart (eds) (1975) *Prologue to Perón: Argentina in Depression and War, 1930–1943*. Berkeley, CA: University of California Press.

Falicov, Tamara L. (2004) 'US-Argentine Co-productions 1982–1990: Roger Corman, Aries Productions, "Schlockbuster" Movies, and the International Market', *Film and History*, 34, 1, 31–8.

_____ De nuestro punta de vista (From our Vantage Point): Young Patagonian Videographers Re-vision the Argentine South. Unpublished article.

Featherstone, Mike, Scott Lash and Roland Robertson (eds) (1995) *Global Modernities*. London and Thousand Oaks: Sage Publications.

Feigenbaum, Harvey (2004) 'Is Technology the Enemy of Culture?', *Interna-*

tional Journal of Cultural Policy, 10, 3, 251–263.

Feldman, Simón (1990) *La generación del 60*. Buenos Aires: Instituto Nacional de Cine y Editorial Legasa.

Félix-Didier, Paula (2004) Personal interview with the author, 17 April.

Félix-Didier, Paula, Leandro Listorti and Ezequiel Luka (2002) 'El nuevo documental: El acto de ver con ojos propios', in Horacio Bernades, Diego Lerer and Sergio Wolf (eds) *Nuevo cine argentino: Temas, autores, y estilos de una renovación/New Argentine Cinema: Themes, Auteurs and Trends of Innovation*. Buenos Aires: FIPRESCI/Ediciones Tanaka, 81–92.

Ferreira, Fernando (1995) *Luz, cámara, memoria: Una historia social del cine argentino*. Buenos Aires: Corregidor.

Frau-Meigs, Divina (2003) ' 'Cultural Exception', National Policies and Globalisation Imperatives in Democratisation and Promotion of Contemporary Culture', Quaderns del CAC, Issue 14; http://www.audiovisualcat.net.publicationsing/Q14france.pdf [accessed 11 August 2005].

Fuchs, Andres (2005) 'Mucho más que cine', *Film Journal International*. 1 November; http://www.filmjournal.com/filjournal/features/article_display.jsp?vnu_content_id=1001349178 [accessed 21 December 2005].

García Canclini, Nestor (1995) *Hybrid Cultures: Strategies for Entering and Leaving Modernity*. Minneapolis: University of Minnesota Press.

García Espinosa, Julio (1997 [1969]) 'Por un cine imperfecto' ('For an Imperfect Cinema'), in Michael M. Martin (ed.) *The New Latin American Cinema*, 1. Detroit: Wayne State University Press, 71–82.

García Oliveri, Ricardo (1992) 'Los años de la democracia', in Jorge Miguel Couselo, Mariano Calistro and Claudio España (eds) *Historia del cine argentino*. Buenos Aires: Centro Editor de América Latina, 167–86.

_____ (1997) 'Opinión por Ricardo García Oliveri: Las tres juveniles películas argentinas que van al festival mardeplatense', *Clarín*, 10 November, 9.

Garnham, Nicholas (1990) *Capitalism and Communication*. London: Sage.

Gemunden, Gerd (2004) 'Letter from Berlin: Report from the 54th International Film Festival', *Film Criticism*, 28, 3, 52–8.

Gerbner, George (ed.) (1977) *Mass Media Policies in Changing Cultures*. New York: Wiley.

Gerchunoff, Pablo and Juan Carlos Torre (1998) 'Argentina: The Politics of Economic Liberalization', in Menno Vellinga (ed.) *The Changing Role of the State in Latin America*. Boulder, CO: Westview Press, 115–148.

Getino, Octavio (1987) *Cine latinoamericano: Economía y nuevas tecnologías audiovisuales*. Havana, Cuba: Fundación del Nuevo Cine Latinoamericano.

_____ (1990a) *Cine y dependencia: El cine en la Argentina*. Buenos Aires: Puntosur.

_____ (1990b) *El impacto del video en el espacio audiovisual latinoamericano*. Buenos Aires: IPAL.

_____ (1995) *Las industrias culturales en la Argentina: Dimensión económica y políticas públicas*. Buenos Aires: Ediciones Colihue.

_____ (1996) *La tercera mirada: Panorama del audiovisual latinoamericano*. Buenos Aires: Paidós.

_____ (1998) Personal interview with the author, 23 July.

_____ (2005) *Cine argentino: Entre lo posible y lo deseable* (second edition). Buenos Aires: Ediciones CICCUS.

Gibson, Edward L. (1997) 'The Populist Road to Market Reform', *World Politics*, 49, April, 339–70.

González, Horacio and Eduardo Rinesi (eds) (1993) *Decorados: Apuntes para una historia social del cine argentino*. Buenos Aires: Editorial Manuel Suárez.

González Acevedo, Juan Carlos (2005) *Che, qué bueno que vinisteis: El cine argentino que cruzó el charco*. Barcelona: Editorial Dieresis.

Gramsci, Antonio (1971) *Selections from the Prison Notebooks*, ed. and trans. Quintin Hoare and Geoffrey Nowell-Smith. New York: International Publishers.

_____ (1982) 'Film as International Business: The Role of American Multinationals', in Gorhan Kindan (ed.) *The American Movie Industry: The Business of Motion Pictures*. Carbondale: Southern Illinois University, 336–50.

_____ (1989) 'International Circulation of US Theatrical Films and Television Programming' in George Gerbner (ed.) *World Communications: A Handbook*. New York: Longman.

Guback, Thomas and Tapio Varis (1982) *Transnational Communication and Cultural Industries*. Paris, France: UNESCO.

Gubern, Roman (1971) *Historia de Cine, Volumen II*. Barcelona: Lumen.

Guerschuny, Hernan and Pablo Udenio (2002) 'Miss Independencia' [Interview with producer Lita Stantic], *Haciendo cine*, 6, 27, 46–9.

Harvey, David (1990) *The Condition of Postmodernity*. London: Blackwell.

Hayward, Susan (1993a) *French National Cinema*. London and New York: Routledge.

_____ (1993b) 'State, Culture and the Cinema: Jack Lang's Strategies for the French Film Industry, 1981–93', *Screen*, 34, 4, 1993, 380–91.

Higson, Andrew. (1989) 'The Concept of National Cinema', *Screen*, 30, 4, 1989, 36–47.

Hill, John (1992) 'The Issue of National Cinema and British Film Production' in Duncan Petrie (ed.) *New Questions of British Cinema*. BFI Working Papers. London: British Film Institute.

_____ (1994) 'Introduction' in John Hill, Martin McLoone and Paul Hainsworth (eds) *Border Crossing: Film in Ireland, Britain and Europe*. Belfast: Institute of Irish Studies, 1–14.

Hoffman, Katja (2005) 'Berlin Film Festival: Fest Funds Team Up to Boost World Cinema', *Variety*, 397, 12, 7–13 February, A4, A10.

Hoskins, Colin, Stuart McFadyen and Adam Finn (1997) *Global Television and Film*. Oxford, England: Clarendon Press.

Iglesias, Fernanda (2001) 'El cine que importa (y exporta)', *Clarín*, 22 September; http://www.clarin.com.ar.diario/2001-09-22/c-01011.htm [accessed 13 November 2001].

Internet Surf (2003) 'Entrevista con Subiela'; http://subiela.tripod.com/entrevistas.html [accessed 25 September 2003].

Jameson, Fredric (1982) *The Political Unconscious*. Ithaca, NY: Cornell University Press.

_____ (1988) 'Cognitive Mapping', in Cary Nelson and Lawrence Grossberg (eds) *Marxism and the Interpretation of Cultures*. Champaign, IL: University of Illinois Press.

Jeancolas, Jean-Pierre (1992) 'The Inexportable: The Case of French Cinema and Radio in the 1950s', in Richard Dyer and Ginette Vincendeau (eds) *Popular European Cinema*. London and New York: Routledge, 141–8.

Johnson, Randal (1987) *The Film Industry in Brazil: Culture and the State*. Pittsburgh, PA: University of Pittsburgh Press.

_____ (1993) 'In the Belly of the Ogre: Cinema and State in Latin America', in John King, Ana M. López and Manuel Alvarado (eds) *Mediating Two Worlds: Cinematic Encounters in the Americas*. London: British Film Institute, 204–13.

_____ (1996) 'Film Policy in Latin America', in Albert Moran (ed.) *Film Policy: International, National and Regional Perspectives*. London: Routledge, 128–47.

Josephs, Ray (1942) 'Argentine Films Show Signs of Leading Spanish Field', *Variety*, 7 January, 91.

Kamin, Bebe (1997) Personal interview with author, 10 September.

Kaufman, Anthony (2002) 'World Cinema Report: Argentina's Next Wave Struggle Sustains Momentum Amid Economic Collapse', *Indiewire*, 20 March; http://www.indiewire.com/biz/biz_020320_Worldcine3.html [accessed 20 March 2002].

Kindan, Gorhan (ed.) (1982) *The American Movie Industry: The Business of Motion Pictures*. Carbondale: Southern Illinois University.

King, Anthony (1998) 'Thatcherism and the Emergence of Sky Television', *Media, Culture and Society*, 20, 2, 277–93.

King, John (2000) *Magical Reels: A History of Cinema in Latin America*. London: Verso.

King, John and Nissa Torrents (eds) (1988) *Garden of the Forking Paths: Argentine Cinema*. London: British Film Institute.

King, John, Ana M. López and Manuel Alvarado (eds) (1993) *Mediating Two Worlds: Cinematic Encounters in the Americas*. London: British Film Institute.

Kriger, Clara (1994) 'Las instancias de comercialización', in Claudio España (ed.) *Cine Argentino en democracia, 1983–1993*. Buenos Aires: Fondo Nacional de la Artes, 290–3.

Kuhn, Rodolfo (1984) *Armando Bo: El cine, la pornografía ingenua y otras reflexiones*. Buenos Aires: Corregidor.

Lange, André and Jean-Luc Renaud (eds) (1989) *The Future of the European Audiovisual Industry*. Bedfordshire: University of Luton Press.

Leandri, José (1984) 'Cuando el cine hace política', *Clarín*, 2 September, 4–5.

Lerer, Diego (1997) '*Comodines* y *La furia* están haciendo historia', *Clarín*, 3 July, 10–13.

_____ (2000) 'No voy a hacer siempre mundo grúa'. (Interview) *Clarín*, 27 November, 6.

Lewis, Colin M. and Nissa Torrents (eds) (1993) *Argentina in the Crisis Years (1983–1990)*. London: University of London, Institute of Latin American Studies.

López, Ana M. (1993) 'Are All Latins from Manhattan? Hollywood; Ethnography and Cultural Colonialism', in John King, Ana M. López and Manuel Alvarado (eds) *Mediating Two Worlds: Cinema Encounters in the Americas*. London: British Film Institute, 67–80.

_____ (2000) 'Crossing Nations and Genres: Travelling Filmmakers', in Chon Noriega (ed.) *Visible Nations: Latin American Cinema and Video*. Minneapolis: University of Minnesota Press, 33–50.

Lowe, Florence S. (1944) 'Washington Hullabaloo', *Variety*, 8 February.

Luka, Ezequiel (2004) 'El mercado del cine en la Argentina: medidas nuevas, problemas viejos', FIPRESCI website, Argentine afíliate, Bulletin 3, August; http://www.fipresciarentina.com.ar/boletin3-%20indies.luka.htm [accessed 11 December 2006].

Lusnich, Ana Laura (1994) 'El Instituto nacional de cinematografía', in Claudio España (ed.) *Cine argentino en democracia, 1983–1993*. Buenos Aires: Fondo Nacional de las Artes, 303–6.

Macnab, Geoffrey (2002) 'Bust and Boom: "It's not all bad news in Argentina. Two groups seem set to ride out the crash – footballers and filmmakers"', *Guardian*, 30 January, 11–12.

Maranghello, César (1992) 'La pantalla y el estado', in Jorge Miguel Couselo, Mariano Calistro and Claudio España (eds) *Historia del cine argentino*. Buenos Aires: Centro Editor de América Latina, 89–108.

_____ (2000) 'Cine y estado', in Claudio España (ed.) *Cine argentino 1933–1956: Industria y clasicismo*, 2. Buenos Aires: Fondo Nacional de las Artes, 24–183.

Marchetti, Pablo (1994) 'Parisier organizo un concurso en el que ningún miembro del jurado forma parte de la industria', *La Maga*, 15 June, 31.

Martin, Michael T. (ed.) (1997) *New Latin American Cinema, Volume One: Theory, Practices, and Transcontinental Articulations*. Detroit, MI: Wayne State University Press.

Martínez, Adolfo C. (2003) 'Entradas de cine, con nuevos precios', *La Nación*, 30 January; http://www.lanacion.com.ar/03/01/30/ds_469913.asp [accessed

30 January 2003].

Martín Peña, Fernando (1998) 'Hay un nuevo cine argentino?', *Film*, 5, 56–7.

_____ (2003) 'Raúl Perrone', in Fernando Martín Peña (ed.) *90 Generaciones/60 Generaciones: Cine argentino independiente*. Buenos Aires: Malba-Colección Constantini, 141–51.

Mathieu, Agustín (1974) *Breve historia del cine nacional*. Buenos Aires: Alzamor.

Menant, Danilo and Ezequiel Siddig (1996) 'Los discursos del poder: Meditaciones acerca la globalización y la soberanía', in *Reflexiones de fin de siglo: Una propuesta desde los jóvenes*. Buenos Aires: Centro Argentina para la cooperación internacional y el desarollo (CACID).

Mestman, Mariano (2003) '*La hora de los hornos/Hour of the Furnaces*', in Alberto Elena and Marina Díaz López (eds) *The Cinema of Latin America*. London and New York: Wallflower Press, 119–30.

Minguetti, Claudio (2005) 'Una golpe de realidad', *La Nación*, 9 May; http://www.lanacion.com.ar.entretenimientos/nota.asp?nota_id=702595 [accessed 9 May 2005].

Moisés, José Álvaro (2002) 'Cultural Diversity and Development in the Americas', Cultural Studies Series No.9, Unit for Social Development, Education and Culture, Organisation of American States; http://www.oas.org/udse/espanol/documentos/1hub4.doc [accessed 11 August 2005].

Monteagudo, Luciano and Adriana Schettini (1995) 'Barajar y dar de nuevo', *Página 12*, 14 March, 7.

Monteagudo, Luciano (2003) 'Last News from the Battlefront', *Elamante.com*, 7 August, http://www.elamante.com.ar/nota/2/2080.shtml [accessed 8 October 2003].

Montesoro, Julia and Diego Batlle (1999a) 'En la orilla del futuro', *La Nación*, 13 June, 4–5.

_____ (1999b) 'Vuelta de página para el cine argentino', *La Nación*, 13 June, 8–9.

Moran, Albert (ed.) (1996) *Film Policy: International, National and Regional Perspectives*. London and New York: Routledge.

Morgan, Michael and James Shanahan (1995) *Democracy Tango: Television, Adolescents, and Authoritarian Tensions in Argentina*. Cresskill, NJ: Hampton Press.

Moro, Patricia (1998) Personal interview with the author, 10 February.

Moss, Nathaniel (1997) 'Ribbon of cinema: *Moebius*', *Film Comment*, 33, 6, 79–80.

Motion Picture Society of the Americas Report, 1944–45, 11, Beverly Hills, CA: Academy of Motion Picture Arts and Sciences, Margaret Herrick Library.

Munck, Ronaldo (1997) 'Introduction: A Thin Democracy', *Latin American Perspectives*, 24, 6, November, 5–21.

Muoyo, C. Adrián (1993) 'Alemania y la Argentina usaron el cine como propaganda', *La Maga*, 23 June.

Neale, Steve (1981) 'Art Cinema as an Institution', *Screen*, 22, 1, 11–39.

Nelson, Cary and Lawrence Grossberg (eds) (1988) *Marxism and the Interpretation of Cultures*. Champaign: University of Illinois Press.

Newbery, Charles (2003) 'Martel Rolling Holy', *Variety*, 16 June, 26.

_____ (2004) 'Quotas give screen time to local pix', *Variety*, 12 July, 12.

_____ (2005a) 'Sparks fly in Argentina', *Variety*, 22 May; http://www.variety.com/story.asp?I=story&a=VR1117923280&c=1447 [accessed 6 June 2005].

_____ (2005b) 'Pic Fund protesters burn 'Maria' set', *Variety*, 24 May; http://www.variety.com/story.asp?I=story&a=VR1117923438&c=1447 [accessed 6 June 2005].

_____ (2005c) 'Local Fare Clicks with Argentines', *Variety*, 10 October, 8.

_____ (2006a) 'Argentina picking up the pic pace: Trapero, Caetano, Others Have Works in Progress', *Variety*, 1 January; http://www.variety.com/article/VR1117935347.html [accessed 4 January 2006].

_____ (2006b) 'Pricey Problem at B.O.: Inflation Batters Argentina', *Variety*, 5 March; http://www.variety.com/article/VR1117939223.html [accessed 18 December 2006].

Newman, Kathleen (1991) 'Latin American Cinema in North American Film Scholarship', *IRIS*, 13, 1–4.

_____ (1992) Cultural Redemocratisation: Argentina, 1978–89', in George Yúdice, Jean Franco and Juan Flores (eds) *On Edge: The Crisis of Contemporary Latin American Culture*. Minneapolis: University of Minnesota Press, 161–86.

Newton, Ronald C (1992) *The 'Nazi Menace' in Argentina, 1931–1947*. Stanford, CA: Stanford University Press.

Nichols, Bill (1994) 'Global Image Consumption in the Age of Late Capitalism', *East-West Film Journal*, 8, 1.

Niosi, J. (1974) *Los empresarios y el estado argentino (1955–1969)*. Buenos Aires: Siglo XXI.

Nowell-Smith, Geoffrey and Steven Ricci (eds) (1988) *Hollywood and Europe: Economics, Culture and National Identity, 1945–95*. London: British Film Institute.

Olivera, Héctor (1995) Personal interview with the author, 15 July.

_____ (2003) 'La nouvelle vague en danger', *Cahiers du cinema*, 578, April, 27.

Oubiña, David (1994) 'El cine argentino en el exterior: Festivales y premios', in Claudio España (ed.) *Cine argentino en democracia, 1983–1993*. Buenos Aires: Fondo Nacional de las Artes, 294–5.

_____ (2006) Written correspondence with the author, 28 March.

Oral History with Robert M. W. Vogel (199 Interviewed by Barbara Hall. Beverly Hills, CA: Academy of Motion Picture Arts and Sciences, Oral History Program, 185.

O'Regan, Tom (1996) *Australian National Cinema*. London and New York:

Routledge.

Paulinelli, María (ed.) (2005) *Poéticas en el cine argentino, 1995–2005*. Córdoba, Argentina: Comunicarte Editorial.

Paxman, Andrew (1994) 'Argentina's Pic Makers Get Subsidy Boost', *Variety*, 10–16 October, 47.

_____ (1995) 'Argentine TV Adds Pic Coin', *Variety*, 10 July, 12.

_____ (1998a) 'Southern Renaissance: Corporate Ventures Multiply Region's Booming Multiplexes', *Variety*, 23–29 March, 43, 64.

_____ (1998b) 'Disputes Stall Cable in Brazil, Columbia', *Variety*, 23–29 March, 52.

Pendakur, Manjunath (1990) *Canadian Dreams and American Control: The Political Economy of the Canadian Film Industry*. Detroit, MI: Wayne State University Press.

Peralta-Ramos, Monica and Carlos H. Waisman (eds) (1987) *From Military Rule to Liberal Democracy in Argentina*. Boulder and London: Westview Special Studies on Latin American and the Caribbean.

Perelman, Pablo and Paulina Seivach (2003) 'La industria cinematográfica en la Argentina: Entre los límites del mercado y el fomento estatal', *Observatorio de Industrias Culturales*, no. 1. Buenos Aires: Centro de Estudios para el Desarrollo Económico Metropolitano.

Pérez, Carlos (ed.) (1969) *La Decada Infame*. Buenos Aires.

Pernasetti, Cecilia (2005) 'Lisandro Alonso' in María Paulinelli (ed.) *Poéticas en el cine argentino, 1995–2005*. Córdoba, Argentina: Comunicarte Editorial, 109–128.

Petrazzini, Ben (1995) *The Political Economy of Telecommunications Reform in Developing Countries: Privatization and Liberalization in Comparative Perspective*. Westport, CT: Praeger.

Petrie, Duncan (ed.) (1992) *New Questions of British Cinema*. BFI Working Papers. London: British Film Institute.

Phillips, Gerald (1988) 'The Return of Hollywood: Fun and Profit', *The Economist* 29, October, 21–4.

Pick, Zuzana M. (1989) 'The Dialectical Wanderings of Exile', *Screen*, 30, 4, 48–64.

_____ (1993) *The New Latin American Cinema: A Continental Project*. Austin: University of Texas Press.

Pinto, Alfonso (1973) 'Hollywood's Spanish-Language Films', *Films in Review*, 24, 473–85.

Podalsky, Laura (2004) *Specular City: Transforming Culture, Consumption, and Space in Buenos Aires, 1955–1973*. Philadelphia: Temple University Press.

Portales, Diego C. (1987) *La dificultad de innovar: Un estudio sobre las empresas de televisión en América Latina*. Santiago: ILET.

Pryor, Thomas M. (1943) 'Argentine Censor Strikes', *New York Times*, 12 December, X5.

Puenzo, Luis (1986) Interview, *American Film*, November, 15–19.

Quintans, Daniel (1997) 'Nuevos directores en cartel', *Haciendo cine*, 3, 9, 36–37.

Quintín (2002) 'From One Generation to Another: Is there a Dividing Line?', in Horacio Bernades, Diego Lerer and Sergio Wolf (eds) *Nuevo cine argentino: Temas, autores, y estilos de una renovación/New Argentine Cinema: Themes, Auteurs and Trends of Innovation*. Buenos Aires: FIPRESCI/Ediciones Tanaka, 111–31.

_____ (2003) 'A Provisory Balance', *Elamante.com*, 1 August; http://www.ela-mante.com.ar/nota/2/2079.shtml [accessed 8 October 2003].

Quintín and Horacio Bernades (1995) 'Conversación en el Maxi', *El amante*, 4, 40, 25.

Raffo, Julio (1995) *La película, cine, y el video: Régimen legal*. Unpublished paper. Buenos Aires.

_____ (1997) Personal interview with the author, 21 July.

_____ (2003) *Ley de fomento y regulación de la actividad cinematografícá*. Buenos Aires: Lumieré.

Rangil, Viviana (2001) 'Changing the Face of Argentinian Cinema: The Vibrant Voices of Four Women', *Afterimage*, 28, 6, 7–17.

Reati, Fernando (1989) 'Argentine Political Violence and the Artistic Representation in Films of the 1980s', *Latin American Literary Review*, 17, 34, 24–39.

Reisman, David (1950) *The Lonely Crowd: A Study of the Changing American Character*. New Haven, CT: Yale University Press.

Ricagno, Alejandro and Quintín (1996) 'Un cine contemporáneo: entrevista a Martín Rejtman', *El amante*, 5, 53, 14–15.

Rich, B. Ruby (1991) 'An/Other View of New Latin American Cinema', *IRIS*, 13, 5–28.

_____ (2001) 'Making Argentina Matter Again', *New York Times*, 30 September, 15, 20.

Robertson, Roland (1995) 'Glocalisation: Time-Space and Homogeneity-Heterogeneity', in Mike Featherstone, Scott Lash and Roland Robertson (eds) *Global Modernities*. London and Thousand Oaks: Sage, 25–44.

Rock, David (1993) *Authoritarian Argentina: The Nationalist Movement, its History and its Impact*. Berkeley: University of California Press.

_____ (1993) 'Argentina, 1930–1946', in Leslie Bethell (ed.) *Argentina Since Independence*. Cambridge: Cambridge University Press, 173–244.

Rodó, José Enrique (1988 [1900]) *Ariel*. Austin: University of Texas Press.

Rodríguez, Jorge Luis (1997) Personal interview with the author, 4 December.

Rogue Pitt, Milagro and Andres G. Schaer (1998) 'Óperas primas: Hacer un cine posible', *Ossessione: Revista de cine*, 1, 2, 50.

Rohter, Larry (2005) 'Floating Below Politics', *New York Times*, 1 May, 16.

Rosado, Miguel Angel (1992) 'Entre la libertad y la censura, 1968–1983', in

Jorge Miguel Couselo, Mariano Calistro and Claudio España (eds) *Historia del cine argentino*. Buenos Aires: Centro Editor de América Latina, 139–66.

Rosemberg, Diego and Eduardo Blanco (1993) 'El disparo contra Fernando Solanas', *La Maga*, 24 March.

Rowland, Donald W. (1947) *History of the Office of the Coordinator of Inter-American Affairs*. Washington, D.C.: Government Printing Office.

Sabat, Cynthia (2005) 'Los de Saladillo: Cine de vecinos', Ciudad Internet, 30 July; http://www.ciudad.com.ar/ar/AR_Nota_2005/0,3813,2381,00.asp [accessed 22 December 2005]

Santos, Rolando (1997) 'El leviatán del cine argentino y las óperas primas', *Haciendo cine*, 3, 9, 44.

Sapere, Pablo (2003) 'El inquisidor: una película maldita', *Cine Fantastico.com*; www.cinefastastico.com/terroruniversal/index.php?id=106 [accessed 30 April 2006].

Schatz, Thomas (1993) 'The New Hollywood', in Jim Collins, Hilary Radner and Ava Preacher Collins (eds) *Film Theory Goes to the Movies*. London: Routledge, 8–36.

Schettini, Adriana (1988) 'La identidad tiene que ser sensata' (Interview with Manuel Antín), *Página 12*, October, supplement, n.p.

_____ (1997) 'El cine argentino entre sombras de la TV', *La Nación*, 24 December, 2.

_____ (1998) 'Subiela ya no espera milagros', *La Nación*, 21 October, 2, sec. 4, 5.

Schiller, Herbert (1971) *Mass Communications and American Empire*. Boston, MA: Beacon Press.

Schnitman, Jorge (1978) 'The Argentine Film Industry: A Contextual Study', unpublished PhD dissertation, Stanford University.

Scholz, Pablo O. (1997a) '... Y Comodines hizo historia', *Clarín*, espectáculos, 24 June, 3.

_____ (1997b) 'El año en que ganó el cine argentino', *Clarín*, 27 December, 13.

Schwartzman, Karen (1995) 'National Cinema in Translation: The Politics of Film Exhibition Culture', *Wide Angle*, 16, 3, February, 66–99.

Secretaria de la Nación (1984) *Plan Nacional de Cultura: 1984–1989*. Buenos Aires.

Secretary of Press, Presidency of the Nation – Facts and Works (1997); http://www.presidencia.gov.ar/bio/libro/libro89i.html.

Secretary of State (1944) September 7, Washington D.C.: National Archives.

Sen, Krishna (1996) 'Cinema Polic(ing)y in Indonesia', in Albert Moran (ed.) *Film Policy: International, National, and Regional Perspectives*. New York: Routledge, 172–84.

Sendros, Daniel 'Paraná' (2004) Personal interview with the author, 20 April.

Sinclair, John (1990) 'Neither West nor Third World: The Mexican Television Industry within the NWICO debate', *Media, Culture and Society*, 20, 3, July,

343–61.

Sirvén, Pablo (1988) *Quién te ha visto y quién TV: Historia informal de la televisión argentina*. Buenos Aires: Ediciones de la Flor.

____ (2006) 'Salvavidas para un cine ahogado', *La Nación*, 23 July, 3.

Skidmore, Thomas and Peter H. Smith (1997) *Modern Latin America* (fourth edition). New York: Oxford University Press.

Smith, Peter H. (1996) *Talons of the Eagle: Dynamics of US-Latin American Relations*. New York: Oxford University Press.

Smith, William C. (1991) *Authoritarianism and the Crisis of the Argentine Political Economy*. Stanford: Stanford University Press.

Solanas, Fernando and Octavio Getino (1973) *Cine, cultura, y descolonización*. Buenos Aires: siglo veintiuno editores.

____ (1997 [1969]) 'Towards a Third Cinema: Notes and Experiences for the Development of a Cinema of Liberation in the Third World', in Michael T. Martin (ed.) *New Latin American Cinema, Volume One: Theory, Practices, and Transcontinental Articulations*. Detroit, MI: Wayne State University Press, 33–58.

Soriano, Osvaldo (1988) 'Opinión por Osvaldo Soriano', *Página 12*, 14 October.

Sosa-Pujato, Gustavo (1975) 'Popular Culture', in Mark Falcoff and Ronald H. Dolkart (eds) *Prologue to Perón: Argentina in Depression and War, 1930–1943*. Berkeley, CA: University of California Press, 136–63.

Sreberny-Mohammadi, Annabelle (1991) 'The Global and the Local in International Communications', in James Curran and Michael Gurevitch (eds) *Mass Media and Society*. New York: Edward Arnold, 118–38.

Stam, Robert (1990) '*Hour of the Furnaces* and the Two Avant Gardes', in Julianne Burton (ed.) *The Social Documentary in Latin America*. University of Pittsburgh Press, 251–66.

Stantic, Lita (1995) Personal interview with the author, 24 July.

Straubhaar, Joseph (1991) 'Beyond Media Imperialism: Asymmetrical Interdependence and Cultural Proximity', *Critical Studies in Mass Communication*, 8, 39–59.

Suárez, Pablo (2002) 'Martín Rejtman: The Surface of Things', trans. Marcela Goglio. *Cinema Tropical Newsletter*, January–February.

____ (2006) 'The Burman Identity', *Film Comment*, May–June, 54–59.

Tarruella, Rodrigo (1993) 'Manuel Romero: Entierro y quema en el día de la primavera', in Sergio Wolf (ed.) *Cine argentino: la otra historia*. Buenos Aires: Ediciones Letra Buena, 25–40.

Thieburger, Mariano and Diego Dupcovsky (1990) 'Reportaje: Octavio Getino', *Contra luz: Revista de cine*, October.

Tijman, Gabriela (1994) 'La TV por cable Argentina es la que más creció en Latinoamérica', *La Maga*, 26 January, 28–9.

Tomaselli, Victor (1998) Personal interview with the author, 20 March.

Torre, Javier (1998) Personal interview with the author, 19 March.

Torre Nilsson, Leopoldo (2000 [1962]) 'How to Make a New Wave', in John King (ed.) *Magical Reels: A History of Cinema in Latin America*. London: Verso.

Torrents, Nissa (1988) 'Contemporary Argentine Cinema', in John King and Nissa Torrents (eds) *Garden of the Forking Paths: Argentine Cinema*. London: British Film Institute, 93–113.

_____ (1993) 'The Cinema That Never Was', in Colin M. Lewis and Nissa Torrents (eds) *Argentina in the Crisis Years (1983–1990)*. London: University of London, Institute of Latin American Studies, 35–52.

Tracey, Michael (1988) 'Popular Culture and the Economics of Global Television', *Intermedia*, 16, 9–25.

Trigona, Marie (2004) 'The Making of Piquetero Televisión', *NACLA: Report on the Americas*, 37, 4, 32–33.

Udenio, Pablo and Hernan Guerschuny (1997) 'Declaración de la independencia', *Haciendo cine*, 3, 9, 18–21.

Universidad de Cine (1996a) 'Rapado', *Informe 1996: Producción Cinematográfica Argentina*. Buenos Aires: unpublished monograph, 53.

_____ (1996b) 'Entrevista con Ricardo Wullricher', *Informe 1996: Producción cinematográfica Argentina*. Buenos Aires: unpublished monograph, 107.

Urien, Paula (1997) 'El año del cine argentino', *La Nación*, 21 September, supplement, 1–14.

Usabel, Gaizka S. de (1982) *The High Noon of American Films in Latin America*. Ann Arbor: University of Michigan Press.

Valente, Marcela (2002a) 'Solanas Returns to Argentina With Camera in Hand', InterPress Service, 12 August, n.p.; http://www.lexis-nexis.com.www.2.lib.ku.edu:2052/universe [accessed 27 June 2003].

_____ (2002b) 'Inventive Directors Conquer Crisis', *Arts Weekly/Film Argentina*, InterPress Service, November 23.

_____ (2004) 'Argentina: An Award-Winning Film Industry Seeks Wider Markets', InterPress Service, 12 April; http://www.lexis-nexis.com.www.2.lib.ku.edu:2048/universe [accessed 11 August 2005].

Vietheer, George C (1972) 'Industry Held Its Own Overseas in Year of Economic Turmoil', *Motion Picture Herald*, 242, 1, January.

Vellinga, Menno (1998) *The Changing Role of the State in Latin America*. Boulder, CO: Westview Press.

Vogel, Robert M. W. (1991) Interviewed by Barbara Hall. Oral History Program, Margaret Herrick Library, 185.

Waisman, Carlos H (1987) *The Reversal of Development in Argentina*. Princeton, NJ: Princeton University Press.

Walger, Silvia (1994) *Pizza con champan: Crónica de la fiesta Menemista*. Buenos Aires: Editora Espasa.

Wasko, Janet (1994) *Hollywood in the Information Age: Beyond the Silver Screen*.

Austin: University of Texas Press.

West, Dennis (2001) 'The Buenos Aires Festival and the renaissance of Argentine cinema', *Cineaste*, 21, 50–3.

Whitney, John Hay and Francis Alstock (1942) Memo signed on 15 June declaring support for the Mexican moving picture industry. OCIAA collection, Motion Picture Division Folder, Box 7, Rockefeller Archive Center, Sleepy Hollow, New York.

Williams, Leslie (1993) Argentine Film and Class-Based Concepts of National Culture: 1930–1935. Unpublished manuscript, presented at UCSD conference on Latin American Popular Culture.

Wolf, Sergio (1993a) 'Cuestión de poeticas: los otros cines argentinos', *Film*, 3, 4–6.

_____ (1993b) 'El cine del proceso: Estética de la muerte', in Sergio Wolf (ed.) *Cine argentino: La otra historia*. Buenos Aires: Ediciones Letra Buena, 265–79.

_____ (1998) Personal interview with the author, 23 January.

_____ (2001) 'El cine bajo estado de sitio', *Clarín*, 11 March, tapa suplemento.

Yúdice, George, Jean Franco and Juan Flores (eds) (1992) *On Edge: The Crisis of Contemporary Latin American Culture*, Minneapolis: University of Minnesota Press.

Zamboni, Fabian (1998) Personal interview with the author, 26 July.

INDEX